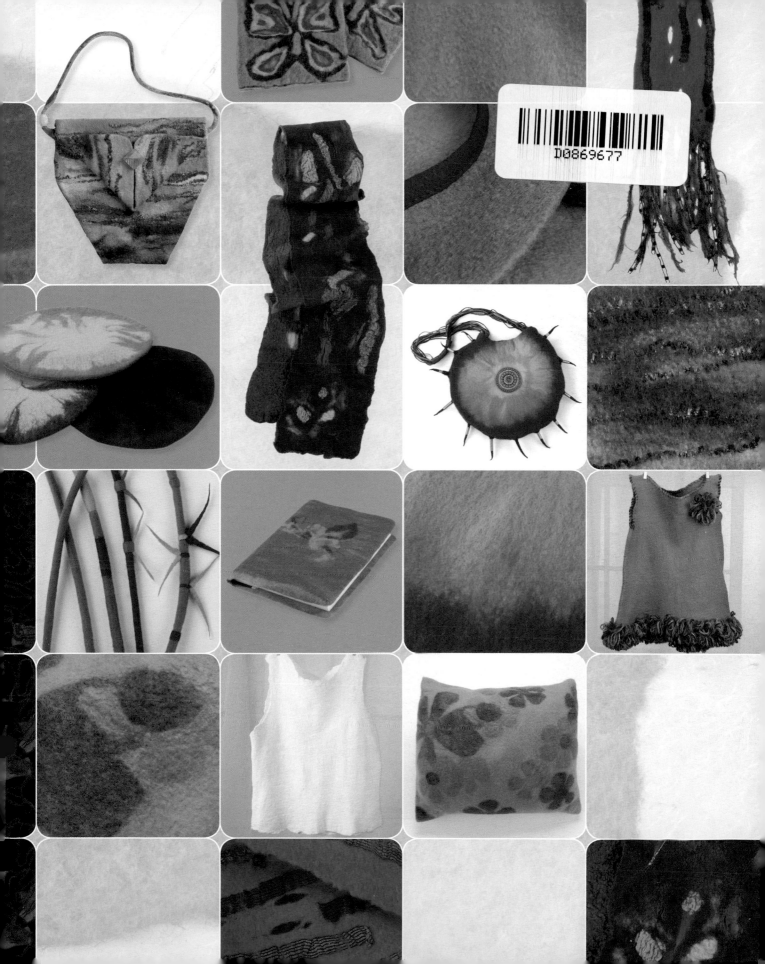

Uniquely Felt

Christine White

||| Dozens of techniques from fulling and shaping
to nuno and cobweb ||| Includes 46 creative projects

Storey Publishing

The mission of Storey Publishing is to serve our customers by publishing practical information that encourages personal independence in harmony with the environment.

Edited by Nancy D. Wood
Art direction and text design by Mary Winkelman Velgos
Cover design by Michael Hagelberg

Cover and interior photographs by John Polak Photography
  except for those noted on page 311
Photo styling by Rory Valentine
Illustrations by Alison Kolesar

Technical editing by Pat Spark
Indexed by Mary McClintock

The information in this book is true and complete to the best of our knowledge. All recommendations are made without guarantee on the part of the author or Storey Publishing. The author and publisher disclaim any liability in connection with the use of this information. For additional information please contact Storey Publishing, 210 MASS MoCA Way, North Adams, MA 01247.

Storey books are available for special premium and promotional uses and for customized editions. For further information, please call 1-800-793-9396.

Printed in China by Dai Nippon Printing

10 9 8 7 6 5 4 3 2 1

Library of Congress Cataloging-in-Publication Data

White, Christine, 1962–
 Uniquely felt / Christine White.
    p. cm.
 Includes index.
 ISBN 978-1-58017-673-6 (pbk. : alk. paper)
 1. Felting. 2. Felt work. 1. Title.
TT849.5.W54 2007
746'.0463–dc22
                2007023531

Acknowledgments

Creating a book of this scope within an eighteen-month time frame was possible only with amazing group chemistry. Editor Nancy Wood deserves tremendous credit for tackling an impossible number of pages full of my passionate tangents and finding the best in those words. She is as bright as she is efficient, and her attention to detail allowed me to write the book I wanted to write. Thanks to Deborah Balmuth, who was solidly behind the concept of the book from the beginning. Mary Velgos and John Polak are not only artistically talented but really fun to work with, and they made the photo shoot days some of the best of the entire project.

Many of the projects in this book were made with the help of others. Sue McFarland worked with me for months, especially on the beginning projects, and Mai Frank made clothing under my direction. Shoemaker Sharon Raymond helped with all things leather, especially the Sun Tote project. Roz Spier, Cathy Rogers, and other feltmakers made contributions that improved the book. Feltmaker Heather Hall has been an inspiration for her steadfast devotion to making the highest-quality felt possible.

Nina Compagnon and Rory Valentine, both former students and now close friends, have been at my side for every step. Nina generously shared her time and helped keep my studio afloat while I wrote. Rory served as the book's photo stylist and contributed in so many ways that it's truly impossible to list them. To Darlene Chandler Bassett for providing stellar personal and professional mentorship for many wonderful years, I thank you.

Beth Beede offered a tremendous opportunity by suggesting my name to Storey as an author and I certainly hope I have lived up to that gift. Beth and her husband, Larry, epitomize the joyfulness possible when we celebrate each other's artistic gifts and share ourselves freely. In that spirit, I offer sincere and heartfelt thanks to all of my feltmaking mentors and students, especially master feltmakers Mehmet Girgic and Jorie Johnson, who have most influenced my feltmaking. For her technical editing and selfless contributions to the feltmaking community, Pat Spark holds my immense gratitude.

Thanks to my loving family. A small bunch to begin with, we lost both my father and my brother-in-law during the time of this project, and writing the book provided the chance to create something promising and new during that difficult time. It's my wish that readers everywhere will use those seeds of hope to grow their individual creativities.

Without any doubt, this book's dedication belongs to my extraordinary husband, who made it possible for me to immerse myself in the project for two years. He built a studio for me in the garage he had hoped to claim for himself and handled everything from meals to meltdowns so I could live between the felting table and the computer chair for many months. He has earned my unlimited love and respect and many, many Sunday NFL games in gratitude.

— Christine White

Contents

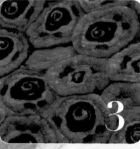

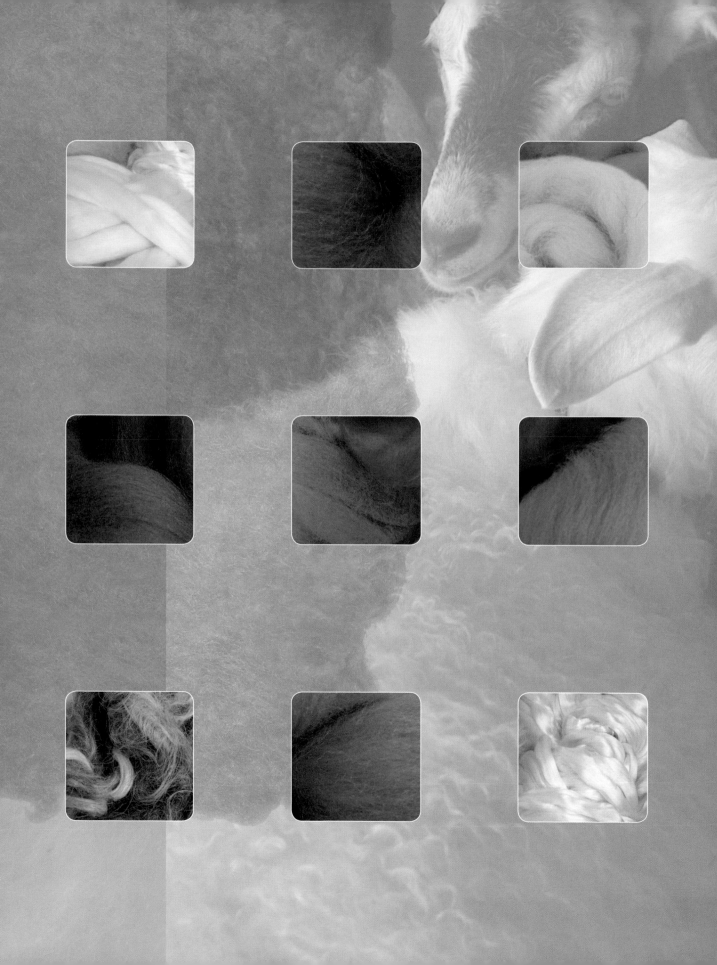

What Is Feltmaking?

Felt has been familiar to most of us from childhood and frequently is associated with warmth and comfort. Boot liners, hats, pool table tops, marking pens, polishing disks, piano key parts — felt is all around us, yet we rarely give it much thought.

People are often surprised to learn that felt can be made by hand using wool and other animal fibers. No wonder! For most people, the word "felt" brings to mind a scratchy, colored sheet sold for under a dollar at the craft store. Unlike Scandinavian countries and much of the Asian continent, the United States has no tradition of feltmaking. But older generations might remember the soft, flannel-like felt that was around prior to the man-made polyester felt that is so widely available today. That soft felt was made of 100 percent wool. The renewed interest in natural fibers is leading many to rediscover the comforting and remarkable versatility of this fabulous fabric.

What is it that makes felt and feltmaking so alluring? Is it the connection to ancient cultures and distant lands?

The tactile pleasure of touching and working with soft wools? The surprise of seeing a loose pile of fibers melt together into a flowing fabric or a one-of-a-kind work of art? Felt appeals to many people for a variety of reasons, but it seems to boil down to two simple but powerful things.

Feltmaking is a forgiving and flexible process. Anyone can learn to make felt in a matter of minutes. It's easy enough for even small children to do, so it's a wonderful activity for parents, teachers, and babysitters.

Feltmaking is at once deceptively simple and endlessly complex. Feltmaking can be much more sophisticated than most people realize, so it's also a perfect medium for creative people who seek a challenge. In fact, there are so many subtle things to learn in feltmaking that some artists have chosen lifelong careers as professional feltmakers.

No wonder felt has such a wide appeal. People of all ages love to be pleasantly surprised, and felt delivers the magic trick — *every* time. But the best part is that you are the magician, and you can learn as little or as much as you like. You can do a little and your felt will still be a beautiful success. You can do a lot and fall under the spell of feltmaking's endless depths. Either way, it's all in these pages, waiting for you.

Is It Felt?

Felting or feltmaking? Needle felting or nuno felting? What does it all mean? It's no surprise that people are often confused by these terms since feltmaking has been relatively unknown in the United States until recently.

It helps to understand that this confusion has arisen partly because of timing. Two very popular techniques have recently arrived on the craft scene in the United States: *fulled knitting* (knitting something and then shrinking it in the washing machine) and *needle felting* (poking loose wool fibers with a barbed needle to mat them into a shape). Although both techniques were developed far more recently than true feltmaking, the fulled knitting in particular has come to be called felting because there was no common term in usage.

So what is "true feltmaking"? Felt is defined as a nonwoven cloth that has been pressed or matted together without any internal structure (stitches or weave). Feltmaking (also called wet felting or traditional felting) is an ancient process that involves these actions:

- beginning with a pile of loose wool fibers
- adding a little soap and water
- pressing the fibers until they hold together as a cloth
- vigorously working the cloth to shrink and strengthen it

FELTING DEFINED

Fulled knitting: The process of knitting something with wool yarn, usually with large, open stitches, then shrinking it by throwing it into the washing machine. This process, commonly called felting, is actually fulling. It's based on the same idea that has been used for centuries by weavers: slightly shrinking and tightening premade cloth to improve its insulating quality.

Feltmaking: The ancient process of beginning with loose wool fibers, adding water (and, more recently, soap), then pressing the fibers together, followed by a more vigorous working of the cloth to shrink and strengthen it. Also known as traditional felting or wet felting.

Felting: A word that can mean either fulled knitting or the ancient feltmaking process.

Needle felting: A process in which sharp, barbed needles are poked down through loose fibers, entangling them into a dense mat. Initially used in industry to create padding and factory felts, the process has been adapted by crafters, doll makers, and other fiber artists surface embellishment, "painting" with wool, and for sculpting felted figures. Also called dry felting. (*See pages 16–17.*)

Nuno felting: A technique, named by Polly Stirling in the mid-1990s, that involves felting loose wool fibers into cloth, usually silk. The fibers travel through the weave of the cloth and entangle on the back side; as the fibers shrink, a strongly textured felt/fabric hybrid is generated. Europeans first developed something similar, called laminated felting, in the 1980s.

Cobweb felting: A technique in feltmaking in which very small amounts of fiber are used to create an extremely sheer felt that contains holes as a textural effect.

Carved felt: A technique of carving away layers from a thick, durable felt, usually to expose multicolored wool layers within the felt.

Yarn felts: Felted fabric made with preexisting wool yarns, sometimes with small amounts of wool *roving*. These include lattice or *grid felts* (crisscrossing yarns in a grid) and *free lace* (laying the yarn in a freestyle pattern).

Fulled knitting

Feltmaking

Needle felting

Nuno felting

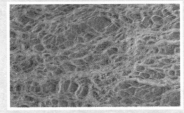

Cobweb felting

Carved felt

Yarn felts

This process dates back to the Iron Age and has been practiced by cultures all over the world. Some areas such as Mongolia, central Asia, Turkey, and Scandinavia have feltmaking histories that have been uninterrupted for centuries. For this reason, the process is understood by their general populations. But the United States is a relatively young country with no feltmaking tradition, so it is not familiar to most Americans.

Ancient Roots

Felting is an ancient process, and many people connect strongly to this aspect. There is something quite powerful about taking one's place in the long line of feltmakers down through the centuries, especially when that ancient process is one that occurred across such vast regions of our planet.

We can never know exactly where and how felting began, but legend has it that a human ancestor once packed wool into his sandals for comfort. The presence of moisture (rain, puddles, sweat) and miles of walking naturally produced a kind of felt. Whether or not this is true, once the herding of sheep and other wool-bearing animals became common, there were numerous opportunities to notice how wool mats together when the fibers are warm and damp. The kind and quality of

This madder-dyed, felted saddle from the interior mountains of Turkey is like others made in the eighteenth century.

felt, as well as which felted objects were made, depended on what animals were being raised and the needs of the people. In many ways, feltmaking became integral to human survival. In cold northern climates, felt provided warmth, while in hotter regions, thick felts insulated people from heat and wind.

Felted fabric is thought to predate woven or spun fabric. Among the oldest examples of felt are 3,500-year-old hats found in Scandinavia. A felted saddle, other horse adornments, and a felt swan from the Bronze Age (1400 to 500 BC) were found in the Pazyryk tombs in the Altai Mountains of northern Siberia. Around 1000 BC, a nomadic people known as the Scythians traveled in groups or tribes across vast distances of Eurasia by horseback. They ranged from Germany

and Italy in eastern Europe all the way across central Asia to far eastern Mongolia, taking their feltmaking with them.

Asian Countries

Today, regions in Mongolia, Kyrgyzstan, and Turkey are recognized as having a long, uninterrupted history of feltmaking. Although most of us have never visited these remote countries, we have heard of the gers, or yurts, made there. These round, tentlike, traditional dwellings consist of a collapsible wooden frame covered with sturdy felt. In some regions, the yurt is fitted with a brightly colored

red door. Both men and women are feltmakers in these areas, although farther west in Turkey, primarily the men make the traditional felted carpets.

In the 1990s, an interesting trend began. Teachers and volunteers from abroad started traveling into the small villages of these countries to help the people preserve some of their ancient techniques, at the same time creating a sustainable local economy for their families and villages. Ironically, this often means that modern-day feltmakers, dyers, and weavers are teaching natives modern applications of ancient techniques.

Scandinavia

The countries of Scandinavia also have a long history of feltmaking. While nomadic Asian peoples are known for their large, flat pieces of felt, such as carpets and yurt coverings, Scandinavians have a tradition of making three-dimensional clothing shaped to fit the body. Thick felted boots, hats, and mittens provide protection against a long, cold winter. Finland, Norway, and other Scandinavian countries are now among those leading the way in modern feltmaking techniques and design.

From left to right: Kazakh falconer's mitt and hide-soled boots; mohair sikke hat made by Mehmet Girgic (see page 125); Bhutanese rain hat made from yak hair. (Photos on these pages are courtesy of Beth Beede, from her collection.)

Kazakh children display a felted rug made in the local tradition.

A variety of breeds, such as this Shetland sheep, can often be seen at regional county fairs.

Europe and England

Without attempting a comprehensive history of feltmaking in Europe and England, it is at least interesting to note the once-popular felted beaver hat. Dating back to the fourteenth century, these hats were produced from felted beaver fur everywhere from England to Holland to Spain. When European beaver populations were exhausted, the beaver pelts were imported from North America. Rabbit fur also became a popular source material for hats, with the majority of rabbit fur produced in Belgium. Feltmaking continues in Europe and the British Isles, with Hungary hosting international gatherings for feltmakers for the past 25 years.

Australia and New Zealand

Like the United States, Australia and New Zealand are relatively newly formed countries. Although their felting tradition is more recent, both countries boast talented feltmakers. This would appear to be a natural outgrowth of the well-supported national sheep industry in these countries.

Sheep arrived in 1788 with the first English settlement sent to Australia. The climate proved to be ideal for raising them, and by 1838, a flock of Merino sheep — widely known then as Spanish sheep — had landed in South Australia. Initially, the sheep were raised for their meat, but today Australia produces most of the world's fine Merino wool. Merino is the most popular wool for modern feltmaking because it is soft and felts quickly.

The United States

Feltmaking began in the United States sometime in the 1970s, at a time when soft sculpture and macramé were popular. Early fiber artists and craftspeople often made soft, textural felt that was incorporated into mixed-media artwork. For years, feltmaking was mostly something people briefly explored, much like tie-dye. As feltmakers began to work in greater numbers, they eventually helped to define felt as a separate medium unto itself.

In the past 10 to 15 years, the medium has exploded in popularity as American felters catch on to this fabulous goldmine of creative opportunity. What could be better than a material that not only lends itself to a quick afternoon of play, but can also offer a lifetime of professional study?

Most people are truly shocked when they realize how sheer and light and drapable felted clothing can be or how texturally interesting, artful, and colorful

felt is. We've simply had no precedent for anything like it. When this delightful surprise is coupled with the fact that felt is made from a natural, sustainable material that is both gentle on the earth and of a familiar softness and feel from our childhood, it is very easy to understand the immediate appeal.

Although American feltmakers are still learning volumes from our European, Australian, Turkish, and Asian counterparts, American feltmaking is poised to truly take off in the next couple of decades. No doubt this will forever change the common perception of felt as a stiff, scratchy, man-made fabric found in a craft store. The sheep have been patiently waiting for their chance to show us what they're made of!

Creative Freedom

When you make felt for the first time, it seems like some sort of magic has happened right before your eyes. When you make felt for the fiftieth time, it still feels like magic. And when you make felt for the five-hundredth time, its magic seems even more powerful because you know that this is no fluke, that you are involved in a dance, a dialogue. Although you can guide the process, it will still ultimately

result in something beyond your control — something brand new that is both random and predictable. This fabulous duality is the essence of making felt.

Most people find that feltmaking is very freeing. You really can't make a mistake — potential errors are easily transformed into successes. Without a doubt, this is one of the secrets of why feltmaking is so appealing. While it is possible to become very precise by measuring shrinkage rates, aligning the wool fiber in particular ways, and so forth, you don't need to know any of those things to participate fully in the process. Quilters, knitters, and weavers especially seem to enjoy the free-form aspect of feltmaking as a welcome break from the precision of pattern design and counting stitches.

Feltmaking allows you to find your own way through the creative process. Because there are so many ways to reach the same result, it's very easy to experiment on your own. In fact, you probably already have all of the equipment sitting around your house that you need to get started. Feltmakers are famous for discovering their own "perfect little tool" — for instance, a corrugated plastic lid, old pantyhose, or a cat litter mat. No doubt you will soon be eyeing the things around your house in a different way.

How Does It Work?

Felt is alive, and every wool speaks a slightly different language. This may sound daunting because there are hundreds of types of wool, not to mention other animal fibers. But there is one simple key to unlocking the language: Hold still and listen. In feltmaking, *listen* usually means *feel*. Experienced felters understand this, and beginners, with practice, soon understand that hands and fingers will know what to do.

Many types of animal fibers will felt. (*See the box on the facing page.*) In the broader definition of felt as "a sheet of matted or fused material," even things like plant material and man-made fibers might be included. Traditional feltmakers work with wool partly because it is and always has been readily available in many parts of the world. But it also happens that, of all the animal fibers, sheep's wool

is particularly well suited for *entangling*, due to the overlapping scales on the surface of the fibers. Many types of fibers have overlapping scales, but it is the well-developed (even exaggerated) texture of wool scales that makes it felt. It helps to understand how fibers move around on a microscopic scale, since those movements often hold the key to why different wools behave in different ways.

Imagine a box of pinecones with tightly closed scales. If you shake the box, the cones will jiggle around and bump into each other, but not much else will happen. If you try this with a box of fully opened cones, however, at least some of them will begin to clump together. Sitting alone, each cone's scales open in the same direction. But as they move around in space, they come into contact from all different angles and begin to tangle. With wool, the process is much more dynamic because the fibers are not dead, static strings but lively little "worms" with an energy all their own.

Specifically, wool fibers have an internal, elastic core surrounded by a sort of outer cortex. During the feltmaking process, the outer part of the fiber softens in response to warm, soapy water and also to the heat from the friction of fiber-to-fiber contacts. This softening allows the whole fiber to behave more dynamically as it moves, releasing some of its stored

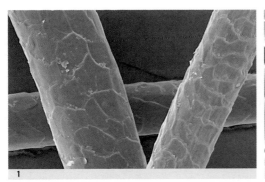

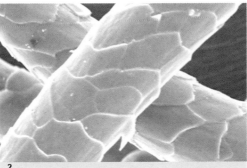

1. This magnified photo of unfelted wool shows the scale structure of the fibers.

2. When wet, the scales on the fibers open up, causing the fibers to lock onto each other. (Photos courtesy of Electron Microprobe/SEM Facility, Dept. of Geosciences, Univ. of Massachusetts.)

Fibers That Will Felt

(Other Than Sheep's Wool)

camel	Short fiber. Can be slow to felt; often mixed with silk or wool fibers. Baby camel hair is the softest.
llama	Excellent felter; choose low *guard hair* content for least shedding. Readily available from local farms.
alpaca	Same as above. Both alpaca and llama fibers are somewhat slippery to work with, so they are sometimes mixed with wool fiber.
mohair goat	Good felter. Very fast as an embellishment because the long fibers attach to other wool and to each other quickly.
Cashmere goat	Very good felter; very fine and soft. The most expensive of the luxury fibers, so it's often mixed with silk or other fine-quality wools.
yak	Downy *undercoat* that felts well. Tail fiber is like horsehair and can be used as embellishment.
Angora rabbit	Makes a lovely, strong, and very soft felt, but too many guard hairs will result in shedding. Expensive, so often mixed with fine wools.
beaver	Once prized for making hats, the soft undercoat felts into a dense, durable, waterproof felt with a silky sheen. Rarely used today.
dog	The hair of some breeds felts better than others. Sometimes felts faster in a lower pH, so skip the soap (or add a little vinegar) when experimenting.
cat	Very slippery with a tendency to shed. Best when "trapped" in a soft wool mixture with fine (small-diameter) wools.
human hair	Dreadlocks!

Two Stages of Feltmaking

Although feltmaking is one continuous process, there are two distinct stages. In each, the wool behaves in a unique way. The first of the two is called, a little confusingly, the felting stage. The second is the fulling stage.

Felting

Simply stated, the felting stage is the beginning of the process, when you lay down fiber, saturate the pile with water, and press the fibers into contact with each other. They begin to entangle with each other, but they do not completely lock down. At the end of this stage, the fibers become a sort of infant felt, still fragile and easily pulled apart. Felt at this stage is called *prefelt*. Although the original loose pile of fiber has flattened, the dimensions are about the same — no shrinkage has occured yet.

Normally, you proceed to the next stage of feltmaking (fulling). Otherwise, the prefelt dries to a fluffy felt that is not strong enough to function as fabric on its own but is nonetheless quite valuable to feltmakers. This prefelt material, when cut into strips and shapes and added to other projects, can be used to embellish your work. You can never have too

elastic energy; this results in increased tangling.

When moving through a pile of wool, fibers will migrate toward their root end, because this is the direction of least resistance against the scales. Once they migrate around the pile and begin to entangle, they can't move backward — at least not very easily. But although they are trapped, the fibers are still somewhat elastic.

Once the fibers start holding together, many beginning felters will stop felting. To the naked eye, the felt looks coherent. But experienced hands can feel the trapped air pockets and elasticity still present in the fibers. Depending on the felt's intended use, this might be fine. For a more durable felt that will not stretch, however, it is necessary to keep working the felt to further the process.

many prefelts. They are fabulously fun to layer over each other and with other loose wool to create endless color combinations. Prefelts are like gold to feltmakers, and it's often a sad truth that — when you're right in the middle of creating the perfect design — whatever color or thickness of prefelt you need will not be in your stash. So the time you spend making prefelts is never wasted.

Newly available to feltmakers, factory-made prefelts dramatically speed up the wet felting process. They come in a limited selection of colors but will make routine projects go much faster. The most interesting prefelts are always the ones you create yourself, because no one can exactly duplicate your choice of colors and patterns. They take more time to make, but handmade prefelts will always add value to a piece of felted art or clothing. Your choice of which prefelts to use depends on your goals for a given project, as you'll see in chapter 4.

Fulling

At prefelt stage, the fibers have started to entangle but are not yet locked down tight. To make a piece of finished felt, you need to continue on to the second stage: fulling. This process involves shrinking and strengthening the fragile prefelt into a strong, permanent felt. As the fibers lock down, air pockets collapse and the felt fabric becomes denser as it becomes smaller.

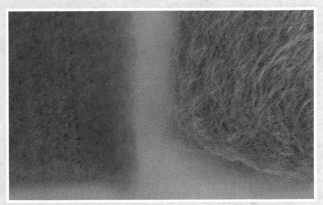

Needle-punched factory prefelt (left) has a more uniform appearance than handmade prefelt (right).

READY-MADE PREFELT

In Europe, where feltmaking is common, some mills have begun to recognize the demand for 100 percent wool products and are now producing colored prefelt sheets of varying thicknesses (weights). There are many benefits to using these "needle-punched" factory prefelts, and each weight serves a different purpose.

- Sheer, lightweight prefelts are great for embellishing fine felts and nuno where the goal is to keep the end product light.
- Medium and heavy weights are better for thicker projects like blankets, clothing, and home decor items.

The time savings is tremendous, and factory prefelts make it very easy for anyone to quickly make nice-looking felt with an even thickness.

During needle (dry) felting, fulling is accomplished by physically poking the fibers with needles to ensnare them more and more tightly. During traditional (wet) feltmaking, the felt is rolled, dropped, scrunched up, kneaded — sometimes even thrown and beaten! The extent of physical exertion one undertakes during fulling depends on the kind of felt being produced. The harsher punishments like throwing and beating are used only in special cases at the very end of the felt-making process. The truth is that wool will respond to your touch, no matter how light. This is the key to understanding fulling. Your hands have a tremendous amount of power over the fibers — everywhere you touch the wool, it will full a little more there than elsewhere.

Slow rolling produces a consistent high quality in felts composed of more than one layer. This is because the different layers have time to meet and entangle evenly inside the wool pile. However, nuno felts are made with only one layer of wool, so kneading and tossing them is an appropriate way to full them. Each case is unique. Whatever the method, the goal of all fulling is to create a stable felt that shrinks evenly in all directions.

❝ *Fulling Magic*

For those of you who dread the fulling process, I'll let you in on a little secret: Fulling is where the wools really give up their secrets. You can never predict exactly how a wool will speak, and this is the great challenge of becoming one with your medium — even if it's for a single afternoon.

When I'm felting alone, especially with a new wool, I enjoy a kind of meditation when I get to the fulling process. Fulling is a conversation between you and the wool. Close your eyes as you feel different sections of the wool with your fingertips, palms, and thumbs. Keep your mind open but out of the way. You may be using the same wool used by thousands of other felters, but it is a new conversation each time, and this one is all yours.

Many beginners — and even some experienced felters — consider fulling to be the most grueling, physically exhausting, boring, and downright painful part of feltmaking. If you've never been shown how to watch the wool for the right clues, or how to stand the correct way, or how to properly use your tools, then fulling will be much harder than it needs to be. But the mythical difficulties of fulling are easily dispelled by a little advice about the proper posture (*see page* 39), and the right approach to the wool.

Fleece to Felt

Some felters take a special pride in felting wool from sheep they have raised themselves. Regardless of whether you felt with commercially prepared wool or your own local "whole-grain" *fleece*, it's interesting to learn a little about the journey wool has made.

It all begins, of course, on the sheep. Shepherds who raise animals for fiber are aware of the extra care needed to protect the sheep's woolly fur, called fleece, from gathering too much vegetation as it grows. They will often cover their animals with coats made of light canvas, knit jersey, or other material. Raising healthy, disease-free animals on the proper diet creates superior, strong fleece. Each breed of sheep grows a unique type of fleece. (*See pages* 94–96.)

Shearing the Sheep

Depending on the animal and the breed, sheep are sheared one or more times each year by a specially trained sheepshearer. Prior to the shearing, the fleece is often quite dirty. Some sheep raised for meat tend to have spongy fleece that is the same length all over the sheep. Many fiber sheep tend to look more like beasts with individual curls, also called *staples* or *locks,* hanging down. Often the wool is of varying lengths on different parts of the body. Individual locks that are washed, but still intact and not brushed out, are valuable. They are used for embellishments and sometimes dyed for doll hair.

Cleaning the Fleece

Once the fleece is sheared, *skirting* takes place to remove any undesirable parts. Then the fleece is washed to remove dirt and *lanolin,* a grease secreted by the sheep's glands. Natural fleeces that first appear to be dark beige will often become brilliant white when washed. The amount of dirt that is washed away is often very surprising — in some cases up to 40 percent of the total weight of the fleece. This depends on the breed; for instance, Merino sheep have fine wool that is tightly packed and contains quite a bit of grease, whereas Romney sheep

These fleeces, top to bottom, are from the following breeds: Leicester Longwool, Karakul, Columbia, and Norwegian Pelsull (Götland type).

have a more open fleece that is coarser and contains far less grease. What's left after skirting and cleaning is referred to as the *yield* of a particular fleece.

Although it isn't absolutely necessary to research information about sheep breeds, the more you learn about the fleece you're using, the better you will ultimately understand how the fibers behave in your felt. And it's great fun talking with shepherds and learning how very different sheep breeds can be. One of the best ways to do this is to visit your local county or state fair and wander into the animal pen area. Most people are more than happy to point out the virtues of their particular breed, and they're often interested in your experience felting the wool, too.

Processing the Wool

Once the wool is washed, the staples are *picked* to open them up (like brushing out a curl). The wool is then usually brushed or *carded* into an evenly distributed sheet of wool (called a *batt*) or into a rope of fiber (called *sliver* or *roving*). These options are known as the *wool preparations*. Large amounts of fleece are processed at mills, but fiber enthusiasts also like to do this preparation on their own using *hand cards* or a *drum carder*. (*See page* 34.)

In a processing mill, wool is fed onto a series of different-sized drums. Each drum is covered with metal teeth that brush the fibers into a thin, continuous sheet of wool. If the wool is taken off the machine at this stage, the thin layers are stacked to make batts, which are like puffy blankets. This thin batting sheet is later gathered into a tighter rope form if it is to be made into roving or is earmarked to be spun. If the latter is the case, the roving is *drawn* (thinned out) and spun into *singles*. These singles are then *plied* together to become yarns. Roving is much more commonly available, because most hand spinners prefer this type of preparation.

Commercial roving is also known as *combed top,* meaning the roving has been combed, leaving fibers of equal length. Combing stretches the fibers, removing their *crimp* (natural waviness), which is why commercial top seems longer than natural wool fibers from the same breed. Spinners love the extra length for processing roving into strong yarns. Feltmakers usually prefer batts because the wool is much faster to lay out. Also, the fibers are more randomized, as opposed to the perfectly straight, combed roving. The random orientation helps the fibers entangle better right from the beginning.

Nonetheless, commercial Merino wool roving is the most common wool used by U.S. feltmakers, primarily because it felts very quickly and is readily available in many colors. Batts of many types of wool are available online, but request a sample first to evaluate the cleanliness and quality of the fiber. Although they are harder

Airy batt fibers (left) are more randomized than roving fibers (right), which have been uniformly combed.

Orientation of batt fibers (top) versus roving fibers (bottom).

to find, you might come across short-fiber batts. They're made from wool that has been purposely cut up into smaller pieces before it's carded out into batts. This preparation results an extremely fast-felting wool that seems to almost melt together with very little work. The downside is that the finished felt can pill more easily.

In many spinning mills, the wool arrives washed and dyed, and the process begins with picking. There are a number of small, family-run processing mills throughout the country that support the fiber community. (*See* Resources.)

Many people who raise a few animals or buy select fleeces at a fair will send out the fleece to be made into clean batts or roving. This type of mill also has the advantage of returning the fleece in its natural state of crimp, since the fibers are not chemically altered during cleaning. This is desirable for a feltmaker who likes to retain the material nature of the fiber as she's working.

What about Dyes?

Wool is a protein fiber and is best dyed with acid dyes. Often misunderstood as a complicated or dangerous process, dyeing with acid dyes simply means that the dye molecules adhere in an acidic environment, often with the addition of a little vinegar or other acidic substance. Protein fibers are the opposite of plant fibers, such as cotton and linen, which break down in an acidic solution and respond best to dyes with a higher pH. There are many types of dyes, and some can be used on all fibers. (*See* Resources.)

When purchasing wool that has been dyed, wet it to see if the colors run. A small amount of color run will occur with hand-dyed wool, and unless you are felting something with regions of pure white wool that may stain, it won't hurt anything if some dye comes out during the felting process. But dyed wool that continues to bleed strongly is a sign of amateur preparation.

Just for Fun

If you want to test out what needle felting is like, try making a simple felted ball. These make great Christmas ornaments or cat toys — or make them smaller for beads or earrings.

What You Need

- one 38-gauge felting needle
- a piece of flat upholstery foam about 1" thick
- about 1 oz. of carded wool fiber, primarily one color with bits of contrasting color for decoration

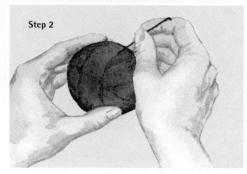

Step 2

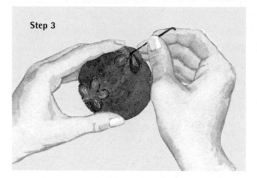

Step 3

What You Do

1. Work with a strip of wool (in your primary color) about 1" to 2" wide and 14" long. Lay it down on the foam pad and roll up the end of the strip lengthwise until you have a small tube about ½" wide. Fold in the ends of the tube to create a rounded shape. Continue rolling and folding in the loose ends to keep the round shape. When the ball is about 1" wide, start wrapping the wool around the center at an angle, as though you were winding a ball of yarn. For a nice, smooth surface, roll the wool tightly and avoid twisting the fiber.

2. When the wool bundle is the size you like, needle gently all over it to secure the fibers on the surface. When the ball is holding together well, you can add additional strips of wool to the surface to make the ball bigger. Needle each additional layer to the ball.

3. Add surface design by needling bits of contrasting colored fiber to the surface of the ball. Lay the wool in any pattern you desire. In the example shown, petals have been shaped from short wisps of wool. Contrasting colored fiber can be added in the center, as well as leaves or other elements.

4. If you want the balls to be very smooth and firm, wet felt them by dipping them in a bowl of hot, soapy water. Gently massage the balls in your hands until they are firm. Otherwise, simply needle felt all over until the surface of the ball is evenly covered.

Sharon Costello

Sharon Costello is an accomplished fiber artist with years of primary experience in hand-spinning, weaving, and knitting. While raising her own sheep, she became fascinated with feltmaking and began to explore many different felting techniques. Since then, through classes and instructional videos, Sharon has taught people of all ages across the United States and beyond, spreading the word about the magic of working with wool. Sharon is best known in the felting world for her vessels and needle-felted figures.

In addition to creating art and teaching, Sharon is also a natural-born organizer who brought hundreds of felters together in the first nationwide feltmaking conference in America. The "Felters' Fling" is held in Williamsburg, Massachusetts, every two years. For more information on what Sharon is up to these days, visit her Web site. (*See* Resources.) To learn a bit more about needle felting, try the sample project Just for Fun, directions and pointers compliments of Sharon.

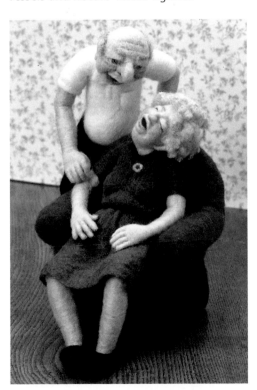

NEEDLE-FELTING POINTERS

- Felting needles come in many styles that differ in gauge, cross sections, lengths, notch (or barb) depths, spacing, and metals. Gauge numbers are similar to those of sewing needles — the bigger the number, the finer the needle.

- Felting needles work better with fiber that has been washed and loosely carded into batts or roving. Avoid using combed top or fiber from extremely fine breeds. Medium to coarse wool batting is the best choice.

- **Warning!** While needle felting is simple and fun, felting needles are very sharp! They are not appropriate tools for young children. Neither felting needles nor wool fiber is sterile, so wash your hands if you prick yourself, and do not share felting needles with others.

Sharon loves "to explore the relationships of two people interacting with each other in everyday life." *Afternoon Nap*, New Zealand Romney and Merino wools, needle felting and wet felting. Each figure is about 15" high.

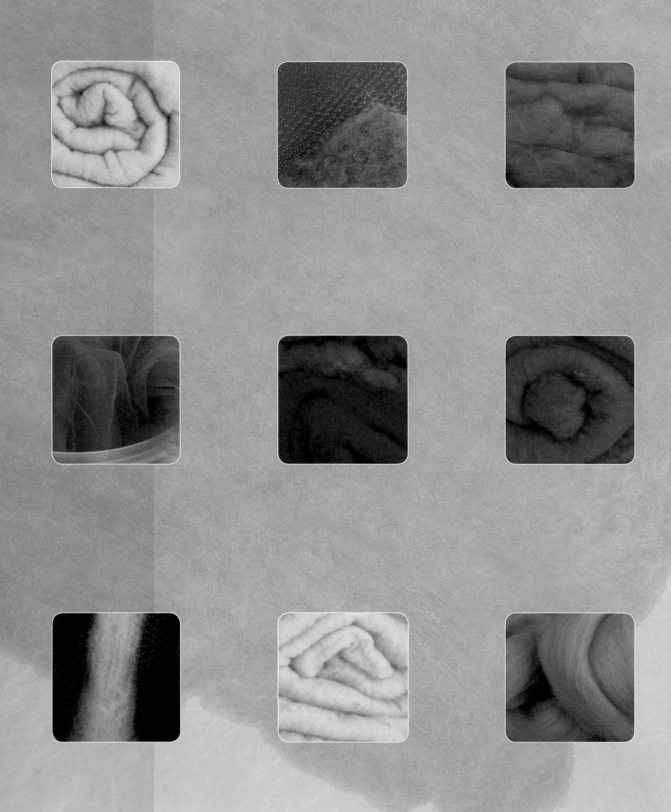

Collecting the Tools

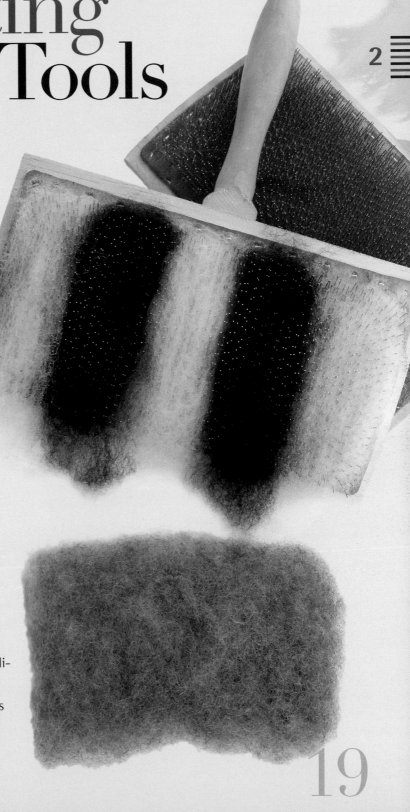

2

Your collection of felting equipment can be as spartan or as elaborate as you wish. You actually need only wool, water, and a small amount of soap to make felt — and even the soap is optional in certain situations. But most felters enjoy building a collection of tools over time as they gain experience and discover various techniques.

Feltmaking is a very broad medium. You can make everything from thin garments to thick, sturdy rugs; from three-dimensional bags and hats to outdoor sculptures. It should come as no surprise that certain tools will better serve you in one technique than they will in another. Yet, because people often learn one felting technique at a time, there seems to be confusion when comparing methods and tools used by different felting teachers. This variety is simply a result of the breadth of possibilities within the feltmaking process.

Some of the most common questions people ask are about procedures: Which

GATHER YOUR GEAR

You'll develop your own specialized list, but for now here are the basic felting supplies:

- a rolling mat (a piece of solar pool cover, bubble wrap with the smaller bubbles, or a bamboo mat) large enough to accommodate your project

- fine tulle netting (or mosquito netting) slightly larger than the rolling mat

- a working sheet of 4 mil plastic slightly smaller than the rolling mat

- a few small sponges

- a towel

- a nonbreakable container (a ½-gallon thermos, a plastic food storage container, or a small dishpan) one-quarter filled with warm, soapy water

- a second nonbreakable container to hold waste water or to carry saturated felts to the sink

- a ½-cup measuring cup

- a rolling bar (a foam pool noodle, a piece of corrugated plastic plumbing pipe, a wooden dowel, or even a saturated rolled-up towel)

- elastic ties (cut-up strips of spandex cloth) or large rubber bands

- a black waterproof marker

- a measuring tape

- a calculator

- a scale that measures ounces

soap is best? Why do you use a bamboo mat instead of bubble wrap? What's the difference between a polyester curtain covering and tulle netting? Shouldn't the water be hotter to felt? The answer to all of these questions is ultimately the same: It depends on the situation.

If you are felting a light, drapable, luxurious scarf, you will felt only one layer or maybe two very, very thin layers of fine wool fibers. The situation is different if you are making a thick, sturdy rug from six layers of coarser wool fibers. In the first case, you are essentially felting a single plane of fiber; in the second case you are felting a large volume. As you might imagine, the fibers move and encounter each other differently in each case.

Felting a larger volume of wool requires more pressure to compress the fibers into contact with each other. Therefore, you would use a bamboo mat to distribute pressure evenly and give you more leverage across your thick pile of wool. Felting a thin, delicate layer of wool requires a light touch and tools that are nonabrasive. In this case, you would use a polyester curtain instead of the rougher tulle fabric appropriate for other projects.

The key to keeping everything clear in your mind is simple: Think about the fiber itself. What is happening at the various stages in the process, and what are you trying to accomplish? As you progress or skip around through the book, you'll easily see why the tools may change a bit with each application. It's not nearly as confusing as it may sound at first. The fact that all of these tools work is the key to your freedom, because with time, feltmakers discover they obtain faster or better results with certain tools compared to others. Only your own experimentation will tell you which tools you like best for the job at hand. A favorite pastime of felters is swapping stories about which tools they like and why. Whatever works best for you is the correct thing to use.

Soap

Soap serves a number of purposes during the feltmaking process. Most importantly, it swells the scales on fibers so they can entangle, but it also helps fibers migrate and allows your hands to move across the surface easily without disturbing it. For most types of felting, soap is used only during the first steps, but it can also act as a buffer against too much abrasion during later stages. You needn't use a lot of soap in feltmaking, unless you're making a thick, durable felt that requires extensive physical work during the fulling stage.

An easy way to picture how different fibers respond to soap is to imagine two people shampooing very different types of hair. One has very fine, wispy hair that falls straight and may be slightly greasy. This hair type lathers easily but can be weighted down if too much conditioner smothers the fine hair shafts. The other person has coarse, curly hair that is dry and somewhat rough. This type of hair takes more soap to lather and absorbs more conditioner because the individual hairs are larger and rougher. With this in mind, it's no surprise to learn that different wool fibers will respond in different ways to soap and water.

What Kind?

Each feltmaker has her own opinion about which soap is the best to use, whether it's olive oil, liquid, bar, flake, or goat's milk. The truth is that any soap will work — I once used shampoo at a craft fair demonstration — but certain soaps are definitely better in certain situations. Through experience, you will learn which different wools and combinations felt best in different types of soap.

Olive oil soap gel has been popular-

" Soap Facts

Soaps are like cheeses — some are hard, some are soft, some dissolve more easily than others. One of my all-around favorite felting soaps is a simple glycerin bar because it works in all of the various feltmaking techniques. I buy inexpensive, unscented bars at the dollar store and keep them on hand around the studio.

If you felt on a regular basis, it's difficult to beat olive oil soap. The types of fats that occur in olive oil soap are different than those in soaps made with palm kernel or coconut oils. As a result, olive oil soap never vigorously lathers like the others.

Although a lack of suds is usually a plus when felting, it is not ideal for teaching beginning classes, especially with children. If people can't see suds, many will keep adding more soap until they slow down the felting process by coating the fibers — rather like putting too much conditioner on your hair and forgetting to rinse it out.

fibers like Merino. When felting coarse, large-diameter fibers, a sudsy soap can be very effective in the wetting-out stages because it helps break the high surface tension that initially repels water.

A good, sudsy lather is also desirable during the later fulling stages of some types of hat-making and boot-making procedures. In these situations, the soap serves a different purpose — the lather acts as a protective barrier around the felt piece, preventing abrasion as you vigorously rub it on a washboard or with fulling tools.

It's a good idea to use liquid soaps when teaching children — a watermelon-scented variety is especially popular — but it's critical to remain in charge of the pump bottle. All pump-style liquid soaps work, but some are extremely thick and concentrated, so always start with a very tiny amount in the water.

If you teach or make felt anywhere outside your own studio or home, be aware that a water's *pH* can vary significantly depending on where you are. (*See* About the Chemistry, *page* 23.) If the felt seems to be taking a long time, yet

ized by felter Chad Alice Hagen (*see page* 87), whose recipe calls for dissolving grated bits of the bar soap in hot water. The result is a substance that is great for your skin, has a wonderful scent, and works especially well with fine wools like Merino. This soap is often preferred by production felters who make soft wearables. Commercial olive oil soap bars are milled, a process that makes the soap hard and silky, but you can make a softened gel from these bars as well. Many varieties of olive oil block soap are available, including Greek, Turkish, Spanish, and French, but you can also buy it closer to home at any health food store.

Experienced felters like the fact that olive oil won't create "whipped cream" like high-detergent soaps; therefore, they won't have to waste time when rinsing it out. A fluffy cloud of suds will slow down or stop the felting process by preventing the fibers from making contact. But this is usually only a problem with fine

SOAP GLUE

A concentrated solution of soap can be used at various steps to help seams and embellishments adhere better. Tiny dabs of it here and there can work wonders — it acts just like glue! To make it, add a few hearty squirts of liquid soap or olive oil soap gel to a small amount of water. Another option is to let a bar of glycerin soap sit in about ½ cup of water. The exact proportions aren't important, but it should feel slimy.

you're working with familiar and predictable wool, water pH is often the culprit. This problem is usually easily solved by adding more or less soap than usual, but it doesn't hurt to carry another type of soap with you as a backup, or even a small box of powdered water softener. Liquid dish soap is usually not a first choice because it is so concentrated, but try it if nothing else is working. A bottle of dishwashing soap sitting in the back of the classroom just might save the day.

How Much?

Some felters first saturate their wool with water only and then add soap later. Most, however, mix soap and water in a container and use that to wet out their wool. How much soap do you add to the water? If you make the same kind of felt in the same studio with the same wool and the same water on a regular basis, you will discover your own reliable recipe or ratio. In the absence of a set formula, however, it is useful to learn how to answer this question no matter what the soap or the water pH. Here are some pointers:

- Always add the soap to the water, not the other way around. You'll create less foam that way.
- Fill your container partway with warm water.
- With *dry* fingers, dip into the water and notice how it feels when you rub your fingers together.
- Stir in a few drops of liquid soap or lather bar soap under the water.

- Again with *dry* fingers, dip into the mixture and rub your fingers together. This time they should feel slightly slippery. If they don't, add a little more soap, but keep in mind that the feeling is a subtle one. Better to have less soap and add more later than to have too much and start over.
- While you're felting, keep a small dish with soap and water within easy reach. Whenever you need to add more soap, just dip your fingers into the bowl.

Keep in mind that you can always adjust things because there are no mistakes in feltmaking. It's better to err on the side of too little soap, but even if you accidentally create a pile of whipped mashed potato trails or a thick, gooey film across your felt, the worse thing that can happen is that the process simply stops. All you have to do is go get a tub of clear, warm water and sponge off the excess, rinsing the sponge with each wipe.

About the Chemistry

Soap is *alkaline* and has a high pH value relative to the wool fibers. Soaps range from a neutral pH of 7 to around 10, and wool is around 4 to 5. The farther away from this 4 to 5 pH range the conditions are, the more unstable the wool fiber becomes. As the pH of the wool rises, the alkalinity causes the scales on the wool to open and begin to swell, which promotes entanglement of fibers and is desirable to a point.

The optimum pH environment for felting is said to be somewhere around 9 to 10, but if the pH rises higher, the environment becomes too caustic for the fibers — they will swell and distort so much that the scales begin to break off. Wool will actually disintegrate and fall apart in pH values of about 12 or higher. Don't worry, with common soap you'll be fine; just keep in mind that there is a balance to be maintained between too much soap and too little.

This disintegration also takes place in an extremely acidic environment. A carrotting process was used in hat making, mostly in the 1700s. The purpose was to increase the *feltability* of individual fibers in fur felts, primarily beaver, but also rabbit and other fur fiber. Mercury salts and an oxidizing agent, like hydrogen peroxide, were combined with a very strong acid. This toxic concoction was applied to the tips of the fur fibers while still on the pelt. The acid solution broke down the protective keratin covering that surrounds the fiber and allowed the scales to swell open and roughen so they could tangle. The name "carroting" arises from the fact that the mercury solution turned the fibers a bright reddish orange. The toxicity of the process and its effect on the hat makers is the source of the phrase "mad as a hatter."

Because soap is harsh on wool, never leave the soap in your felt. After the fulling process, rinse your projects completely until you're certain that all of the soap is gone. Students often ask whether they should rinse in cold or hot water, and it doesn't much matter. If you've done your job and completely fulled the felt, it will not be shocked by a change in temperature at this late stage of the process. I usually suggest warm water because the soap dissolves more easily and just feels better on your pruned, tired hands.

The question often arises as to whether you should rinse out the soap if you're not finished with a project and must let it sit overnight or longer. Soap is never good for the wool, but if it's in an early, fragile state, you may do more harm by handling and rinsing the felt. Sometimes even the pressure of your hands squeezing out water will felt one area more than another area — it's no disaster, but you will want to avoid this if possible. If the felt will be sitting around for a week or more, fold it up in tulle netting and very gently rinse it.

If you want to highlight the smooth texture on a flat, unembellished felt — a sophisticated Merino/Tencel or Cashmere blend scarf, for example — you can give it a final acidic rinse to truly reset the alkaline pH inside the felt back to a proper acidic one. Some feltmakers feel there is a difference in the reflectivity and *sheen* on certain pieces when they do this. The sheen is a function of light reflecting off smooth fibers with their scales closed down, so you wouldn't expect to see much of an effect on rougher wools or less fulled projects. Here's how it's done:

- Try soaking any tightly fulled, fine-fibered felt in a small dishpan of lemon juice and water. You need only a capful or a teaspoon or two of juice in about a gallon of water. Vinegar is often used instead of lemon juice, but I don't like the smell of it. Either will work.
- You need to leave the felt sitting in the lemon juice or vinegar solution for only 5 to 10 minutes, but it won't hurt anything to let it stay in the dish-pan overnight if you forget about it.

Screens

Although some felters prefer not to use any type of protective screen, most use a netting of some sort. The netting serves the purpose of holding the fiber and any surface design (yarn, prefelt, or other embellishment) in place during the initial stages of felting. This is especially important when you are first saturating the fibers. Feltmakers who prefer not to use netting don't like the feeling of something between their hands and the wool, and people who make felted beads would have little need for netting.

Tulle Netting

Tulle netting can often be preferable, for several reasons. It provides not only a protective covering at different stages as you felt, but also the perfect amount of gentle friction that keeps the process moving along. This friction becomes very useful later, during fulling. It's best to use tulle fabric with smaller holes as opposed to large, scratchy holes. Tulle pieces that are well used become soft and provide even more precision — much like having finer grades of sandpaper at your disposal.

Tulle also makes a sturdy wrap or sling if you need to pick up the delicate felt for some reason. You can simply roll it up in the tulle, even when dripping wet, to carry it over to the sink or an out-of-the-way table. This is an important function, because you shouldn't pick up the felt by itself at this stage — it's too susceptible to stretching apart. The weight of the water and gravity can pull a newly constructed felt seam wide open if you're not careful.

Polyester Curtain

Polly Stirling, the American feltmaker who pioneered the nuno felting technique (*see page* 231), teaches students to use a polyester curtain, such as an inexpensive drapery sheer. This type of cover works

nonskid
rug mats

tulle

pool noodles

bamboo mats

beautifully for nuno felt. Even the finest tulle is a bit too rough for the nuno technique, which uses very small amounts of wool felted onto an existing fabric. Here you don't need the extra friction of the tulle to help move the fibers through a many-layered pile of fleece because there is only one layer and the felting process happens very fast.

Other Netting

Some felters use mosquito netting, window screening, or the slippery-shiny material in basketball and football jerseys. Any similar material you have lying around will probably do. Whichever material you choose, try to have a lot of it on hand. For flat felts, use a piece that is larger than the dimensions of the wet wool so the rough edges don't catch on your loose wool fibers. Aim for a piece that fits around your intended felt like a wide picture frame.

Rolling Mats

Now let's look at one of the most interesting pieces of felting equipment: what you will use to roll your felt. During the initial felting stage, rolling mats help to distribute both water and soap throughout the fiber pile, saturating everything and pushing the fibers into contact. During the fulling stage, rolling mats continue to act

as a protective layer around the developing felt, but they also set the boundary conditions for the *fiber dynamics* (how the fibers move and interact).

It helps to know that fulling is what determines the strength and consistency of your felt. Whether or not a piece of felt sags out of shape with time, puffs up, or remains rock hard is all a result of what happens during the fulling process, so the equipment you choose is important. Almost any kind of mat or covering will work to make a piece of felt. But making good-quality, stable, consistent felt requires you to think about what materials you're going to wrap around the felt as you work it.

Think of it this way: The rolling mat is an extension of our hands. Our hands aren't large enough to cover all of the felt at once as we full it. The mat serves to distribute the energy of the rolling across all parts of the felt simultaneously. Of course, the fibers on the inside of the roll felt a little differently than the fibers on the outside, which is why you stop and reroll the felt upside down and in the opposite direction. Also there is a vertical component to the fulling that is important to consider when selecting your mat — you want something that will help you push down through all those layers.

For a large volume of wool with many layers, you need a mat that will provide a strong framework around your fiber. A sturdy, heavy bamboo mat or slatted wooden mat will work with you as you press down through the layers, distributing your energy along the entire dimensions of the pile. But if you need a protective covering for the first part of a delicate type of felting, like cobweb felt, that same wooden mat would be overkill and too cumbersome. Serious felters are usually armed and ready with a good collection of mats in different sizes and of different materials.

Bamboo and Plastic Mats

Felting books often call for felters to use a bamboo mat, but sometimes people are confused as to exactly what is meant by that. Does it make a difference if the mat is truly bamboo or not? Should the shape of the slats be flat or matchstick? The bottom line is simple: All types will work. However, true bamboo is superior because of its resiliency and its ability to remain intact in a wet environment without rotting.

The smaller and rounder the individual bamboo pieces are, the smoother the rolling will be. Imagine yourself riding along on a large factory conveyor belt. Hundreds of small rolling cylinders would provide a smoother ride than bumping along on a few large ones. Small-diameter matchstick-style mats are even better than the larger flat-slatted, split-piece mats. Whatever mat you choose, make certain it is sewn well with many running threads holding the bamboo together. If not, your mat will be in pieces soon after your first couple of projects. Use the lightest material you can find that will still accomplish what you need. Experiment until you find something you like.

You can adapt bamboo window shades by removing the hardware and securing the loose strings so the bamboo slats don't fall out. Or you can try the felt-backed bamboo floor rugs popular in home decor, but they are tricky. Their polyester felt backing strongly wicks water away from the felt you are making, which can create unnecessary problems. Saturating the backing helps, but it's better to use something without any backing at all. In general, it's best to use a rolling mat that lets water drain out slowly through its cracks. This way the felt remains saturated, but excess water can be squeezed out as the process progresses.

We use a couple of different bamboo mats in the studio. The workhorse is a 4' by 6' light-colored mat with a white cheesecloth backing, bought at an imported goods store. The one we call "the Cadillac" is an 8' by 10' bamboo mat found in the basement of a store in the Chinatown district of New York City.

For large, one-time projects like murals, yurts, community felting, and working with a school or an entire classroom, the large, inexpensive plastic blinds sold at discount stores work nicely. You will still have to remove the hardware and secure the binding threads, but they're a great way to lay out a very large piece of felt and allow many people to participate at the same time.

Turkish master felter Mehmet Girgic uses very large, thick mats made from a type of woven rush that is native to his country. (*See page* 125.) The mats resemble thatched roof material and have a lot of rebound and resiliency. These are important qualities for traditional Turkish felters because their felt rugs begin as very large piles of wool; for instance, a finished 3½' by 4½' by ¾" felt rug begins as a volume of wool measuring 6' by 9' by 14"! The rebounding motion of the thick thatch helps to plunge a minimal amount of soap and water through the pile while providing a strong vertical motion during the long felting process. Another feature of the mat is a covering of tough canvas at one end that can be wrapped around the diameter of the large roll. This covering helps hands and feet to grip the slippery rush material when it's wet.

Bubble Wrap

First a clarification: Most felters say "bubble wrap" when they are really talking about a solar pool cover. Initially, some clever feltmaker discovered that the clear, plastic bubble wrap we use as packing material made a good rolling mat. But because it tends to capture and retain some of the soapy water and also breaks down with rigorous use, people soon began using a more permanent and sturdier kind of bubble wrap: the material in blue plastic solar blankets used to cover the surface of a pool. The bubbles on a pool cover don't break down as easily and the plastic is more rigid than packing material. The covers are recyclable, just like the real bubble wrap, as long as there is no chemical residue on the plastic.

Pool covers used to be expensive and only available from pool stores, but during the late spring months, you can find clearance prices at the discount chain stores. Sometimes you can buy them online. (*See* Resources.) You can usually get someone to donate his or her used cover, but be forewarned: When a request gets passed around by word of mouth, you may find yourself suddenly inundated with covers. Storage then becomes a problem, as even one cover is very large!

Why use bubble wrap instead of a mat? It's lightweight, inexpensive, and waterproof and works well for many types of felting. By using a sheet of plastic along with the bubble wrap, you can obtain even more versatility by fine-tuning how much the bubbles press onto the felt at different stages.

Nonskid Rug Mats

Some feltmakers like to roll their felt with the nonskid matting used beneath rugs. One advantage to these mats is that water runs through the hole patterning and doesn't pool inside the roll. All types are useful in their own way. The flat, lacy type (also sold as shelf liner) is the best choice for thin, felted garments. The puffy grid type works better for slightly thicker felts because the thicker pile of wool benefits from some vertical motion and will felt a little faster.

Other options include the patterned plastic mats from India, Turkey, and other countries that are used as seasonal outdoor patio floor rugs. These portable mats are also available from pet suppliers since they are commonly used in animal pens at dog shows.

Try anything you might already have that is similar. Remember, the key is to try different tools for different things from time to time. If you get stuck in the mindset of using only one kind of mat or tool, you may miss out on a chance to improve your feltmaking skills, especially when working with a new kind of felting technique.

Stair Treading

Stair treading is sold by the linear foot at home improvement stores and can be used to help full your felt later in the felting process. Small squares of it can be used alone as a fulling surface for small projects like cording or purse handles where you need to roll something rigorously against a rough surface to toughen and harden it. For making smaller felts, some felters lay a sheet of stair treading in the bottom of a wide, flat baking dish and use this setup as a portable felting station, since it also holds water. This becomes even more useful if you can locate a very broad, shallow pan like those used in commercial kitchens.

Rolling Bars

When you're ready to roll your felt, you'll want to wrap it snugly around some kind of rod or bar. The best all-around rolling bar I've found is a Styrofoam pool noodle, available seasonally in department stores. It's a good idea to have a couple of different diameters for different types of feltmaking. Different lengths are also useful to accommodate projects of different sizes. The noodles are good for the same reasons bubble wrap is useful — they provide a little give and have a bit of a rebound, which helps the fibers move in all directions.

Very smooth plastic tends to spin around in the roll, especially when rolled up with plastic sheeting. For this reason, the faceted variety of pool noodle works a little better than the type that is completely round. There is also a kind that is shaped like an asterisk; although it can sometimes be used late in the fulling process, it's not the best choice because not

enough of the noodle is in contact with the felt.

In general, larger-diameter rods are better for nuno felting because the felt does not have to fold over on itself as many times as it would with a smaller rod. In nuno felting, a small amount of fiber is carefully placed in a single layer or in a deliberate pattern onto preexisting fabric, so you must be careful not to disturb the arrangement by distorting it during rolling. In traditional feltmaking techniques, the whole fiber pile responds coherently as one volume instead of trying to peel apart, so a wider range of sizes can be used.

Larger objects make even better rolling bars for advanced garment projects in nuno felting. Look for a very large but hollow plastic pipe or cylinder to use for this purpose. You can create one by riveting two tall plastic trash cans together at their bases. This 2'-diameter rod allows you to wrap the fragile nuno garment only once or twice around the center, minimizing the disturbance of the sparse fibers. Let your imagination lead you to make the tool you need.

For smaller rods, try using a simple wooden dowel, a broom handle, or a length of PVC pipe. All of these will work, but the hard rods are better for fulling and finishing. It's the same as with a bamboo mat: You are able to apply a lot of pressure very evenly across your felt, which leaves a smooth, professional finish without any ripples. You might prefer to use two different rods at different stages of the process. The felt is accommodating and insists that *you* decide for yourself!

Other Options

You can also try things like dryer vent tubing, ribbed plastic plumbing pipe — anything you find that you think might serve your purpose. Glass washboards are useful for fulling thick felts in later stages of feltmaking, when your hands are feeling worn out. In general, an irregular surface (ribbing or treading) that is not too sharp will help move the process along.

Additional Equipment

As you develop your own style and techniques over time, you'll no doubt collect your own set of useful items. However, here are a few standard items you'll want to have on hand.

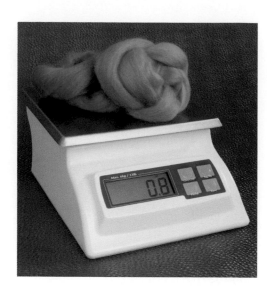

A Scale

You'll need some sort of weighing scale to keep track of how much fiber you're using. Most written projects will be based on using a certain number of grams or ounces of a given type or color of wool, and it's important to be accurate. It's also a good idea to weigh your wool and separate it into halves or quarters when you are making large projects or three-dimensional projects that have two sides and are later joined. This practice will help you keep the wool more evenly distributed throughout the layers and is also recommended for production feltmakers who produce a repeatable line of clothing or other products for which consistency is important.

Try to buy a scale that is accurate to tenths of an ounce (0.1 ounce) and converts between ounces and grams. The maximum weight the scale allows will vary, but you will generally not need to weigh amounts over 8 to 10 pounds unless you intend to create large artworks. Therefore, your best bet is a scale with a lower weight limit that has better accuracy measuring small amounts. If you can't find an appropriate scale locally, look online or on e-Bay for postal scales. Diet scales work if you don't need to be as accurate, but these scales generally show weight in fractions, which will not be as helpful as decimal-based scales.

Handling Water

Water is a primary ingredient in feltmaking, so you'll need a range of materials to help you manage it. Examples: a small container to hold your warm, soapy water as you felt and a larger container on hand for dumping out cold water and draining your project into from time to time.

Just about anything will do. Try a small plastic dishpan, small- to medium-sized buckets, an insulated plastic thermos (to keep water warm), or plastic food storage containers with high sides (to help control splashing). Keep a few old towels nearby and a couple of smaller table sponges to keep spills from becoming waterfalls onto your floor. A waterproof apron will also come in handy.

Marking and Cutting

Another standard part of feltmaking is measuring and drawing templates. Keep a ruler and calculator handy, as well as a pencil and sketchpad for calculations. Use a black, waterproof marker to outline the template on plastic, but test the marker first (write on the plastic and get it wet) to make sure it won't bleed onto your project and stain the wool during felting. Also, have a pair of small, sharp scissors on hand, in addition to a pair of regular-sized scissors.

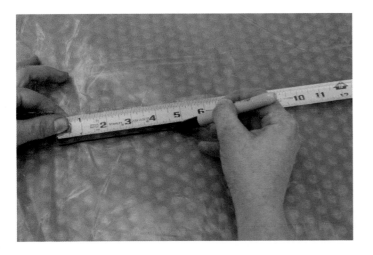

Plastic

The amount of plastic you use is up to you. Some feltmakers prefer not to use it at all, but because it can be wiped down and used over and over again for months, it's actually quite energy efficient compared to using natural cloths, which must be laundered.

The weight of plastic will depend on what you intend to make and how you set up your space, but begin with a roll of 2 mil plastic and a roll of 4 mil plastic. Heavy 6 mil weight is used by some felters as an underlayer to protect tables and other equipment, but it is generally too stiff to be used during the felting process itself. As a general rule:

- 1 mil and 2 mil are most typically used for nuno felting, cobweb felting, and making fine, thin garments with fine wools. This thin plastic is gentle enough not to disturb the arrangements of sparse fiber that are required with these types of felting. It can be used in conjunction with bubble wrap, as it will protect the felt initially yet is thin enough to let the bubbles begin their work of "massaging" the felt.
- If you want a very thin barrier (when rolling extremely small amounts of wool), use 1 mil plastic.
- 4 mil is a general working plastic, sturdy enough to be used as table covering and as plastic worksheets but still pliable enough to be useful as a resist and template material.

- When you need a lot of support around the wool pile, 4 mil plastic is a good choice. Three or four layers of batting will become rather heavy when wet and will sink down between the bubbles before the layers have a chance to hold together well. The heavier plastic prevents this.

- Whatever plastic you use, try to recycle it for as long as possible. Rinse the smaller pieces after use and find a convenient place to hang them to dry. If they are stacked when wet, they tend to trap moisture and begin to smell from mold.

Sewing Tools

Because you can make seamless fabric with felt, you may not need to sew a stitch. However, depending on the project, needle and thread could come in handy. You might need to occasionally baste some items in place before you felt them. A felting needle (the same kind that's used in needle felting) can also be used to tack things down. Embroidering designs or handsewing embellishments such as ribbons or beads on finished felt might also appeal to you, so stock a sewing basket accordingly. Lastly, keep an ironing board and steam iron on hand for finishing and shaping.

Specialty Tools

If you are interested in blending your own colors or making your own custom wool — for instance, adding some Alpaca wool to some locally raised Corriedale — a carding tool is highly recommended. Hand carders (*pictured on page* 19) work well for small-scale projects, or you might want to invest in a drum carder (*pictured below*).

Washboards can be used in the final stages of fulling on thick felts, but be careful. They will abrade the felt's surface if you "scrub" your project on them. Instead, try rolling your felt up and down the grooves. Glass washboards work particularly well but are sharper than they appear, so protect your fingers!

If you become interested in making shaped hats, slippers, or boots, you may want to invest in hat blocks or shoe forms. (*See* Resources.)

drum carder

A Space of Your Own

Feltmakers always seem to be discussing how they set up their felting space, and it's something beginners commonly ask about. It helps to talk to more experienced felters, who can tell you what to avoid when setting up your own space. No doubt you'll create something based partly on advice and partly on your own experience and creativity. Don't worry about planning it out too much in the beginning; you can adapt it as you go along.

To help get you started, there are some good pointers to keep in mind, regardless of the particulars of any given space. The most obvious thing is to think of the space in terms of the physical layout and the equipment you have. However, if you felt often over time, you will find that feltmaking is a physical process that can take a toll on your body. Although not as obvious, it's useful to think of your work space in terms of the least amount of stress and work for your body. Sometimes this layout becomes obvious only after you've worked a while in the space. But if you begin with this consideration in the back of your mind, you will be ahead of the game as you accumulate equipment and build the areas of your felting space.

As for stocking your workshop: Because of the different sizes and shapes of each project, the biggest variation in equipment is probably the size of your fulling roll, which might include a mat, bubble wrap, plastic, tulle, or polyester curtain. For example, you might need a long 2' by 8' strip of bubble wrap for one project (say, a table runner) and then need a 5' by 9' piece for a larger project. You might need tulle one time and a polyester curtain the next time.

Don't worry, we'll include a list of recommended materials for each project. You don't need fancy equipment, but you will need a few variations and sizes. You can gather the equipment for each project as you come to it, or you can purchase a 25' roll each of 2 mil and 4 mil plastic, about 12 yards of tulle, and a very large piece of bubble wrap (about 6' × 20'). Then you can cut different sizes as needed.

Designing a Studio

For the ideal studio, the essential ingredients are as follows:

Sink. A deep, industrial-sized work sink would be lovely, but it really doesn't matter as long as you have hot water and a sink basin large enough to rinse out your projects.

Felting table. You'll be spending a lot of time at the felting table, so it's worth taking the time to set it up properly. Since you'll be reaching forward a lot to work on your felt in the center of the table, a raised table is a must to save your back — unless you are short, in which case a standard height might be fine. This is something that will become clear as you work. If you start having back pain, it's time for an adjustment. Ideally, the table-top should be level with your hip bone.

Many felters use hard-topped, plastic office tables that fold up. Two 6' tables placed together along their length make a nice-sized felting table. You can raise them by cutting eight identical pieces of 1½" to 2" PVC pipe and slipping them onto the table legs. How long you cut them depends on your height, but a general recommendation would be to cut the pieces to 10" lengths and take care to make sure they are all the same. Other-wise, the table won't be level.

added PVC pipe

If the table is to be semipermanent, duct-tape the two tables together. It's also a good idea to form a protective bumper around the table, for the dual purpose of capturing water and soft-ening the table's edges (your hip bones will thank you). Using pool noodles (cut lengthwise) or presplit pipe insulation, duct-tape the padding along the edges of the table, then drape the table com-pletely in 6 mil plastic. Cover that with a large, table-sized piece of bubble wrap, or just use the size of bubble wrap you need, depending on the project.

Supply tables. Although it is very tempt-ing to fill every open space with fiber and other things, it helps to keep an extra, dry table nearby for setting aside and organizing your current working project. Especially if you are making two-sided or three-dimensional projects, you may need to lay one section aside and won't want to prematurely get it wet on the felting surface. You will probably also need another side table for laying out your active supplies while working. Here's where you would draw your templates, lay out your colors, and weigh the wool.

Other possibilities. Again, you will find your own way to create the space that works best for you, but here are some other ideas to get you thinking.

- Display your wool on shelves where you can see it all and where it will be exposed to light and activity in the room. This will help deter moths, a liability for every feltmaker.
- Some felters organize their wool by color; others by wool type. Open bins, plastic cubes, or storage tubs can be arranged on shelves. Wire shelving is also an option.
- At least one strong shelf unit is advisable for bigger equipment like steamers, sanders, and sprayers. Plastic wastebaskets or hampers are a good way to store pool noodles, smaller bamboo mats, and rolls of plastic.
- You may also want a special bin or area for your yarns and embellishments. For instance, you can keep yarn in baskets on a table. Another option is to slip hanks of yarns and specially dyed fabrics through the open-ended compartments in a plastic shoe storage bag, then hang it from a door, a long metal bar, or a closet rod. A rod also comes in handy for hanging yarns, garments-in-progress, and prefelt sheets clamped into pants hangers.
- Your floor doesn't *have* to be totally waterproof if you felt with small amounts of water, but if you can swing it, it's advisable. Rug making and working with larger felts and coarser wools sometimes result in more water in the studio. Use thick rubber mats and nonskid surfaces wherever possible.
- As in any art studio, light should be plentiful and as true as possible. Daylight bulbs show colors well but don't give out a lot of light. Fluorescent bulbs are available that have a strong output and show true colors even at night, so shop around.
- If you plan to teach, leave clear open pathways to the sink area, which will be used by everyone.

- When designing a felting studio, follow the triangle concept used in kitchen design. In kitchens, the counter/sink, stove, and refrigerator are laid out in a triangle, to support how you move through the space. This same triangle concept can be applied to setting up a felting studio, with the three points being your felting table, supply table, and sink.

INSECT ALERT

Clothes moths and carpet beetles are the two biggest threats to your wool stash, so you should know how to identify them and do your best to prevent them. With both insects, it's the larvae that do the damage, feeding on organic material including wool and anything made from wool. Holes are the problem in wool clothing, but in wool fleece, an additional concern is the presence of eggs scattered throughout the loose fiber.

If you see a moth that doesn't fly well and scurries away when exposed, get suspicious. If you see larvae or insect casings throughout a batch of wool, it's time to throw it out. Seal it in a plastic bag before removing it, to avoid spreading the infestation.

A good preventive measure is to store your wool in well-lighted and well-ventilated areas. Moths prefer dark, undisturbed areas of the wool, so it also helps to move the wool around frequently. Infestations are difficult to eliminate, but there is plenty of information online to guide you. Check your stash frequently.

Short on Space?

What if you really want to start felting but don't have an extra room? First of all, it's a misconception that you need a very big or very long table to felt. Many people learn to make long felt scarves in tiny city apartments with almost no counter space. Where there's a will, there's a way.

One approach is to scroll up bubble wrap on each side of the wool, unrolling just one side at a time as you work. You can lay out the wool in one pass, then work back the other way when you wet the wool. Reverse and scroll back the other way for the next step, and so on. It may not be possible to view your entire design at once, but you will learn the feltmaking process just as well as the person with a large table — and you'll be a more adaptable feltmaker because of your tough beginnings!

Whatever the size of your table surface, use heavy plastic and lots of towels. You don't need lots of water or soap to felt. Just wet things out slowly. As you'll learn, you start from the center and dribble small amounts of water on your felt, pressing the water into the wool as you move out toward the edges. You have total control over how much water you apply, and there's no need to have it spilling over your bubble wrap onto the table or floor. Until you get the hang of it, though, keep small sponges nearby and a bucket on the floor.

Posture

Proper posture is essential when felting. It is often difficult to remember when under the spell of the wool, but try to stop frequently to stretch. Find alternate ways to work parts of the project, if possible, so you can take a rest from standing. For instance, you can try rolling felt in bubble wrap with your feet.

Remember, the best felt is always made slowly, so don't be in too much of a hurry to hunch up and work hard with clenched shoulders and a determined jaw. Instead, think about how your body can become a smooth sequence of moving parts designed to move the felt in the way you desire. For example, instead of pushing down toward the table with your upper body as you roll your felt, move your arms into a fork-lift configuration, moving across the roll of felt, parallel to the table. The weight of your dedicated arms is all the felt asks for. Put your body in place properly and let gravity and grace do the rest.

The illustration on this page shows a way to position your body that will help eliminate the upper body stress. Not only that, you will actually be able to perform body stretches while fulling. This is great for anyone with back problems. I find that I can full for hours with no pain, despite having undergone a spinal fusion operation! If your body hurts, find another way.

Felting Machines

The popularity of commercial felting machines has exploded in the last year or so. "Should I buy a felting machine?" is now one of the most common questions people ask. Feltmakers have always designed homemade felting machines. Perhaps one of the first was the Mongolian camel! More recent versions are clever contraptions built by engineering-minded people, some of whom have written instructions on how to build your own. (*See* Resources.)

The main differences in using a machine have to do with speed, the tactile experience, and your intended interaction with the wool. A felting machine can really save some work and time, depending on what kind of felting you do. For instance:

- Production felters who make thin nuno felt find the rolling machines to be true time savers.
- Many small farms now use machines to quickly turn their own fleece into blankets and pads.
- Machines can be useful for anyone who creates mural-type work, especially with children.
- Some feltmakers claim that these machines save wear and tear on the body, such wear and tear may result from incorrect felting posture. (*See page* 39.)

Still, it all comes down to personal preference. Some professional feltmakers insist on working with their hands so they can respond directly to cues from the fiber as they full — cues that change with every piece of felt they make. But production felters, if they are to be successful, must closely manage their felting time. When making multiple pieces of one type of product, an intimate relationship with the wool is not as important.

Others prefer to use a machine for only a particular part of the process. The machines are currently very popular on small farms with folks who are looking for diverse ways to market their own animals' fiber. The results may not be superdurable felts that are well crafted, but they let us experience the animals and the small farm in a direct, organic way that is very appealing.

There are different types of felting machines available, but most are divided into two types: flatbed and rolling machines.

- Flatbed machines are often made by hand in someone's garage or basement and involve a large wooden board, door, or other type of horizontal plane that can be lowered with a pulley system. Feltmaker Larry Beede and others have also created smaller, lighter-weight, more portable models based on the same design.
- Rolling machines are the ones more commonly offered for sale. They work by nestling a wetted felt, rolled up in a mat or bubble wrap, between two long rollers. A third roller bar is cranked down onto the felt roll, holding the mat in place and applying slight pressure.

No doubt American felters will learn much in the next few years as our international communication grows so rapidly through the Internet. It will be very interesting to see how the machines and the feltmakers who use them evolve over the next few years.

rolling machine

FEATURED ARTIST
Pat Spark

American feltmaking owes much of its strong foundation to Patricia Spark of Albany, Oregon. Although she began as a tapestry weaver, she turned to feltmaking in 1975 and found that she could complete her artistic works in a shorter amount of time in her new medium. Because Pat has felted continuously since then, she is an invaluable source of information on all aspects of feltmaking in the United States, something that is perhaps unique. As an art professor for many years, she taught design and color theory, and she incorporates these concepts into her feltmaking workshops. In particular, her felted watercolor technique teaches students how to build a complex image on their felts.

Pat's list of accomplishments is a long one. While living in Sweden, she studied Scandinavian feltmaking and was responsible for bringing this three-dimensional seamless technique to the United States. (*See chapter* 6). She has lectured and met feltmakers from many countries and is truly a worldwide ambassador. In addition to monitoring the well-known Feltlist on the Internet, she publishes the North American Feltmakers Network newsletter three times a year and maintains the most extensive online database known about all things felt. (*See* Resources.) If you have a question about felt, simply ask Pat Spark.

Inspired by flowers in her garden, Pat felted prefelts onto a blended color background and then used needle felting to add detail. *Tulips 1*, Merino wool dyed with acid dyes, 26" × 26".

3

Beginner
Projects

I t's time to get your hands on some wool! This chapter contains some simple projects that let you get a feel for how wool changes into felt as you handle it. You can make these projects on their own, just for the experience, or make them with children. How you finish them depends on your goal. You can felt the whole thing to completion, whether it's a bamboo stick, cord, snake, or whatever else you want. Or, if you intend to felt some of the cords, rolls, and shapes onto something else later (for instance, a hat), you will leave one or both ends unfelted.

The cording projects are based on something like a jellyroll. If you bake, you know this refers to a flat layer of pastry topped with filling and then rolled up into a log-shaped form. As it turns out, this is also a very creative way to make colorful felt ornaments and accessories. Jellyrolls that are at least 1" or more in diameter can be sliced to make beads or buttons. This method of rolling the felt can be adapted to make felted cords, spikes, handles, and other things. The common thread for all of these variations is that the felt must be very hard in order for it to keep its shape when it dries. Also, the harder the felt roll, the longer it lasts when it's cut open (for buttons, for instance).

Once you know how to make cording, you can apply the technique in several ways. For instance, you can fashion cords and loops to use as fasteners on a bag or a garment. As you envision a new closure or fastener, it helps to play with a bit of thick yarn or rope first. You may even want to get a book on knots and duplicate them with felt cording. The fun part is realizing that you can create loops within the cord by splitting it into two strands that rejoin again farther down. In this way, it becomes possible to create felt chains or belts. Another option is to separate the

wool roving into many strands that hang free, like the arms of an octopus. This shape makes a fun attachment that can be felted onto hats, and it can also be an unusual and pretty way to tie a shawl or jacket closed. The possibilities are endless.

Felted closures, like loops, ties, and any frog-type closure, will usually be felted to a primary project later. You can plan for this by leaving one end of the felted cording dry, something called a *brush end*. (*See* Attaching Cords and Spikes *on page* 47.) If you won't be attaching a cord or closure, felt the cord all the way to the ends. If you decide later that you want to attach it, you can always sew it, thread it through a hole, or invent some other way to attach the cord.

Cords and fasteners are also wonderful things to make with children, who often take great pride in making the cords as hard as possible, especially when challenged. With younger children, get the cord started for them first and then let them roll it. Sometimes they'd rather just make a lot of cords in different colors, moving on to the next one while the first is still soft. No problem. These are never wasted; it's easy to come back later and felt them down hard, if you wish.

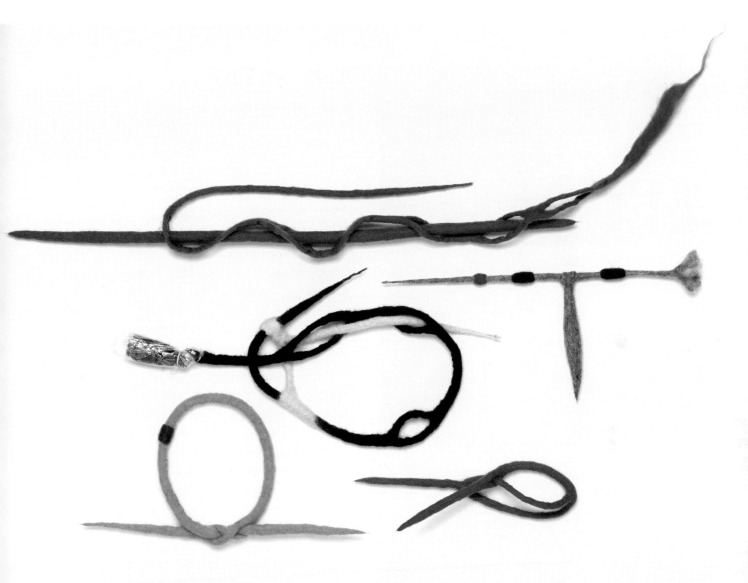

Cording

These first projects are a bit like a meditation. The process will yield something useful, but it's really more about being in the moment. It's such a simple thing to make a straight little woolen cord, but as you create it, notice how the wool feels in your hand and how it's changing every second. The first steps are the same for most of the cording projects; then, read on for the different things you can make from them. These projects require only a minimum of felting supplies, listed on the right.

What You Need

- a small bowl, one-quarter filled with warm, soapy water
- a towel
- a small square (10" × 10" or so) of black stair-treading material or a small bamboo sushi mat
- about 0.5 oz. of Merino wool roving (your choice of colors)

Step 1

Step 2

Step 3

Step 4

What You Do

1. Lay out the towel as a working surface. Tear off a piece of wool roving approximately 10" to 12" long.

2. Drag the piece of roving through the bowl. Wet out the wool completely and squeeze out the excess water as you go.

3. Without pressing, begin to roll the wet wool very lightly between your palms, the same way children make clay snakes. Gradually form a rounded, ropelike shape. Pressing too soon will cause cracks. The fibers need a little time to respond to the shape you are making.

4. Roll the wool more vigorously when you feel it stiffening, but stop often to stretch it back out. Alternating these actions will harden the felt. Roll the wool inside a sushi mat or against stair treading to make it rock hard. From here, continue with the variation of your choice.

Cord Variations

Thin Cording. If you want thin cording to outline the edges of garments or to make jewelry like necklaces or bracelets, simply use a little less wool by splitting a piece of roving down the middle lengthwise. Experiment to find the thickness you like. Slow, steady rolling and stretching will make the finest, smoothest cord. You can make one solid cord or split it into two or more parts with internal loops. By using many feet of roving, you can create a very long, sturdy felt rope.

ATTACHING CORDS AND SPIKES

If you plan to felt cording or spikes to another project later, make a dry brush at the end you want to attach. Do this by leaving about 1" to 3" of dry roving at that end while you wet out the rest of the piece. The brush end looks something like tree roots, and you want to keep the roots pointed outward and away from each other.

Attaching a spike to a flat felt surface

Attaching a spike along a seam

To attach a cord or spike, splay out the brush end in a radial pattern on a project that is still prefelt — when the fibers are coherent enough to act as a main fabric but still soft enough to accept the fibers of the brush end. Felt the brush end to the project in the same manner as any other felting process. If the brush is a different color from the project, a pool of color will show at the base of the cord or spike; otherwise, you won't see the join.

A spike or cord can be added to a flat felt surface or along a seam. For a cleaner look, snip the tiniest possible hole in the project, pull the cord or spike through the hole to the right side, and felt the brush end to the inside. If you are attaching several cords or spikes, baste each one to keep them in place while you felt. Remove basting stitches only at the end of felting.

Attaching things at just the right stage can take some practice. Long, heavy attachments tend to droop when wet, pulling and stretching out their own areas of joining. So, start with small spikes or cords and work up from there.

Attaching a spike from the back through a hole

Snakes. This project is very popular with children, especially when forked tongues and stripes of colored wool or metallic threads are added. For stripes, wrap bits of brightly colored wool and small amounts of thin metallic threads around the dry roving before you wet it. For a tongue, lay a bit of red roving inside the main piece of long roving, letting it hang out the end (keep in mind that it will become very long when wet). Later, as you felt the main snake body, you can rub the red wool to flatten it into a strip and notch it with scissors.

Braided Cords. Weave two or three ropes together to create custom drapery ties or other home decorating elements. How about using braided felted ropes as an unusual garland at holiday time? Wool isn't harmed by weather, so you can even use it to decorate outside areas of your porch or patio.

Octopus Tassel. Create this decorative embellishment by splitting one end of a long strip of dry roving into many strands. As you felt the roving, work the strands individually so they felt separately. Felt tassels can be used as very beautiful closures on a coat or cape. Use complementary colors on each side of the garment and tie the "legs" to secure clothing.

Spikes. Spikes are a popular attachment with feltmakers, and many people find them addictive to make. They're texturally interesting and can add some attitude to an otherwise boring hat or bag. Spikes are meant to be attachments, so you will always have a brush end. (*See* Attaching Cords and Spikes *on page* 47.) If you're attaching the spikes from the back through a hole, keep the hole as small as you can to keep the felt around the base of the spike from stretching out. The tighter the felt, the more it will support the spike and keep it erect. Spikes can be attached along seams and at an angle.

For a handbag with attitude, attach a row of spikes along the outer seam.

Bodacious Bamboo

The idea here is to make a stiff stalk of wool bamboo, then add banded nodes and leaves in contrasting colors. The nodes and leaves are not felted to the stalk but can be moved up and down and positioned to your liking. A collection of these stalks looks lovely displayed in a flower vase.

What You Need

- a small bowl, one-quarter filled with warm, soapy water
- a towel
- a small square (10" × 10" or so) of black stair-treading material or a small bamboo sushi mat
- about 0.5 oz. of Merino wool roving in three contrasting colors

What You Do

1. Start the cording. Follow steps 1 to 4 for cording. (*See page* 46.)

2. Roll the wool. Keep rolling the wool for several minutes after you think it's finished. Wet felt always feels stiffer than it really is, and often a stalk that seems tall and stiff when it's wet will droop like a wilted tulip when it dries.

Step 3

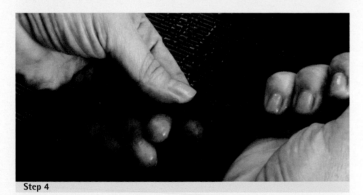

Step 4

Step 5

3. Add the bands. To make the banded nodes that will attach the leaves, firmly (but not *too* tightly) wrap a strip of roving in a contrasting color around the stalk widthwise. Wet the banding right onto the stalk and roll the whole thing on the treading and between your hands to firm the band and begin to shrink it down a bit.

4. Felt the bands. As soon as the band seems to be holding together and getting firm, stop rolling it and slide the band up and down the felted bamboo stalk a few times. This will felt the *inside* skin of the band to itself and prevent it from completely felting right onto the stalk; remember, you want to be able to move the band. Repeat steps 3 and 4 a few times until you've added three or four banded nodes along the stalk.

5. Add the leaves. Lastly, using another contrasting color, create tiny bamboo leaves. Wet and roll a little bit of wool between your fingers to stiffen the points, then slip one end of the wool under the node bands. You may need to use a pin to push the wool up through the tight band. Some bands can be left on their own, without leaves, for accent color.

6. Air-dry. Lay the project out flat and allow it to air-dry before you put it on display.

BAMBOO TIP

If you want to make very long stalks, felt them around armature wire or very thin dowels. As with any smooth surface you want to felt over, wrap it first with masking tape or roughen the surface somehow to give it some "tooth." This will allow the fibers to attach more easily to the support; otherwise, they will just felt to each other in a ring that spins around the wire.

Looped, Beaded Handle

Now that you know how to make a basic cord, let's get fancy! By adding loops and beads, you can make a decorative handle that can be attached later to a handbag or purse. There are endless variations to this idea, but we'll walk you through a simple version to get you started. (The handbag pictured is a folded version of the Everybag on page 143.)

What You Need

- a small bowl, one-quarter filled with warm, soapy water
- a towel
- a small square (10" × 10") of black stair-treading material or a bamboo sushi mat
- a strip of Merino wool roving about 45" to 55" in length
- optional: additional colors of wools and yarns
- a few colored beads with large holes
- plastic wrap

Project Notes

- Before you begin, measure how long you want the finished handle to be, based on where you want the bag to hang. Add to that measurement about a quarter of that length again to allow for some shrinkage.

- Plan ahead as to where you want each bead or other split in the handle to be. You will wet the wool and felt the cord as you go, but you need to stop at each bead location to split the roving while it's still dry. Take care to keep the last 3" to 4" dry so you can form the second brush end.

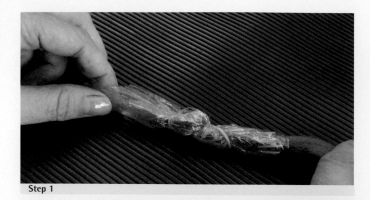

Step 1

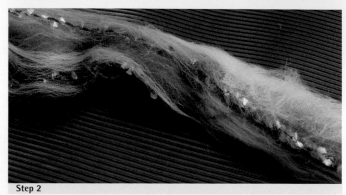

Step 2

Step 3

Step 4

What You Do

1. Wrap the brush end. At one end of the dry, loose roving, wrap about 3" in plastic wrap to keep it dry. Secure it with a small rubber band. This will be one of the brush ends for attaching your handle to a handbag later.

2. Add embellishments. Gently wrap any contrasting wool or yarns along the length of the cording before you wet the wool.

3. Start the cording. Follow steps 1 to 3 for cording (*see page* 46) but do not wet out the wool completely. Instead, wet out a few inches of the roving at a time as you move along the length. Gently press and roll the roving as you go.

4. Place a bead. When you reach a spot where you want a bead, split the dry portion of roving in two. Felt each side of the split separately (while keeping the ends dry), then slip a bead onto one or both sides.

5. Continue felting. You can rejoin the roving and tease it gently back together to leave no trace that it was split. Or, to make our version, felt each side of the split separately. Don't worry about felting the handle down tight yet. You can set the basic shape of it with the loops and beads in place, then go back to felt it hard later.

6. Join the halves. Split the roving again if you want to add more beads; otherwise, join the two halves of roving and felt them until you reach the last 3" to 4" of the handle. Wrap the dry end in plastic wrap as you did with the first end.

Step 5

Step 6

7. Felt the cord. Now work on hardening the handle by rolling it on the stair treading. Don't forget to stop often to pull lengthwise on the handle. This stretching helps the hardening process. When you think the handle is hard enough and if you don't intend to attach it to something right away, let it dry. Don't be surprised if you have to work it more later; when wet, felt always feels harder than it does when dry. Simply wet the felt again and continue to harden it.

Loop Variations

There are endless possible variations when making loops. If you want a loop without beads, you make it essentially the same way as above — by splitting the roving, then wetting and felting each side. Slip a couple of fingers inside each loop to work it well. Looped cords make interesting belts, ties, necklaces, or decorative elements to use as attachments on other work.

Bolo Ties

Bolo ties are traditionally worn in the American West, usually by men. However,

the bolo design can be used in a number of ways, such as on a purse flap. Think of it as a dressed-up drawstring. Bolos make great closures, but they are equally interesting as jewelry, especially when combined with metal hardware. To make a simple bolo, you'll need about a yard of cording and a metal crimp. Light-colored aluminum crimps, available at hardware stores, look particularly nice with felt, especially in modern designs.

Make the cording thin enough to force two cords through the crimp. Any number of knot configurations can be used to keep the cords from slipping. For inspiration, check out a book on knots. Remember that the crimps add weight, so use as small a crimp as possible for your purpose.

" *Hardware Treasure*

Many artists will know what I'm talking about when I say that a trip to the hardware store is one of the best ways to spend a rainy Saturday afternoon. You are guaranteed to score treasure as you wander through aisles full of wing nuts, bolts and clips, magnets, metallic strips, and other items just waiting to be creatively paired with felt. I always spend more money than anticipated, and if you're like me, you'll need to be accompanied by a guardian who will cut you off.

Jellyroll Trivet

The Jellyroll Trivet is essentially a big, fat cord made with an assortment of wool, then sliced open to reveal the colors. You start with flat layers of roving, roll them up, and then keep adding roving to the outside until you build up a nice, fat caterpillar. After wetting and felting it, you'll reach the exciting moment of cutting it open — and voilà!

Gorgeous, colorful, bull's-eye slices can be used in a variety of ways. Skinny jellyrolls can be sliced to make beads or buttons; string those slices on a strand of thread or yarn, and you will have a beautiful mobile or curtain. The slices of a fat jellyroll can be stitched together to make a trivet. I strongly recommend making a small practice jellyroll before taking on a larger one. You'll be surprised how much the rolls compress!

What You Need

- a dishpan of warm, soapy water for small rolls; work in the sink for large rolls

- a surface on which to roll; stair treading is best, but you can use bubble wrap or a mat for a large roll

- tulle netting
  For a small roll: about 10"–12" square
  For a large roll: about 18"–24" square

- spandex strips or knee-high panty hose to tie on the tulle

- Merino wool roving in at least five colors; choose high-contrasting colors for the most vibrant patterns
  For a small roll: about 2 oz. total, 10"–12" long strips
  For a large roll: 3–8 oz. total, 18"–24" long strips

- a large pair of scissors or an electric knife

- a long craft needle

- a spool of strong thread

- beads (optional)

Project Notes

Merino wool works best for jellyrolls because it felts together fast. You can use different preparations (roving or batts) and even mix them together, but be aware that they compact differently:

- Merino roving comes in many colors and works well, but it has already been combed out in one direction and flattened. To get the layers to felt easily, spread it out into thin, sheer webs as you layer it onto the roll.

- Batting will stick to itself easily and is easy to layer, but it's lofty and full of air. So, keep it compressed as you roll it up.

With either one, the idea is to keep the dry roll tight while you add layers; otherwise it will collapse in a big mess when you wet it out. The best way to keep the roll snug is to wind the sheer webs of wool completely around the roll at least once so they attach back onto themselves. Think of them as a bandage that is very sheer. Squeeze the dry roll in your hands after every few layers to keep it compacted.

What You Do

1. Lay out the wool. Decide which color(s) you want in the center and lay out the wool in sheer layers. If you're using roving, spread out each strip into flat sheets. If you're using batts, the wool is already in sheets, but peel them into thinner layers. Pile up at least six to eight layers. If you use one central color, you'll get a round bull's eye. Or you can alternate two colors to get a more subtle, textured spiral.

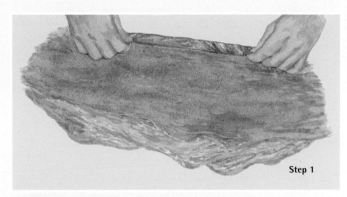

Step 1

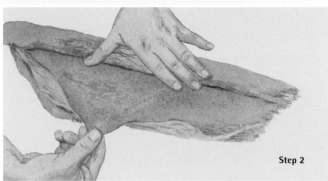

Step 2

2. Start rolling. Roll the layers together, just like a pastry jellyroll. Stretch the outermost parts of the fleece into a fine web to create a sheer bandage that keeps the roll together.

3. Continue the layers. Set the roll aside for a moment while you spread out your next layer of colored wool; then wrap the roll in this layer. Again, allow the sheer web of wool to wrap back around the roll onto itself, like an athletic bandage. Repeat many sheer layers of one color so it will show prominently; otherwise the layers will be only a thin line of color when the roll is felted.

4. Wrap it with tulle. When all of the wool has been wrapped into the roll, wrap the tulle very snugly around the roll to hold everything in place; then tie it at both ends with spandex strips or panty hose.

The tulle will keep the roll from collapsing into a flat pile when you saturate it.

5. *Get it wet.* Once the roll is wrapped, submerge one end in warm, soapy water. Saturate it through to the core by gently pressing water into the center of the roll with your hands. Try not to change the cylindrical shape too much as you do this. Continue wetting the roll until it is thoroughly saturated but not dripping.

6. *Gently start rolling.* Keeping the jellyroll wrapped in the tulle, begin to *very* gently roll it on the stair tread or mat. During the first minute or so, you're only trying to get the roll back into its original round shape. Don't press down on it yet; just gently rock it back and forth. If your net is slippery and you can't get it to roll very well, wrap the whole thing up in a damp towel. If you apply too much pressure too soon, you'll form cracks in

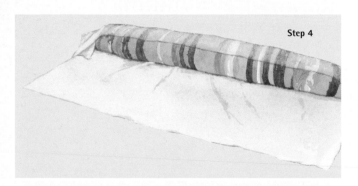

Step 4

Step 6

the roll. Avoid this by building pressure gradually as you roll. If cracks do appear, just fluff the wool back out in those areas and continue with less pressure.

7. *Apply more pressure.* Soon the roll will be moving along nicely and you can apply a lot more pressure. Take your cue from the wool and use more pressure as soon as you feel the roll get harder. Press down firmly, so you'll be felting all of the way to the middle of the roll. Stop often to test its hardness by touching or squeezing the felt and to stretch the roll out lengthwise. Remove the tulle at any point after the roll is holding together.

8. *Take it all the way.* Now you're in it for the long haul. To felt to the middle of the roll and make it hard enough for buttons or a trivet, you'll need to roll it for a few hours. You certainly don't have to do this all at once. Just plunge the roll into hot water whenever you begin again (or whenever you want to speed up the fulling process). You can roll it on a towel while talking to friends or watching a movie. When your arms get tired, wrap the roll in a towel and roll it on the floor with your feet. Roll until you think you can't stand it, and then roll some more. If you're making a large roll, once it's fairly sturdy, you can use a wooden board to increase the pressure and save some wear and tear on your arms. *Note:* Some people felt a small roll

Step 9

first, then add more wool layers and felt those on. Try it this way, if you like.

9. *Cut the roll.* When you think you've rolled enough, it's time to cut the roll. Use a pair of big scissors on smaller rolls or an electric knife on larger rolls. It will take some practice to make even cuts. Sometimes holding the roll in a vise or stabilizing device will help. Cut the roll into perfectly round shapes or at an angle, as when slicing Chinese vegetables. Angled cuts work best on rolls that have been felted very, very hard.

10. *Set the slices out to dry.* This is usually a beautiful and proud moment! Small rolls might be dry in about a day, while large rolls might take as long as three days.

11. *Sew the trivet.* When the slices are dry, use a long craft needle to sew them together into the trivet shape you desire. Dress it up by using decorative thread or by adding small beads at the end knots or in between the slices themselves.

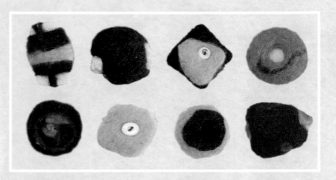

SPEAKING OF BUTTONS . . .

There are many ways to make interesting felt buttons, limited only by your imagination. The examples shown here, created by Loyce Ericson, include felt-covered beach glass, felt-covered twigs, little felted balls, small pads of handmade felt layered on top of each other, and, of course, jellyroll buttons. You can also make thin felt to use on the homemade fabric-covered buttons found in craft stores. What other things can you think of? Try incorporating metal, wood, and other interesting bits from your junk drawer!

CANNOLI BEAD BARRETTE

Felted jellyrolls can be sliced on the diagonal to show off even more of their colors. The roll should be very hard if you intend to cut it this way because you will be exposing even more of the center surface. Make cannoli by felting a thin jellyroll made up of a few highly contrasting colors. Cut the jellyroll into beads with angled cuts on both ends and glue them securely onto a barrette to make a unique hair ornament.

" *Cover It with Felt!*

Making felt over simple objects is an appealing way to brighten an entire room, and an ideal project to do with children. Whether you need a quick paperweight for Father's Day or a stunning, contemporary centerpiece for a dinner party, these things can be made in a flash. You can cover almost anything in felt, if you're determined enough. People have tried felting around trees, chairs, rods and poles, branches, pipes, flowerpots. . . . Who knows why felters do it? Perhaps there is something comforting about swaddling things in felt — and the felted object somehow becomes more personal and familiar.

Balls

Of all of the different felt items displayed in my home, these felt-covered balls probably draw the most comments. Everyone seems to love them: men, women, and kids; felters and nonfelters. They are extremely fast and easy to make, have a homey appeal, and go surprisingly well with any sort of decor, from formal to playful to special holiday settings. Add a string to create a hanging ornament. What's the secret of their appeal? Maybe it's the memory of all of those gumballs . . .

What You Need

- a dishpan or sink filled with warm, soapy water
- Styrofoam balls in various sizes
- one or two pairs of queen-sized pantyhose (leg portion only)
- pieces of tulle netting large enough to wrap around each ball (optional)
- decorative yarns, especially types with high wool or mohair content (optional)
- a couple handfuls of Merino wool (batting, roving, or both) per ball in a selection of colors

Project Notes

When selecting Styrofoam balls to felt, avoid the white or green ones used by florists. They are messy to felt because they flake apart so easily. Look instead for the hard, smooth, white balls found in craft and fabric stores. Consider using an assortment of sizes to make your arrangement more interesting.

What You Do

1. Apply the wool. Cover each ball by spreading and wrapping sheer sheets of wool around it like a bandage or by rolling the ball into a sheet of wool on a table. Make sure each layer is wrapped all the way around on itself so it will felt well. This is also how you keep the layers tight as you add more wool. Keep in mind that the first few layers won't show, so use a color that isn't important to you. As you wrap the ball in wool, mix colors to create a nice watercolor effect. Keep the layers as tight as possible until the ball feels well padded. There is no magic number of layers; whatever you try will probably work just fine as long as you have good coverage.

2. Embellish. Now add yarn to embellish, if you wish. Hairy mohair yarns felt into the wool quickly, and if you wrap them around the circumference a few times, they help keep the wool on tight. You can use acrylic-based novelty yarns, but since the fibers don't contain any wool, they will not readily felt in on their own. Spread thin strands of wool across the yarns here and there to hold them in place. Set each ball aside until you've made as many balls as you want.

3. Tie up the balls. When all of the balls are wrapped, stuff them one at a time into the legs of the pantyhose. (*Hint:* The pantyhose legs stretch open better if you wet them first.) It can be difficult not to disturb your wool design as you insert the balls, but with practice, you'll get better. Begin by gathering up the pantyhose in one hand, just as you would when putting them on your foot. Carefully stuff the first wool-covered ball into the toe and tie it off snugly before stuffing the next one. Continue this way until all of the balls are inside. Don't tie so tightly that you can't get the knot undone, unless you don't mind cutting the pantyhose apart later.

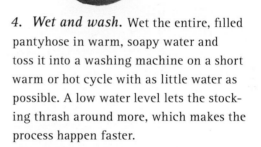

Step 3

4. Wet and wash. Wet the entire, filled pantyhose in warm, soapy water and toss it into a washing machine on a short warm or hot cycle with as little water as possible. A low water level lets the stocking thrash around more, which makes the process happen faster.

5. Rinse and finish. If the felt feels very puffy after this first cycle, you can run it again. If not, rinse out the soap. Then toss the whole sausage string into the dryer for a few minutes. Or you can work the felt even harder by hand through the stock-

GETTING FANCY

If you want to make more complicated designs, work each ball by hand initially to keep from disturbing your fiber placement. Just wrap it first in a piece of tulle. Wet out the wool and work the surface by first rubbing gently, and then a little harder when you feel a skin begin to form. Stuff the balls into a stocking to finish the felting in the washer and/or dryer, if desired.

ing. It depends on whether you want the felt on the balls to be tight and finished or soft and fluffy. After rinsing, remove the stocking. The wool will often stick to the nylon, so you may need to slowly but firmly peel it away. Hold the design down with one hand to prevent it from ripping off the ball.

6. *Let the balls dry.* Drying time will vary depending on how many layers of wool were used. If when the balls dry there are yarn bits hanging off them, you can sometimes bead them to make the balls even more interesting. One of my favorite ball designs came out of a big, loose flap of wool that didn't felt in with the rest of the fleece. I stretched it into a long, spiky spiral and added a slider bead to it. Use your mistakes to improve your designs. What happened along the way stays between you and the wool.

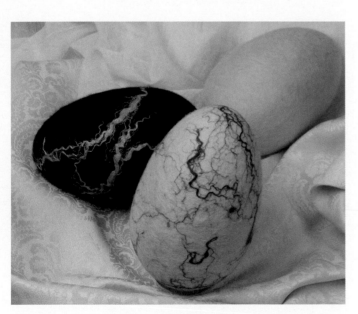

IDEAS

Cover a rock or a large pebble for a fantastic, brightly colored doorstop. This is a great gift for a child to make for a teacher or a family member, and it's guaranteed to be displayed for a long time. Good idea for a rainy day: Let a child decide what you will felt over together. How magical it is to don the robes of the Wizard and Alchemist and change everyday household objects into felt!

Eggs and Stones

These large felted eggs make marvelous gifts at any time of the year, but look for the oversized eggs (or other plastic shapes) at the dollar store around Easter. Put a line of them on the mantle or let a few lie around on a large coffee table. Trés chic!

The process for felting eggs and stones is the same, except that the objects you cover may be too large for stockings. These are better felted by hand than in the dryer. Just cut a piece of tulle netting as large as you need and secure it with a rubber band or a tie to keep the net taut around the wool as you wet it and work it. Remember that the net provides a lot of friction, so don't rub too hard in the beginning or you'll be too rough. Go slowly until you get the hang of it, and be sure to keep dipping the whole thing into hot water as you felt.

Andrea Graham

Ontario resident Andrea Graham is a perfect example of someone who fell in love with feltmaking and wasted no time in making a career out of it. Since beginning to felt professionally in 2002, Andrea has been working to establish her own body of work while maintaining an ongoing quest for professional instruction. She recommends committing yourself to learning from those you admire, even if it means traveling to study with them. *(See Resources.)*

The work by Andrea shown here is part of her *Lemoine's Point* series. These pieces begin as a wet felted "canvas" in which she lays out her rough composition. She then needle felts the details. The finished piece is about 36" by 30".

On a fulled, wet-felted background that contains her basic composition, Andrea uses needle felting to add depth and dimension. *Lemoine's Point,* blended wools (Merino, Romney, mixed-breed batt) and yarns (wool and synthetic), 36" × 30".

4

Learning the Basics

No matter what project you want to make — be it placemats, slippers, hats, or clothing — the basics of feltmaking are the same: You select the wool, build it up in dry layers, add water to felt it, then work it for a while to full it. During the fulling process, the wool shrinks. As you begin to create your own patterns, you will learn to allow for that shrinkage. This chapter shows you the fundamental steps

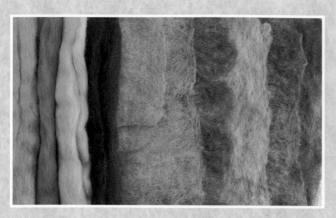

CUSTOM COLORS

If you're short on time, you can buy ready-made needle-punch prefelts to use for embellishment. (*See Resources.*) These materials can be handy in a pinch, but the color choices are limited. Making your own prefelts allows you to experiment with the process, custom blend your own color shades, and make felt that is different from what anyone else would make. You'll be surprised at how well some colors mix. This photo shows four colors of roving (beige, pink, gold, and dark brown) that have been mixed with a hand carding tool to form a range of earthy colors.

of making flat felts from start to finish. Once you know the basics, the rest is a matter of adapting the process to make what you want.

Because it helps to make something specific when introducing shrinkage rates, we will use placemats as our starter project. They are made from Merino wool roving with added embellishments cut from prefelt. As described in chapter 1, prefelt is partially felted material that will hang together enough to be cut into shapes but is soft enough to felt onto other prefelts or background wool. First we'll make the prefelt sheets for the embellishments, and then we'll start again and go all the way through the process with a placemat. Reminder: Prefelt does not shrink from its original size because it isn't fulled.

" Plastic Works

Many felters lay out their wool directly on the bubble wrap, but I recommend using a *working sheet* of 4 mil plastic that is slightly smaller than your piece of bubble wrap. Having the extra plastic underneath is useful for a number of reasons.

- Working plastic keeps the loose fibers from sinking down between the bubbles when you first get the wool wet. Until the fibers reach the skin stage and become prefelt, the plastic supports them. Later, the plastic can be removed.

- The plastic also works well as a "serving tray" for transferring a project off the table at any time during the process. When making berets, I often lay out a number of them dry, stacking them up like pancakes with the protective working plastic between them. This serving tray idea is also useful in classes, where multiple students are laying out two sides of a project and need table space.

- In advanced projects, two sheets of working plastic, pressed together when wet, will form a vacuum around whatever you're making and act as a set of giant spatulas. This is very useful when you want to flip over a big, wet garment with delicate seams.

Making Prefelt

Making prefelts is a good way to get familiar with the process and your equipment, and whatever you make is bound to be useful in a later project. As you make them, try layering different colors together to get a feel for how the colors mix and how to control shading. This will also make your designs look more sophisticated because the colors will have more depth.

The thickness of the finished prefelts will vary depending on how thickly or thinly you lay out the wool. Thin prefelt has the advantage of melting into

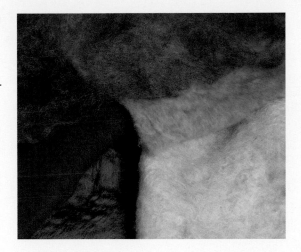

Step 1

Step 2

Step 3

Step 4

WORKING WITH ROVING

Roving is the wool preparation most commonly available to felters. Primarily Merino, roving felts quickly and is available in a wide range of colors. But it does take a little getting used to. Mostly it's a matter of practice, and making prefelts is a perfect way to practice laying out fleece. Here are some tips:

1. *Make sure the roving is completely untwisted* before you try to pull it apart.

2. *Individual fibers are about 3" to 5" long* in commercially prepared Merino fleece. If you hold your hands closer than that, you won't be able to separate the fibers; so, keep your hands a few inches apart.

3. *Work with small amounts of roving at a time.* This is the most important way to gain control over how evenly your wool is laid out. Tear off a length of roving about 12" to 18" long and split it down the length. Some felters split it a couple of times until they have only a wide ribbon of fleece instead of a big, fat rope. This helps control how much fiber can be pulled off.

4. *Pull out small bits of roving* or use your fingers to hold the fleece down as you pull the roving away. Do whichever way feels most comfortable to you.

background felt without leaving a ridge, but it will be strongly colored by the background wool. (If it's too thin, you can put two layers of prefelt on top of one another.) A thick prefelt will retain its color but may feel as if it is in slight relief on the finished felt.

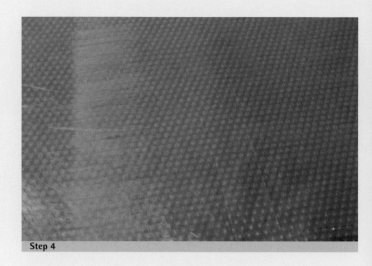
Step 4

Before and After

Template Size: 24" × 24" •

Finished Size: 24" × 24"

Shrinkage Rate: none

What You Need

- basic felting supplies (*see page* 20.)
- 1–2 oz. of Merino wool roving

Set It Up, Lay It Out

1. Organize your space. Lay down your bubble wrap (bubbles facing up) followed by a sheet of working plastic. Collect your supplies.

2. Make a template. Because there is no shrinkage when making prefelts, you don't need to calculate shrinkage. However, you will need some outline to go by when you lay out your wool to ensure that the piece is big enough for you to cut out the shapes you need and perhaps have some left over to add to your prefelt collection. Use a black marker to mark the corners of a 24" by 24" square directly in the middle of your working plastic. Use these measurements as a guide for laying out the wool.

3. Measure out the wool. Once you've selected your wool, divide it evenly in half. Because you will be laying it out in two very thin layers, dividing it evenly first will help you construct two layers of the same thickness. Just for fun, you can make each layer a different color or alternate the colors from side to side. The more important thing, though, is to pay attention to keeping the layers even.

4. Lay out the first layer. Begin at a corner and lay the fiber down in rows that overlap by about one-third. Remember to work with only a small amount of wool in your hands. Each row should be thin enough to see through (positively wispy!), but keep them as even as possible in thickness. Large thin areas could result in holes or weak spots. The ends of the roving should not extend past the edges of your template. Practice stopping just a fraction of an inch before the exact edge of your pattern line because the wool will spread out when you wet it.

5. *Lay out the next layer(s).* When laying out any fleece, it's better to use multiple thin layers instead of one or two thick ones; thin layers felt together better. Lay the wool fibers of the second layer perpendicular to those of the first layer. As an experiment, you can add more wool in a third layer on only half of your prefelt sheet, again changing the direction of the fibers. This will give you a thicker prefelt on one side, which means the fiber colors will mix a little differently when placed on background wool.

Step 5

Wet It Out

6. *Add water.* Fill a bowl or thermos with warm, soapy water. Lay dry tulle netting over the wool, with the edges extending beyond the wool on all sides. Use a little cup to pour a small amount of the soapy water at a time onto the center of the pile. (*See box below.*) Working with wet, soapy hands, slowly spread the water outward. Saturate the wool without disturbing the fibers or moving the tulle. Imagine pressing the water through the pile, all the way to the bottom.

Step 6

ADDING WATER

The phrase "wet it out" describes well the most effective way to add water to your dry, layered wool. It's best to *wet* the project from the center *outward* with small amounts of water at a time. Why does this matter? Using too much water can slow down the process. When using fine wools like Merino, you can actually float the wool fibers apart, creating holes in the nice, even layers you worked so hard to make. One of the most common beginner mistakes in felting is using too much water.

Tip: After pouring a cup of water onto the fibers, place a small square of 4 mil plastic over the spot. Slide your soapy hands across the plastic without sliding the plastic itself. This will immediately spread the water without disturbing the fibers.

7. Check the tulle. If the tulle is pulling up from the fibers, you probably need a little more water and possibly a bit more soap. When saturated enough, the tulle becomes almost invisible and looks like it has melted into the wet wool. Also, a little soapy puddle will form when you press down on the wool with your hand, yet it will seem to suck back into the wool a bit when you take your hand away. (Felters call this "The Swamp!")

8. Check the soap. If you don't see or feel any soap in the wool, try adding a little more by smearing a very small amount of soap on your hands and patting the wool firmly through the netting. This action gets soap right down in between the fibers where you need it — but beware. Too much soap on fine wools like Merino will suffocate the fiber scales like too much heavy conditioner on fine hair; use just a little at a time and avoid applying it directly to the wool. Take care not to stretch or slide the tulle around as you do this. It should be stuck to the wool as if it were glued. The job of the tulle at this point is to keep the loose fibers locked and immobile so they don't float apart.

Felt the Wool

Okay, it's time to get the fibers to interact. Please keep in mind that these next steps are subjective and a little difficult to describe. It's something you have to feel and do a couple of times; but don't worry, it will work for sure. Some felters press harder than others; sometimes the water is

TRUST YOUR HANDS

Check for thin areas across the entire prefelt. Your hands are more accurate for this than your eyes; with practice, you will become very good at finding areas with too little wool. Keep your palms wide open and use the entire surface of both hands to feel for thin spots. Keep them side by side and move them as a pair across the felt in little steps. If you feel a thin spot in one of the layers, you might see it if you look; however, learn to let your hands decide. Soon you'll be working on projects with more layers, which can't be effectively checked by sight. Add little bits of fleece to cover the thin spots.

colder or the wool is a slow felter or there are other factors. Because of this, it's not possible to give exact times for doing each step. Just try it.

9. Apply pressure. As you're pressing down, move all around the project a few times. Again, do not move the wool itself, but lift up your hands each time before putting them down in another spot. It's important to involve the whole pile of wool, not just the surface layer, so imagine that you are pressing straight through to the table.

10. Gently vibrate your hands. Now apply a different kind of pressure by gently vibrating your hands in place while pressing down. This controlled vibration should not disturb the position of the fibers or the tulle. With your hands together, slowly move all around the piece, working a little at a time. Keep your hands in one place long enough for the fibers to respond to the heat and vibration (at least 20 to 30 seconds).

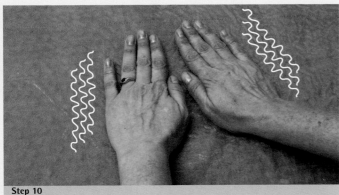

Step 10

Step 11

They are beginning to swell and migrate a bit, and some of them are finding their way up through the tulle. Take a moment to very slowly peel back the tulle, but be sure to hold the felt down directly behind the tulle as you go. (Failing to do this with embellished felt will often pull the pretty yarns and other things right off!) Test for a skin by pinching the felt. (*See* The Pinch Test *below*.) If it's not ready, simply replace the netting and continue working the areas that are not yet holding together.

11. *Keep going!* Continue working all around the wool for a few minutes. A common mistake is to rub mostly in the center of the wool pile instead of out along its edges. In any piece of felt, fibers always migrate toward the center of the pile, so keep your hands along the edges more so than in the middle. This will help the whole felt come together evenly. Otherwise, the middle will start forming a skin before the edges do, and the outermost fibers will remain loose and unfelted.

12. *Check the tulle again.* Soon you'll begin to notice little pills coming up through the netting. This is a good sign — the fibers are telling you something.

THE PINCH TEST

The goal of the felting stage is to get the fibers saturated and lightly connected to one another. You'll know you've achieved this when the felt behaves as a coherent piece of delicate fabric rather than a bunch of loose hairs. The best way to check this, called "testing for skin," is to lightly pinch the wet fibers between your thumb and forefinger. Are the fibers beginning to hold together? You'll know they are if you've left a tiny, hairy tent where you pinched (you can easily just pat it back down). If you can do this all over the piece, you have a prefelt.

Step 14

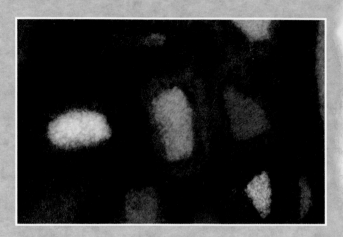

ADVANCED TIP

Try using thick prefelts on the back of your yardage in a planned pattern to allow their ghosts to felt through. This use of background prefelts will increase the subtlety and depth of your designs. Notice the halos around the prefelts in this felt.

KEEP IT WARM

If you are making a very large prefelt sheet, your felt may get cold as you're working. If you can keep the piece warm, felting occurs much faster. (The same is true when fulling.) It's not effective to just add warm water to sopping wet, cold felt. Instead, use your sponge to remove much of the cold water before adding new warm, soapy water. While doing this, keep the tulle in place.

13. *Expel the water.* Once the entire piece is felted, it will feel like a soggy paper towel. Don't ever lift up heavy, wet prefelt by its edges, because the water and gravity will stretch it out and could even rip it apart. Instead, roll the felt up loosely in the tulle, carefully lift the whole thing into your dishpan or the sink, and press out all of the water.

14. *Rinse out the soap.* If you'll be using the prefelt soon (within a week or so), there's no need to rinse out the soap. If you're saving the felt for later, keep it wrapped in the netting long enough to rinse out the soap by pressing clear warm water through the felt. Pressing or lightly squeezing is okay, but never wring your felt. Although it's best to use prefelt dry, it can be damp when you use it as long as you brush its surface a bit and raise some loose fibers.

15. *Let it dry.* Prefelt is still fragile at this stage, so it's best not to hang it on a line or use clothespins. Instead, gently drape the prefelt over the back of a chair or across a drying rack. Better still, if you have the table space, leave it flat to dry. You now have a sheet of prefelt!

How Much Shrinkage?

If you compare your finished prefelt to the template you used, you'll see that it didn't shrink. Shrinking happens in the fulling stage and is part of what makes the fabric strong. Shrinkage can vary quite a bit depending on the type of wool, the number of layers used (less wool = more shrinkage), and other factors.

Even the direction you lay out the fiber matters, since fibers shrink more along their length. When you lay out only one layer of wool roving (as with some later projects), you will allow for greater shrinkage in the lengthwise direction of the wool. When you build two layers of wool, one horizontally and one vertically, the felt will shrink more evenly. With three layers, the felt will shrink more in the dominant direction of the fibers.

When using Merino roving, a good rule of thumb is to figure that a piece of felt, when fulled, will shrink by about a third when you use three solid layers of wool. This formula is sufficient when you're making a project where the final size doesn't have to be exact, such as the placemat on the next page. In the next chapter, you will learn how to make a test swatch to determine a wool's shrinkage rate.

HOW MANY LAYERS?
The number of layers you build for a sheet of flat felt will vary depending on the project. What type of felt you are trying to create? Do you want it to drape nicely or be stiff? What kind of wool are you using? Unlike in a recipe, there is not always a magic number of layers. We will make suggestions with each project, but with experience, you will learn what works best for you.

DOING THE MATH
For the placemats in this chapter, let's aim for a fairly standard finished size of 13" by 18". If you allow for the wool to shrink by about a third, how do you calculate the size of the template? It's easy: multiply the desired finished dimensions by 1.5.

Desired finished width of 13" × 1.5 = 19.5" for width of template
Desired finished length of 18" × 1.5 = 27" for length of template

Note: This formula works as a shortcut for sizing a template only when the shrinkage rate is about a third (33%). Later we will get into other ways to calculate template sizes.

Placemat

Now let's go through the entire feltmaking process, start to finish. Think about your background colors and decide whether you want your placemat to be abstract or pictorial. Multiple colors of loose wool result in a melted, watercolor-like effect. If you like this look, choose more than one color for the placemat background. Prefelts retain the sharp lines of their shapes, so think about them as pattern elements or pictures when designing your mat. Use prefelt sheets to cut out embellishments for your placemat. You will be building three layers of wool for this project.

Before and After

Template Size: 19½" × 27"

Finished Size: 13" × 18"

Shrinkage Rate: 33% using suggested fiber

What You Need

- basic felting supplies (*see page* 20.)
- steam iron (optional)
- prefelt sheet(s)
- about 2 oz. of Merino wool roving in one or more colors

Project Note

We used a pool noodle as the rolling bar in this project.

Set It Up, Lay It Out

1. Organize your space. Set up your work area with the working plastic on top of your bubble wrap or mat. To make a placemat with our finished dimensions, draw a 19½" × 27" template directly on the working plastic or on a separate piece. If you want a different size, refer Doing the Math (*in the box on page* 71) to calculate the template size.

round off the corners

19½"

27"

Layer 1

Layer 2

Layer 3

Step 2

2. Lay out the background. Lay out the wool. (*See steps 4 and 5 of* Set It Up, Lay It Out *on pages* 66–67.) Divide your wool into three piles before you start, and lay out three layers of fiber instead of two. The fibers in each layer should be perpendicular to those of the layer below.

3. Add the embellishments. Now comes the fun part — decorating your felt. Cut up dry prefelt sheets to make any design you want. These pieces will shrink by a

Step 3

Fulling the Felt

The fulling process involves pressing, squeezing, rolling, throwing, and otherwise working your wool to get it to shrink. There are many paths to achieving a finished felt, and the particulars will vary from project to project, person to person, and teacher to teacher. Watch any experienced feltmaker during the fulling stage and you will see the process come alive.

Now it's up to you to guide the wool, to control what is happening *inside* the pile, not just what you see on the surface. This is what makes truly excellent felts. In time, you will find your own way to "speak" to the wool and respond to the constantly changing material in your hands. Turn up the dial on your sense of touch and let's go.

third, just as the background wool will, so cut the shapes larger accordingly. Gently brush the fibers on the back side of the prefelt (to help them attach to the background wool), then lay them directly onto the loose wool layers. Fibers added on top of prefelt (like the brown fibers on the green shape) won't blend in as much.

Wet It Out, Felt the Wool

Follow the steps for wetting and felting the wool on pages 67–70. When you reach the point of rinsing the felt, leave it wrapped in the tulle and gently squeeze out the cold water. Now get some fresh, hot water for fulling and it's time to move on to the shrinking stage.

4. Wet it out. Unroll the felt. Remove the plastic, pattern and working plastic, but keep the tulle on the felt for the time being; it now becomes useful in a different way. During the felting stage, its job was to protect the loose fibers from moving around too much. Now, the slightly rough texture of the tulle provides a little friction, which helps the fibers move toward each other and begin to lock down. Use your dipping cup to add fresh, hot water until the felt is slightly beyond damp, but not dripping. You can use a little soap if you wish, but it's not as important in the fulling stage except in particular cases.

5. Begin rolling. Lay the noodle at one end of the felt and roll up the netting, felt, and bubble wrap together around it. Secure the bundle with elastic ties. The roll should be snug, but don't worry about

SEE WHAT HAPPENS

Experiment! It's interesting to use a variety of sizes and shapes to see what happens after the piece has been felted. You will learn a lot about how much a shape changes. For example, how much detail is retained on a pointed star? How large do the prefelt shapes need to be to give you the finished size you want? Invite the element of surprise!

Step 5

getting it as tight as possible. If your roll loosens, stop and reroll it — you'll soon get the hang of it. Using correct body posture (*see page* 39), move the roll back and forth on the table for about four minutes. There is no set time for how long to do this. Stop as often as you like to check your felt, to see if it looks or feels different. However, not much is likely to happen for the first couple of minutes.

6. *Rotate the felt and keep rolling.* After four minutes or so, open the roll and turn the whole thing (netting, felt, and bubble wrap) 90 degrees to the left or right before rolling it all up again. Repeat step 5, for the about the same amount of time, then open the roll and look at your prefelt embellishments. They should look like they are melting into the background wool; if not, just keep rolling and check them again in a few moments.

7. *Rotate the felt again and keep rolling.* Keep rotating the contents of the roll in the same direction, by 90 degrees, each time you open it to check the felt. Soon the surface will start looking different, slightly tighter. You're watching for when

FULLING TIPS

- Felt shrinks in the direction that you roll it or work it. The idea is to roll for a while in one direction, then roll for about the same amount of time in another direction. This helps to shrink the felt down evenly.

- Be kind to your back. As you get into the dynamics of fulling, don't forget to check your posture! You'll last a lot longer and enjoy it more if you aren't wearing out your back. Check the posture suggestions on page 39.

WHAT IF IT WRINKLES?

Try not to roll up your felt too tightly. Snug is good, but super-tight will cause wrinkles. It helps if you can lift the entire roll up slightly off the table as you roll it up. Some wrinkles are inevitable, though, so check for them each time you unroll your wool. Most wrinkles disappear on their own, but when you find one, you can simply flatten it with your palm. The only thing to beware of is going too long without checking your felt, in which case a small wrinkle might grow into a large, permanent crease. With experience, you'll worry about wrinkles less and develop little tricks to avoid them.

all parts of the felt behave as a tightened fabric. Make sure all parts of your prefelt designs are sticking well; apply a dab of soap with your finger, if needed. When the felt begins to tighten and shrink, you can move to the next step.

8. *Use your hands.* As soon as the felt feels strong enough, set aside the bubble wrap, the plastic, and the noodle. Roll the felt for a few minutes more with the netting wrapped around it (to keep the felt from sticking to itself). Then full the felt by rolling it directly with your hands, to feel how the wool behaves. Continue to roll it from different directions as before, adding a small amount of hot water to keep the felt damp and warm. Working on

Step 8

a damp towel provides a nonslip surface and a little additional friction.

9. Shape the wool. Now is the time to start shaping the felt, before the fibers lock down too tightly. This means keeping the edges straight and making sure the felt shrinks down evenly on all sides. Use the flat, open palm of one hand to create a wall along one side of the felt as you roll it past your palm with the other hand. (*See* Corral Those Fibers! *at right*) Immediately, the felt's edge will begin to straighten and become more even in thickness. As you roll and rotate the felt, set the edges on each side. Repeat each side a number of times, as repetitive motion is needed to influence the way the fibers come together and to set a memory in the wool.

10. Stretch it out. Although it seems counterintuitive, *gently* stretching the felt is an important part of fulling that will help harden your felt. Why? Stretching pulls the fibers backward slightly, which gives them a second chance to lock down more tightly when you begin rolling again.

11. Keep going and listen to the felt! Alternate stretching, rolling, and rotating the felt in different directions. Move your hands back and forth all across the felt and don't work too long in one area or direction. Stop often and look at your felt. When it begins to look tight and approaches the size of your finished placemat, you're nearly done.

12. Rinse and dry. When you feel you're done fulling, rinse the felt to remove all traces of soap. On a flat surface, press the felt into shape with your hands and let it dry. For a more professional, finished look, iron the felt while it's still damp. However, you might prefer the natural, pebbly texture of finished felt.

" *Corral Those Fibers!*

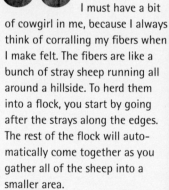

I must have a bit of cowgirl in me, because I always think of corralling my fibers when I make felt. The fibers are like a bunch of stray sheep running all around a hillside. To herd them into a flock, you start by going after the strays along the edges. The rest of the flock will automatically come together as you gather all of the sheep into a smaller area.

Fibers that are not corralled early will keep trying to escape and won't lock down in the same way as fibers in the middle of the felt. You will end up with felt that is tight in the middle, but with loose, scalloped edges along the sides.

The goal is to felt your piece as evenly along the edges as in the middle. You accomplish this by framing the felt with your hand along the edges as you roll it. Since fibers naturally migrate toward the center, it's more important to take care of the edges first. Any stray fibers moving outward will encounter your hand and be forced to turn back toward the center. Exactly where you put your hands matters a great deal to the fibers.

When Is It Finished?

This is one of the most common questions we all ask ourselves when felting. You will ask it every time you work with a new wool or a wool mixture, or when you're not sure of the shrinkage rate. Experience helps, but there are a few guidelines to go by, especially with well-known wools like Merino.

- For one thing, you can measure it. For the previous project, you know the felt should end up as a 13" by 18" placemat, so if it's at least that small or smaller, you're probably finished.
- When you don't know the shrinkage rate, give it the "size change" test: Stretch the wool to see whether it's easy or difficult to distort. If the shape changes some but the overall area of the felt remains the same when you tug on it, it's probably finished. If the shape changes and the overall size grows, continue to work it.
- Keep in mind that some wools are more elastic than others. Even when a finished felt feels fairly immobile when stretched, sometimes the shape will change a little bit. The thickness of the wool sometimes plays a part in this.

" Fulling Is Personal!

Because the shrinking part of feltmaking seems so magical, we are inclined to think of that as the whole show. But felt really does shrink differently depending on how you full it. That hidden complexity is part of what makes feltmaking so fascinating.

As you complete different projects and gain experience with your hands, you'll begin to see this for yourself. There are many different ways to felt, but there are also reasons for using one method over another. You could take the approach that "it doesn't matter how you do it, because they all work," and certainly you will achieve felt that shrinks. But that may not be the best way to make high-quality, professional-looking felt.

It's useful to finish the fulling process with your hands on the wool if you can. This is the mark of an experienced felter and the way to monitor the very subtle changes in the late stages of feltmaking. It's not only easy to learn this, it's fascinating.

Table Runner

Your own handmade table runner can make a personal statement in your dining room — and you can make a custom runner for any occasion. Be it for a baby shower, a birthday, Halloween, or the holidays, it's easy to create a themed design. If you need one extra fast, use ready-made prefelt. We list the colors we used to give you an idea of the wool amounts you need. But, by all means, make this project personal with your own blended colors and special yarns.

Before and After

Template Size: 18" × 72"

Finished Size: 12" × 48"

Shrinkage Rate: 33% using suggested fiber

What You Need

- basic felting supplies (*see page* 20.)
- a needle and white basting thread
- a steam iron (optional)
- 1 square yd. of medium-weight black needle-punch prefelt
- ¼–⅓ yd. each of pink and orange prefelts (needle-punch or handmade)
- 1 skein of Berroco HipHop yarn or other thick-and-thin "homespun" yarn
- 2 yds. of very thin black wool yarn

Project Notes

- The following instructions assume that you have the prefelt you need already made and ready to use. If you don't, either use needle-punch prefelts, or follow the instructions in this chapter for making prefelt. (*See page* 65.) In that case, you would use about 5 to 6 oz. of black Merino wool roving to build two layers on the template.

- You will probably want a narrow rolling mat and rolling bar to accommodate the narrow width of this project. If you have more than one pool noodle, for instance, you can cut one in half.

- The exact amount of shrinkage will vary a bit depending on the number and size of decorations and thickness of wool. Unless you need an exact finished size for the runner, this shouldn't matter.

What You Do

1. Organize your space. Lay down your bubble wrap (bubbles facing up) followed by a working sheet of plastic. Collect your supplies.

2. Cut and baste the background prefelt. Cut the square yard of black prefelt into two 18" by 36" pieces. With the two lengths abutting but not overlapping, baste the ends together lengthwise to form a long piece that is 18" by 72". When basting, use a contrasting color of thread and don't knot it at the ends. Instead, double back on your first stitch to lightly secure it at the beginning and leave a long tail at the other end. This allows the felt to shrink freely without

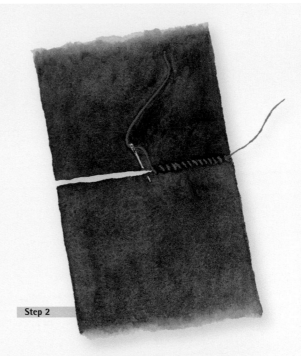

Step 2

interference from the stitching. Leave it in until the felt has been fulled.

3. Seal the seam. Wet this seam with soapy water and gently felt it together by rubbing it carefully with your fingers.

4. Lay out the design. Use the photo of the table runner as a guide to lay down the yarn, or make up your own pattern. You can cut pink and orange prefelts into imperfect squares and rectangles and then layer them over and under the yarn. The thinner black yarn was added last to give the design more dimension.

5. Wet, felt, and full. The rest of the work is the same as for the placemat. So, lay the tulle netting over the project and follow the instructions on pages 74–76. Here are some other pointers:

- Try not to work the middle of the table runner very much during fulling. Focus instead on working the edges with the flat palm of your hand. (*See* Corral Those Fibers! *on page* 76.) Because the runner is long and narrow, corralling the outer fibers will be sufficient to help shrink the runner evenly and to prevent the edges from scalloping.

- When the fulling is completed, pull out the basting thread, snipping it as needed.

- After rinsing the felt, iron it while it is damp and leave it flat to dry.

Variation
Mosaic Scarf

The instructions for this project can be used to make a mosaic scarf. Just recalculate the dimensions for the width and length you desire. This is a great project for using up a lot of old prefelt scraps. Create your own design or check out mosaic tile craft books for design inspirations. The smaller the prefelt squares, the more intricate the mosaic. However, keep the squares at least ¾" in size if you want to preserve their square shapes; otherwise they are likely to shrink into rounded dots.

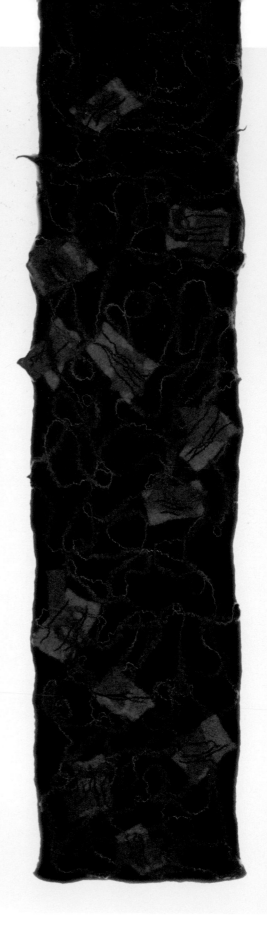

Citrus Picnic Blanket

This comfy blanket is perfect to tote around for a summer picnic in the park or a day at the beach. Or make one in red, white, and blue for watching Fourth of July fireworks! The felt is sturdy but so lightweight you won't even notice it in your bag. Because of the large finished size, this project is best made with medium- or heavy-weight factory-made prefelts.

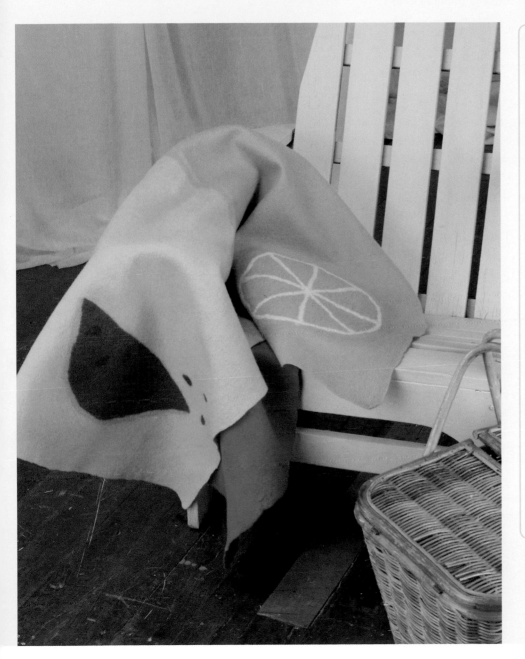

Before and After

Template Size: 6' × 6'

Finished Size: 4' × 4'

Shrinkage Rate: 33% using suggested fibers

What You Need

- basic felting supplies (*see page* 20.)

- a sewing needle and thread for basting the background squares together

- a felting needle and small piece of foam (optional)

- 1 square yd. each of orange, yellow, green, and fuchsia medium-weight needle-punch prefelts for the background

- 14"–16" squares of each of the above colors for the fruit designs

- a few yards of white wool yarn for the lemon

- bits of brown wool for the watermelon seeds and navel on the orange

Project Notes

- When using prefelt for the background, you don't need a template. However, you will need plenty of space to lay out and work the materials.

- Use 2 mil plastic for this project instead of 4 mil. Since you are working with prefelt sheets instead of loose fibers, the project doesn't need the protection of 4 mil.

- Baste the prefelt patterns onto the background with a needle and thread until they are securely felted in place. Better yet, use a felting needle (the same kind as for needle felting) to punch through both layers (embellishment piece and background). Position a small piece of foam beneath the background layer to serve as a pincushion for the needle.

What You Do

1. Organize your space. Lay down your bubble wrap (bubbles facing up) followed by a working sheet of 2 mil plastic. Collect your supplies.

2. Lay out the background. Baste the four colored background squares together and felt the seams as in step 3 of the Table Runner. (*See page* 79.) The assembled prefelt background will be about 6' by 6' before felting and about 4' by 4' after fulling.

3. Lay out the design. Cut out the fruit designs in the approximate proportions shown. Remember to allow for the same rate of shrinkage as for the background. Baste or needle felt the designs onto the background prefelt base.

Step 2

Step 3

4. Wet, felt, and full. The rest of the work is the same as for the placemat. So, lay the tulle netting over the project (to help keep the fruit designs in place) and

Step 4

follow the instructions on pages 74–76. Here are some pointers:

- Pay attention to the details on the design to make sure they remain attached during fulling.

- Take care to watch the seams while you felt this project. The seams should be well felted together before you wet out the rest of the blanket. Otherwise the weight of the water in the felt can pull the seams apart. In fact, it's a good idea to use only just enough water to keep the process moving.

- After the seams, the fruit designs are your next priority. As with any surface designs, make sure each piece attaches early on. If you have trouble, add a dab of soap as glue.

- In spite of your best efforts, holes or tears might develop. If so, stop and rebaste them before going on. Still have holes? Well, there's no shame in hand sewing where needed. You might as well use a colorful embroidery yarn and turn a problem into a design feature.

5. *Finishing.* Rinse out the soap, iron the felt while damp, then let it dry flat.

Variation
Baby Blanket

For this lovely, lightweight baby blanket, we fulled plain white prefelt and then basted on nuno felt roses made of fabric and prefelt. (Making nuno felt is covered in chapter 8.) Our starting size was 40" × 50", with a finished size of 28" × 36", so the shrinkage rate was about 30% instead of 33%. This is partly due to the different shape (rectangle versus square), but remember that shrinkage rates are meant as a guide, not an exact number.

Poppy Pillow

Sometimes the best way to learn something is by purposely doing the opposite.
So far we've carefully coached you on how to avoid making wavy edges, but here's
a project where waviness is just what you want. Blend a few colors together for a
truly stunning flower. It's easy to sew the felt right onto the face of pillow. Once
you get the hang of it, you might want to make a whole garden of flower pillows —
what about pansies, buttercups, or cosmos?

Before and After

Template Size: 21" diameter

Finished Size: 14" diameter

Shrinkage Rate: 33% using suggested fibers

What You Need

- basic felting supplies (*see page* 20)
- a 4 mil plastic template of a circle,
  18"–22" across, depending on the size
  of your pillow
- beads or embroidery thread to decorate
  the center of the flower
- a round silk or cotton pillow in a coordinating color
- a needle and thread in coordinating color
- about 2 oz. of Merino wool roving (your
  choice of colors)

What You Do

1. Make the template. If you want the flower petals to extend beyond the edges of the pillow, make your template a little larger than usual. For example, if your pillow is 14" in diameter, you would usually start with a 21" circle to account for the 33 percent shrinkage of Merino wool. For a larger flower, make the circle 23" instead.

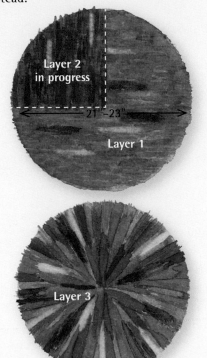

Layer 2 in progress

Layer 1

← 21"–23" →

Layer 3

Step 2

2. Lay out the wool. Divide the wool into three piles. Lay a patch of wool right in the middle of the template (to help prevent a hole). Then lay out the roving in the usual tufts, horizontally in the first layer and vertically in the second layer. For the third layer, lay out the tufts radially, beginning in the center and moving out toward the edges.

3. Wet, felt, and full. Follow the standard directions for felting and fulling. (*See pages 74–76.*) *Exception:* For this project only, break the rules! While fulling, crunch up the wool tightly in your hands any way you wish and ignore working the edges. Let the sheep stray where they will! (*See* Corral Those Fibers! *on page* 76.) Watch the felt as you do this to see what happens.

4. Finishing. When the felt is fulled and puckered in the middle, rinse it out and let it dry. Sew on the center beads or use embroidery thread to make French knots if you prefer. Lastly, tack the felt to the pillow by taking a few stitches in the center and wherever else you like.

❝ *Breaking the Rules!*

We've been repeating the mantra, "There are no mistakes in feltmaking," and the Poppy Pillow is a perfect example. True confession: This idea emerged from a piece of beginner felt that was overfelted in the middle. It turns out that controlling the edges of your felt during fulling is even *more* important when you are making anything circular. In this case the fulling "problem" created a perfect opportunity to make a beautiful flower! It's freeing to learn early on that felt is always able to be recycled somehow.

Frequently Asked Questions

Q *Why cut a separate piece of plastic for the prefelt patterns when you could just lay out the wool right on top of the working plastic?*
A The advantage of having a dedicated template is that it acts like a serving platter. You're able to move your project around independently of your working plastic — something that is useful when rolling a couple of prefelts that are finished at different times. You can also move the laid-out wool at the dry stage before felting, if you need to set it to the side for some reason. However, for small, simple projects, you may wish to draw a template directly on the working plastic. A black marker is best, but test it first to make sure it won't bleed and stain the wool.

Q *How do I make my edges straight?*
A You learn to set straight edges in the felt from the very beginning by framing the felt with your hands as you roll it. However, you can also create straight edges by learning to pile the fibers in a very straight line along the edge of your template at the beginning of the process. Then, during the first stages of wetting out, tuck the tulle or other netting under the edges a bit.

Q *How hot should the water be when I'm felting?*
A Water temperature can vary quite a bit depending on the type of felt you're making. In general, use water that is about dishwater temperature — hotter than tepid, but not so hot your hands are uncomfortable. The hotter the water, the faster the fiber scales lock.

The felting can happen too fast in some cases — for instance, when you've layered a fine, fast-felting wool with a coarser, slower-felting wool. Very hot water would cause the fine wool to quickly felt to itself before the fibers have time to migrate through the pile and mix with the coarser wool. The same is true with nuno felting (*see chapter* 8), where slightly cooler water is used in the first stages to give the fibers time to migrate through the weave of the base fabric.

No matter how hot the water is to begin with, you will always encounter the cooling effects of air temperature. In the winter, when this is more of a problem, begin with hotter water than normal because it cools so quickly on the table. Also, the thinner the felt, the faster the water will cool. The bottom line is this: Very cold water will shut things down; very hot water can shock the fibers. Almost anything in between will work.

Q *How vigorously do I roll the felt? Am I supposed to push down hard while I roll? Does pressure matter when I'm working the felt by hand?*
A It absolutely matters. From the perspective of a tiny wool fiber, your hands are extremely powerful. Every time and every place you touch your felt there will be a consequence. This is what I call having a dialogue with the wool. The wool speaks, but you talk back with your hands. Begin gently and increase pressure as you need to. Steady rolling is best; fulling too fast results in uneven felt. Stop from time to time and look at the felt. Only you can determine what is working. This is something your hands will learn to feel — they possess the intuitive wisdom you need!

FEATURED ARTIST
Chad Alice Hagen

Chad Alice Hagen has been exploring hand-felted wool and dyeing since 1979 and is the author of a number of felt-making books. (*See* Resources.) A popular teacher, Chad travels the country sharing her colorful dyepots and opinions, both dished up with a wry sense of humor.

What advice does she have for new feltmakers?

- Research contemporary feltmakers to learn about those who have gone before you in the field.
- Read about the tradition and history of feltmaking.
- Do your research on sheep breeds, dyeing techniques, and ways to felt.
- Always try to make something interesting that is your own, not a reworked copy of someone else's work.

Working with bits of resist-dyed wool like a puzzle, Hagen often deconstructs and reassembles her pieces. It's not unusual for her to incorporate something from her collection of shells, buttons, rocks, and other found material. Chad lives in Ashville, North Carolina, where she continues to felt, dye, and write.

This unusual work has been felted and resist-dyed, with stones then tied into place. *Driveway Collection 3*, Merino wool and wrapped Lake Michigan limestone, 16" × 54".

Learning about Wool

5

Discovering the many different wools you can use in feltmaking is a great adventure and often a surprise to people. The fact that wool can felt at all is amazing enough, and we often don't think to go beyond that alchemy. But different wools behave very differently and will create dramatically different felts. Quality aside, *any* wool works for spinning and needle felting, but the same is not true for wet felting. The wool you use does matter. It's unfortunately common for people to try felting for the first time and unknowingly using the wrong wool. Because feltmaking is so little understood to begin with, it's no surprise that this occurs.

Early in my feltmaking career, I made the mistake of telling someone who raised a particular breed of sheep, "That type of fleece doesn't felt." She became upset about this and said it wasn't true. I later realized she was technically correct — and that I needed to clarify just exactly what I meant by "felt."

From my point of view, fleece that "doesn't felt" means a wool that might hold together but doesn't compact down into a tight felt — or a wool that entangles slightly but remains patchy. From the perspective of someone new to feltmaking, loose wool that holds together at all qualifies as felt. What's missing is the distinction between felting and fulling. We also need ways to talk about the quality of the felt being made. Since then, I've learned to ask people about the material properties of the wool they've used, since the term "felt" is so subjective. How can we minimize all of this confusion?

We can begin by defining some very basic terms. Feltmaking is part of a broader field called *fiber arts*. The term *fiber* refers to just that — any natural or synthetic fiber, including flax, wool, rayon, camel down, Tencel, dog hair, soy silk, paper, bamboo, Angora rabbit fur, Cashmere, and so on. *Wool* and *fleece* are usually interchangeable terms. However, one confusion is when people think of Polarfleece fabric, a soft synthetic material that has nothing to do with wool. Also, when spinners or weavers talk about *a fleece* (in the singular), they are referring to the raw form of the wool, basically a sheared, dirty wool coat. Sheep are not skinned when sheared, so this is not the same as a *hide. Batts, roving, combed top, locks,* and *yarn* all refer to the physical preparation or form of the fiber.

Breed refers to different types of one particular animal. For example, Merino and Corriedale are two different breeds of sheep that have different types of wool. Sheep are often crossbred to retain different desirable traits of each parent breed. A favorite game of feltmakers is to guess whether a crossbred wool behaves in the way they might expect if they have previously felted with the parent wools. Sometimes it does; sometimes it doesn't. Within a breed, factors such as the age of the sheep and diet can also affect how a particular wool felts. Some breeds seem to be more variable in this respect than others.

Even if you have no knowledge of sheep breeds, it doesn't take long to begin to see the very real differences in your felt. Although you can certainly felt without the knowledge, if you want to experiment with different techniques or create your own wool mixtures, it's a good idea to know the source of your fleece, if possible, and what it looks like before processing.

Materiality

Feltmakers, like all other artists, need a common language to describe their process and share observations and experiences with each other. The feltmaking process is so physical and sensory — and the wools and felts so changeable and different in character — how do we begin to describe this bountiful feast?

The solution lies in a discussion of *materiality:* the physical characteristics of a given material. When describing the materiality of a felt, we might mention things like drape, sheen, roughness, elasticity, hairiness, body, and surface texture. These qualities can sometimes be subtle to the eye but obvious to the touch. Some qualities are inherent to a type of fiber, but some are dependent on the way you make the felt. Drape, for example, is influenced by both the type of fibers and the way you lay them out.

When we are learning the language of felt, materiality goes a long way toward increasing our understanding of the raw materials and the process of feltmaking. It helps new feltmakers understand the types of things to look for in their felt. At the same time, a common terminology tightens communication and allows specific information about felts and wools to be exchanged between more experienced feltmakers.

Finding Wool

People often ask where to find a list of wools that felt. While there are a few guides (we will include some of them in this chapter), there is no single magic list for a couple of reasons:

- Until recently, there simply hasn't been enough general curiosity (outside of

A Dorset sheep snoozes at the New York Sheep and Wool Festival.

industry) about felt or about wools. Since the majority of sheep in the United States are raised in very large flocks as livestock, few of us even think about different sheep breeds in the first place. Our country does not possess the long history of keeping sheep for clothing and shelter that is common in other parts of the world. Sheep here are mostly raised for food, not for the particular qualities of their fleece.

- Sheep breeds, and therefore wools, are variable. Individual fleeces from different animals also vary. The qualities of a given type of wool depend on many factors including the environments in which the sheep are raised and especially their bloodlines and crossbreeding.

Although in the minority, small "spinners' flocks" of sheep are being raised in this country for their fiber. This is a wonderful source of wool for feltmakers. In New England, for example, each state has a sheep and wool festival, which is the best place to see different sheep breeds and learn about various types of wool.

(*See* Resources.) If your state doesn't hold such an event, visit your state fair to see sheep firsthand and see what's available.

Many types of fleece can be purchased online; some feltmakers even search for particular wools on eBay. However, you may not be able to determine the quality of the fleece. This option can be useful, though, as a way to locate small amounts of a particular fleece for experimenting, especially if you live in an urban area.

Testing the Wool

It's a wonderful practice to experiment with wools from different breeds. You will learn a lot by creating fiber mixes to test the feltability and general materiality of the wools. By learning the characteristics of the wools and how they respond during felting and fulling, you can begin to understand wool on an entirely different level. One of the rewards of this experience is figuring out how to create a custom blend of wools that provides *exactly* the type of felt you desire. This is like the difference between a novice cook, who is learning the ingredients, and the master chef, who knows how each ingredient will affect all of the others at different stages.

When considering a particular wool, talk to other feltmakers who have felted with it, if possible. Your best bet, though,

is to try a sample yourself. It's easy to do a quick felting test. (*See pages* 100–101.) This test won't always reveal the whole story, but you can at least learn if the wool will felt. This test will work almost anywhere, and you can pull it off in a few minutes as long as you have access to water. A little soap is useful to speed things along, but you can even do the test without it.

If you have a more serious interest in feltmaking and want to build your knowledge more systematically, the best advice is to make larger samples. (*See pages* 102–104.) Mine are rarely less than a foot square, finished size. With larger samples, you can tell a lot more about the surface characteristics of the wool and how it behaves. More importantly, your projected shrinkage rates will be more accurate. If you take the time to compile and build your own notebook of resources, you will be rewarded with a solid foundation of information that will serve you for years to come. For a peek at some of my research, check out the gallery of swatches on page 98.

A Closer Look at Fibers

In general, felters look for different wool characteristics than spinners do. Spinners value an elastic quality in wool because it creates a nice resiliency in the spun yarn, which results in a nice-fitting garment. Felters, however, usually don't want the wool fiber to behave elastically. The goal in felting is to create an immobile, entangled mass of wool fibers that results in a stable felt. Elastic fibers that spring back apart from one another will work against the felting process. Please note that *crimp* is not the same thing as *elasticity*. A fiber may have many kinks in its structure (high crimp) but not expand and contract particularly well (elasticity). These are two related but separate material properties.

Many spinners also value long-stapled fleece, because the long hairs are generally easier to spin than shorter ones. When felted, however, this type of wool creates a very hairy felt. This is usually not a desirable quality, especially for clothing that is to be worn near or next to the skin.

It's helpful to understand that sheep fleece is composed of three different types of fibers: the *undercoat,* the *outer coat,* and *kemp.* The purpose of the outer coat is to protect the animal from the elements by repelling water and keeping the under-

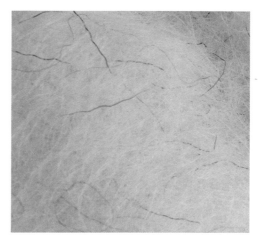

The dark, straight fibers in this white Karakul wool are kemp fibers, which prevent a sheep's fleece from becoming too matted.

coat fibers dry and fluffy. The undercoat fibers lie next to the skin and provide insulation by trapping the animal's body heat. Kemp fibers act as spacers to keep the fleece from becoming too matted, helping to prevent skin diseases.

When most people think of a sheep's fleece, they think of a fluffy, white ball. This is mostly true of the type of sheep we are used to seeing in this country: the crossbred meat sheep or down breeds. Their fleece is very spongy and elastic and will compress easily in your hand if you squeeze it, only to completely fluff back up when you open your hand. In these breeds, the undercoat and outer coat are very similar and will seem to be one.

In many other breeds, this is not the case. The undercoat is usually finer, whereas the outer coat fibers are straighter, coarser, and often hollow inside. Air is more easily trapped in the fine mesh of small-diameter, crimped fibers close to the skin, which helps keep the animal warm. The kemp fibers are

Unlike wool, silk fibers don't have a rough scale structure and can therefore reflect light much better. (1,000× magnification photo courtesy of Electron Microprobe/SEM Facility, Dept. of Geosciences, Univ. of Massachusetts.)

hollow and usually even straighter than the outer coat fibers. Not all breeds have kemp fibers, but they are quite recognizable when they're present because they are very brittle and will break or slip right out of the wool.

Both the undercoat and the outer coat fibers are useful in feltmaking but will generally give different results and felt at different rates. Finer fleece and undercoat fibers have scales that overlap more closely than those of coarser fibers. As a result, they felt faster and tighter than coarser fleece. Because the fiber is small and the overlapping creates a more broken-up texture, fine fibers are often dull in appearance. On the other end of the spectrum, larger-diameter and outer coat fibers often have a sheen or luster because light rays are able to reflect off the broadly spaced scales more easily.

An extreme example of this can be seen with luminous silk fibers. Having no scales means greater light reflection, but it also means that silk doesn't felt. When silk fiber is added to felt as an embellishment, the wool fibers migrate around the silk and draw it into the felt as they entangle.

Felting Wools Chart

Compiled by feltmaker Pat Spark, ©1990 and 2006

As a general guide to understanding more about wools that make good felt, check out this chart compiled by feltmaker Pat Spark. It is based on the Bradford System, a standard measure used in the wool industry based on the size of the individual fiber. The Bradford count refers to the number of hanks of yarn (each 560 yards long) that can be spun from one pound of wool top. (*Note:* The hanks are plural, so an "s" follows each count.) Wools with the higher counts are finer and can be spun into longer, finer yarn. The microns refer to fiber diameter.

The bulleted information is followed by a list of the breeds themselves. As you might expect, finer wools make softer felt, so they are appropriate for next-to-the-skin wearables. Coarser fibers make more durable felts that won't pill and are able to stand up to more abrasion — good for book bags or upholstery, for example. Each wool has its use and its champion. It's exciting to try them as if at a buffet, one by one!

- Fine wool ranges from 64s to 80s (or finer than 80s) = less than 22 microns
- Medium-fine wool ranges from 56s to 62s = 27 to 23 microns
- Medium wool ranges from 50s to 55s = 30 to 27 microns
- Medium-coarse wool ranges from 48s to 50s = 32 to 30 microns
- Coarse wool ranges from 44s to 48s = 39 to 35 microns
- Very coarse wool ranges from 36s to 40s (or coarser than 36s) = 40+ microns

Fine and Medium-Fine Wools

Breed	Bradford Count	Micron Count
Merino	60–80s	22–18
Rambouillet	60–80s	25–19
Delaine	64–80s	25–19
Debouillet (Delaine × Rambouillet)	62–80s	25–19
Cormo (Corriedale × Saxon Merino)	60–64s	25–22
Targhee (Rambouillet × Corriedale)	58–64s	26–23
Polwarth (N.Z. Merino × Lincoln/Merino)	58–64s	26–22
Finn (American-imported Finnish Landrace)	50–60s	32–25
Finull (Swedish Landrace × Finnish Landrace)	50–60s	30–25
Columbia (Lincoln × Rambouillet)	50–60s	31–24
Panama (Rambouillet × Lincoln)	56–58s	28–26
Shetland	54–58s	27–26
Corriedale (Leicester/Lincoln/Merino)	50–58s	34–23
Falkland Island (Corriedale family)	46–58s	34–26
N.Z. Half-Bred (Leicester/Lincoln/Romney × Merino)	50–58s	30–26

This and other useful information may be found online on the excellent North American Feltmakers Network site. (*See* Resources.)

Medium and Long Wools

Breed	Bradford Count	Micron Count
Icelandic, Dual Coated: outer wool (tog fiber)	56–60s	30–27
Icelandic, Dual Coated: underwool (thel fiber)	64–70s	22–19
Blue-faced Leicester	56–60s	30–27
Polypay (Targhee/Dorset × Rambouillet/Finn)	48–58s	32–26
Pelsull (also known as Pelssau or Götland)	48–52s	32–28
Perendale (Cheviot × Romney)	46–52s	32–28
Icelandic	46–52s	32–28
Jacob	44–56s	36–32
Leicester Longwool	40–46s	38–32
Romney	44–48s	36–31
Coopworth (Border Leicester × Romney)	44–48s	36–31
Cotswold	44–48s	36–31
Wensleydale	44–48s	36–31
Border Leicester (Leicester × Cheviot)	44–46s	38–33
Lincoln	36–40s	40–37
Ryaul (Rya Wool)	unknown	unknown
Spelsau	unknown	unknown

Coarse Wools

Breed	Bradford Count	Micron Count
Karakul	36–50s	40+–30
Navajo Churro, Dual Coated: outer wool	36–40s	40+
Navajo Churro, Dual Coated: underwool	62s	23–22
Mongolian	unknown	unknown

Learning What Works

In general, the down breeds aren't very good for feltmaking. Examples of these breeds include Suffolk, Cheviot, Shropshire, Hampshire, Dorset, and Oxford. Some of these wools don't hold together at all, while others will felt and hang together but won't work down past a spongy, springy mat. But these wools, too, have their uses. They are good for spinning and needle felting, and they make good stuffing for figures and sculpture. They can also provide a wonderful internal cushion for other hard-fulling wools, if the intent is to create a chair pad or carpet that retains good internal loft but wears well on the outside. Although it won't felt well, the down fleece can act as loose stuffing between these two outer layers.

Be flexible and patient when learning and talking to others about the best wools for feltmaking. It's easy to see the appeal in soft, fast-felting Merino wool, but don't be too quick to dismiss the coarser fibers and slower-felting wools, especially when creating mixtures. Feltmakers from different countries often prefer different wools. Australians are particularly experienced with Merino wools, while many Finns prefer their native Finnsheep wool. Fine wools are preferred for clothing worn

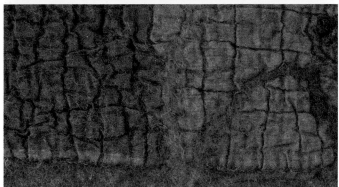

The melon-colored cotton-rayon fabric is the same in each example of nuno felt above. Small-diameter Merino fibers found their way easily through the entire weave of the cloth (top), but coarse Norwegian C-1 blend fibers had a more difficult time and could pass only through certain areas of the fabric's warp and weft (bottom). The resulting elephant-skin texture was a complete surprise and an excellent example of the rewards of experimenting with coarser wools.

close to the skin, but they may felt too fast and be uninteresting for another purpose, such as creating texture in felted artwork. Sometimes using a coarse, lesser-known wool will give a very surprising and interesting result.

The best wool to use depends on what you're making and what you want the wool to do in terms of its materiality. Do you want the wool to be shiny? Elastic? Soft? Figure that out first, and then go find a wool or create a mixture that suits your purpose. Taking the time to felt a sample can make all the difference.

SWATCH GALLERY

Trading samples and notes with other felters is a good idea, especially for a community or guild project. Keep in mind that everyone felts differently and will be at different skill levels. Take a peek inside my studio notebooks for few things I've learned with other feltmakers about different wools.

Fine Wools

Three similar wools (shown below) are very good for feltmaking.

1. Merino. Tight (flat) surface, soft and smooth.

2. Cormo. Soft and not as tight as Merino. Surface is slightly waxy.

3. Targhee. Soft and fine with nice drape.

Other Samples

Navajo Churro. Strong felt. Dual-coated fleece also used for rugs and yarns.

Manx Loghtan (rare breed from the British Isles). Distinctive color (*loghtan* means "mouse brown"). Fast felting and similar to the more common white fine wools.

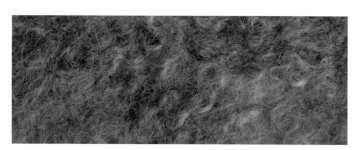

Adult Jacob. Sample made from uncarded locks to preserve crimp texture and color variation. Jacob sheep are multihorned, multicolored, and often spotted. Compare this sample to the Jacob swatch below to see how fleeces can vary within one breed.

Jacob with white silk. Slightly fuzzy surface; good drape if laid thinly. The addition of silk to this fleece gives an interesting "oatmeal" texture, attractive for felted garments.

Suffolk. Down breed, spongy fleece. Not good for wet felting.

Karakul. Very fast felting and coarse. Dual-coated fleece with a softer undercoat and longer straight guard hairs. Also has kemp fibers. Makes hairy felt good for rugs, boots, and outdoor sculpture.

Shetland lamb. Fine wool that feels rougher than Merino but makes a similarly tight surface. Strong and durable felt.

Wensleydale. Longwool. Very high sheen. Distinctive swirl texture; often used in cobweb felt.

Corriedale × down breed. Poor felter. Spongy, won't full down, uneven felt with weak areas and holes.

Coopworth ram. (This sample is dyed in turquoise blue, but the original fleece was charcoal colored.) Takes a long time to wet out and full, but when finally finished makes a beautiful, durable fabric suitable for upholstery and high-wear projects.

Blue-faced Leicester. Longwool. Takes longer, but makes a felt with a distinctive highly pebbled or pocked texture.

Alpaca. Slippery to felt. Very soft, luxurious fiber that is easy to obtain. Makes a hairy felt with nice sheen and wavy texture.

Hand-Sample Felting Test

Suppose you find a tempting wool source at a county fairground or at a local farm. Before you invest any money, do this quick test to see how it will felt. All you need is the wool (clean or dirty, in any form) and some water. Although this method is not as accurate as making a large measured sample (see page 102), it's very useful for a general indication of the wool's felting potential.

What You Need

- water
- a generous handful of wool
- soap (optional)

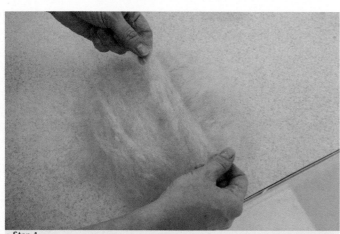

Step 1

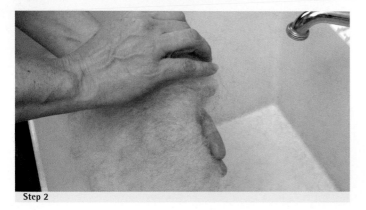

Step 2

What You Do

1. Make some layers. Pull out small amounts of the wool or fiber blend, or if the sample has well-developed locks, separate them into sheer layers that you can see through. Pile up a couple of layers as best you can with however much fleece you have. Keep each layer at a 90-degree angle to the previous layer, and try to keep the layers more or less equal in thickness. It doesn't matter how many layers you have; just build the pile roughly into a 5" to 6" square or rectangular shape that will fit comfortably on your palm.

2. Shape the edges. When you have about four layers or have used all of the wool — and can't see through the pile at all — lightly tuck the edges around the square or rectangle to make it even. Try not to fold under a large amount of fiber; just straighten the edges a bit.

3. Get it wet. Lay the sample flat in the palm of one hand. With a small amount of water cupped in your other hand, sprinkle water over the wool to get it wet without disturbing the position of the fibers.

4. Add soap. Dab a little soap on your palm and spank it into the sample a few times. This quick motion will help prevent the fibers from sticking to your wet hand. If you don't have soap, just wet the pile the best you can.

5. Felt it. Now palm the sample to felt it. Begin by pressing your hands together in a vibrating way, the aim being to agitate the wool without moving the fibers around. Then slowly begin to work the sample by pressing it tightly in your hands.

The Results

Good Felter. If it's a good, fast-felting wool, it will begin to felt immediately. Other felting wools — usually those that are a bit coarser — will take a bit longer but will eventually begin to felt together. Work these samples further by rolling them in your hands, in other words, fulling the wool to shrink it. Sometimes you'll end up with a very tiny sample! But no matter, at least you'll know it felts.

Not a Good Felter. If the fiber just keeps sticking to your hands — even when you've applied soap and worked it for a few minutes — it may not be the best wool for wet feltmaking.

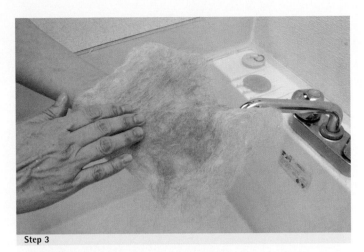
Step 3

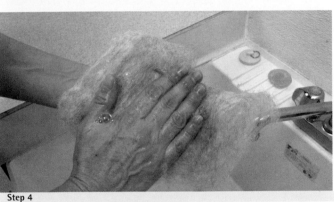
Step 4

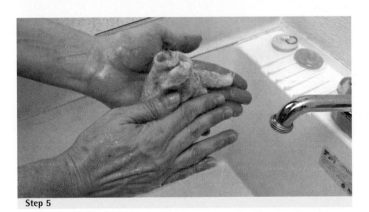
Step 5

Full-Sized Felting Sample

To create a consistent set of felting samples, you will want to felt and full your wools a little more carefully than with the quick hand-sample test. A notebook with an entry page for each sample can keep your information organized. The key bit of information you're looking for is the rate of shrinkage.

Your data will be more accurate if you keep as many factors the same as possible. For example, aim for using the same starting size and the same amount of wool (easiest if you weigh it) with the same number of layers going in the same directions, worked for the same length of time with the same soap. If that sounds like too much trouble, don't worry. It's helpful enough just making a sample before you use a new wool. It's a good idea to make it large enough to evaluate how the felt drapes, especially if you are interested in making clothing with the wool.

Before and After

Template Size: 20"–24" square

Finished Size: varies based on fiber used

Shrinkage Rate: varies based on fiber used

What You Need

- basic felting supplies (*See page* 20.)
- about 2.5–3 oz. per sample of wool, for instance, Merino, Romney, Dorset, Border Leicester, Icelandic, alpaca, or llama, all of which are fairly easy to come by
- plain wool yarn (optional), about 8"–10" long per sample

What You Do

1. Record some information. You never know what details you might need in the future from a sample, so it's a good idea to write down the source and price of the wool, the breed (if known), and the soap used.

2. Organize your space. Lay down your bubble wrap (bubbles facing up) followed by a working sheet of plastic. Collect your supplies.

3. Build the layers. Split the wool into thin strips or pieces. Basically, you want to make a 20" to 24" square of wool with as many layers as you choose. Record the number of layers. Use a ruler to measure the length and width of your wool pile before and after felting.

4. Add a strip of yarn. If you like, lay a strip of colored wool yarn across the top of the pile from edge to edge in one direction. The yarn will help you keep track of which direction you are rolling; with a square sample that's all one color, it's easy to lose track. Also, if you have an uneven number of layers — for instance, one vertical layer and two horizontal layers — it's helpful to keep track of the direction that has more layers. Will it shrink more or less in that direction? Record the direction

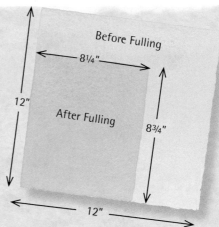

HOW MUCH DID IT SHRINK?

When calculating shrinkage, check how much the sample shrank in length and width, not in total area. Why? When we take measurements for clothing and other patterns, we measure the length of a shirt or its width across the chest, not the total area of the blouse in square inches. When figuring the size of a template or pattern, you generally measure the shrinkage in linear terms. Here's how you calculate the shrinkage rate of your full-sized felting sample.

Before felting: Suppose you laid out a 12" by 12" sample of four sheer layers of an unknown type of wool.

After fulling: Suppose you measure one direction as 8¼" and the other as 8¾". To determine linear shrinkage, divide the after-fulling sizes by the before-felting sizes, then round off to the nearest percentile. In this case:

width: 8.25" (after-fulling size) divided by 12" (before-felting size) = .6875 = .69

length: 8.75" (after-fulling size) divided by 12" (before-felting size) = .729 = .73

Important! The resulting numbers are NOT the shrinkage rates! The numbers .69 and .73 represent the material left on your table, not the part that shrank away. So you must subtract these numbers from 100.

100 – 69 = 31% shrinkage in width

100 – 73 = 27% shrinkage in length

For the best approximation, average these two numbers:

31 + 27 = 61, divided by 2 = 29% average shrinkage rate

Why are the shrinkage rates for length and width different? Many things can affect the rate, but if you roll the same number of times in every direction for the same length of time, the rates should be within about 4% of each other.

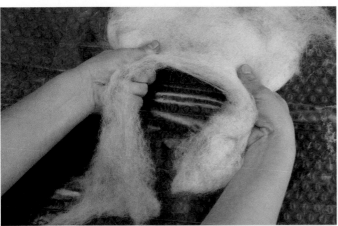

Step 3

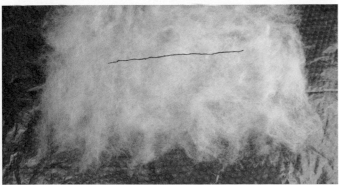

Step 4

Step 5

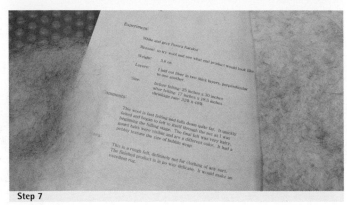

Step 7

SWATCH MANIA

Sample squares are a great way to learn about a wool or a blend of wools, but the samples needn't stay tucked away in a notebook. Here are some other creative uses:

• Use them as mini canvases for needlework or needle felting.

• Create farm animals for a child's room or holiday motifs to string as a garland along the fireplace mantle.

• Sew them together as patchwork for a table runner or floor pillows.

• Cut them into shapes and string them into a mobile to hang from a tree in your yard or garden.

• Combine them with other primitive fabric — chunky yarn knits, painted canvas squares, or leather or suede — to make a designer runner for a foyer or entryway.

of the yarn in your notebook before you felt.

5. *Wet, felt, and full.* Follow the instructions for making felt in chapter 4. (*See pages* 74–76.) To get a true shrinkage rate, you should make the sample perfectly square and roll it for the same amount of time in each direction. You could just approximate this, though. If the sample shrinks differently horizontally than vertically, just average the two shrinkage rates. This shortcut is okay as long as you have laid down an even number of layers so you don't bias the sample in one direction.

6. *Determine the shrinkage rate.* Check the sidebar for how to calculate the shrinkage. (*See page* 103.) Then record this information in your notebook or attach a label to the finished sample.

7. *Record any other relevant information.* Write down anything important that you may have observed when felting your sample, for instance:

• Did the wool seem difficult to wet out?

• Did it felt slowly but full quickly, or vice versa?

• Did you notice whether any unusual textures occurred during the felting or fulling?

• How many minutes did you work or roll the felt?

Making Larger Felt

The projects in this chapter are designed not only to show you how to create some fabulous felt for your home decor, but also to increase your skills in two major areas: learning how to work with large pieces of felt and learning how different wools, wool mixtures, and other fibers behave. Here are some pointers for working with larger flat pieces:

- Weigh and divide your wool into as many piles as you need to build evenly distributed layers.

- Look at your project from all directions as you lay out the wool. If you look across large projects from only one angle, you might be fooled into thinking your layers are even when they aren't.

- Watch your back. It's easy to get so engrossed in the fiber that you don't realize you're leaning way across the table. Protect yourself from back strain by scooting your wool pile closer to your body or walking around the table to work the pile from another side.

- For thin piles of wool or fine fleece like Merino: Buy a new pressure sprayer (designed for pesticide application) from a garden supply store and fill it with hot, soapy water. Use a prewetted paint roller to press the wool down through the tulle or curtain, saturating it with the sprayer as you go.

- For thicker piles of coarse wool, skip the sprayer; it takes too long. Pour soapy water from a cup directly onto the wool and use a plunging motion with your hand to break the surface tension.

- To avoid one side of a large project becoming cold by the time you finish wetting the other side, you can roll up the project as you go. Many felters learn to felt this way anyway because they must work in small, tight spaces. Since you can't view the template all at once, though, it's even more important to weigh and divide your wool so you'll stay consistent in thickness across the project.

- Wear a plastic or waterproof apron to avoid smearing or picking up tufts of wool as you lean over areas of your project.

Merino Bath Mat

This soft Merino rug is perfect for a bathroom or baby's room where there is less foot traffic. As a soft wool, Merino is not the usual choice for rugs, but this cozy mat delivers a big punch of color and is very comfy for bare toes! It works best over carpeting, but if you use it on bathroom tile, just place a nonskid mat beneath it.

Project Notes

- This project lets you practice making and attaching spikes, using prefelts, and handling a large layout.

- Usually a bamboo mat works best for full-sized rugs, but for this soft, thin mat we recommend just using a large piece of bubble wrap or nonskid rug mat.

- The tulle netting should be larger than the wool layout so its rough edges won't snag on the wool fibers and pull them out of place.

- The working sheet for this project can be 2, 3, or 4 mil plastic.

- For wetting out the wool, you can substitute a sprayer and paint roller for your regular thermos and dipping cup.

Set It Up, Lay It Out

1. Organize your space. Lay down your bubble wrap (bubbles facing up) followed by a working sheet of plastic.

2. Draw your template. Draw a 44" by 66" rectangle in the center of your plastic to serve as your pattern. With shrinkage, this will produce a 26" by 40" bath mat.

3. Cut the shapes. From prefelt sheets, cut out whatever shapes you desire. Lay them out inside the rectangle to check their placement. Make a sketch of the design, if you need to.

4. Make the spikes. Now make 30 spikes that are about 2½" long, or the length you like. (*See page* 47.) You might need to make a couple of practice spikes to get the length and thickness you want. (Save any rejected practice spikes for a future project.) Don't worry about shrinkage as you make the spike; what you see is pretty much what you get. Be sure to leave a full circle of dry brush at the end of each spike so it will attach well to both sides of the bath mat. When you've finished the spikes, set them aside.

5. Lay out the first layer. Divide the background wool into thirds, about 6-plus ounces for each layer. Now set two of these piles behind you and work only with the third pile. By weighing the wool or just by eyeballing it, divide this pile in half twice to make four piles of wool for your first layer. Set each pile in the four quadrants of your rectangle. You don't have to measure the quadrants; it's just helpful when laying out large projects to have a guide for how much of the wool goes into each section. Now lay out your

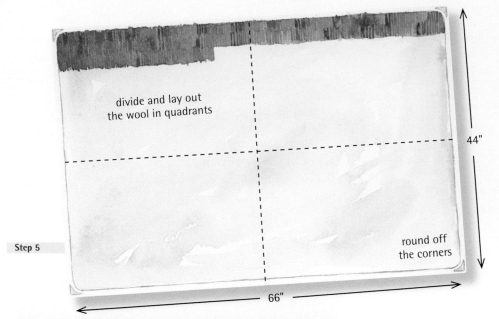

divide and lay out
the wool in quadrants

44"

round off
the corners

Step 5

66"

Step 7

roving in the usual way, with all the fibers going in one direction and slightly overlapping.

6. Lay out the next two layers. Build the other two layers in the same way as the first layer. Alternate the direction of the roving each time. (*See page* 73.)

7. Lay out your design. Refer to your sketches, if need be, and lay out your prefelt design on top of the wool.

Wet It and Felt It

8. Add water. Lay tulle over the Merino, then wet it out. (*See pages* 67–68. *If using a sprayer, see page* 105.)

9. Felt it. Felt the wool by applying pressure and vibrating your hands. Gently lift the tulle from time to time to see how the fibers are holding together. Add more hot, soapy water to the prefelt attachments, if needed. Check the prefelt design elements to make sure they're felting in. If not, add a dab of soap.

10. Attach the spikes. When the felt has formed a light skin, it's time to attach the spikes. Keep a towel right beside you as you do this, because each time you pick up a new spike, your hands must be dry to spread and the position the brushy ends. Here's what you do:

• Use the tulle to gently pick up the bath mat and flip it onto its back side.

- Lay out each spike along one end of the mat, as shown, leaving half of the brush end dry.

- For each spike, place your scrap of tulle and a tiny dab of soap over the half of the brush end spread on the felt. Firmly rub through the tulle in outward strokes that follow the direction of the fibers. Do not rub across the fibers or you'll roll them up on themselves and they won't attach.

- After stroking the fibers for a moment, very carefully check to see if the spike is sticking. Do not pull on it, or it will come right off in your hands. You only want to check that it seems to be attaching, then trust the wool to do the rest.

- Gently turn back the edge of the mat and attach the other half of the spikes to the other side in the same way.

- Follow the same process to attach the rest of the spikes to the other end of the mat.

Full It

Follow the fulling instructions on pages 74–76, with these additional pointers. This project will be a little more complicated to handle because of its size.

- At this stage the felt doesn't need to be dripping wet. All of that extra water just distorts the shape and works against the fibers trying to come together. It's much easier to work the felt somewhere between damp and wet, but do keep it as warm as you can. Otherwise the fulling will take much longer than it needs to.

- You have a big surface to deal with now, so keep in mind that the air will cool the felt faster than with your smaller projects. Minimize the time you let the whole roll sit open.

- Remember to sponge out cold water before adding more hot water.

- Finish the bath mat in the usual way with a good rinse and iron.

Step 10

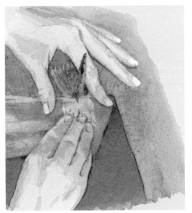

Beyond Merino

Now is a good time to introduce a new set of skills: working with wool and wool mixes other than Merino. Even if you don't plan to work with different wools on a regular basis, trying a few (at least once) will give you a greater appreciation of the wide range of possibilities within feltmaking. Think of it as the difference between having overheard only one topic of conversation versus listening to many viewpoints on many diverse subjects.

Your best opportunity to learn comes from making sample swatches. This is your chance to try out a small amount of a new wool or mixture before committing a huge amount of time and resources. We are all a little bit spoiled by felting with Merino. It *is* a grand wool, no doubt about it! But it is simply not great for everything. The wide, woolly world of felts has so much more to offer us if we have the patience to let each wool speak. For example, a new wool will likely take longer to wet out, seeming to shed water forever before it gets wet. This is typical of coarser wools but only seems frustrating when you compare it to working with Merino, which wets out fast. These coarser wools have their own stories to tell.

In this book, some projects are made with a Norwegian mixture — a medium-coarse wool blend called C-1 (actually a blend of three wool types that are similar to Corriedale wool). This blend mixes very well with other wools, is fantastic for upholstery, and is also a good candidate for anything structural (vessels or sculpted hats, for instance). However, felting it can be a challenge. We've dubbed it the "toddler wool," because you will be taken for a ride — like an unsuspecting, kindly babysitter — unless you are prepared to wipe all traces of Merino out of your mind.

For the first few minutes of felting, C-1 stubbornly sheds all of the soapy water you give it, coming up dry in your hands. What's going on? The answer is straightforward enough: The fibers are much larger than Merino fibers and they just take longer to saturate. You must break the surface tension and use *a lot* of soap, something you know not to try with Merino or you would smother the fine fibers. If you know this secret about C-1, though, the toddler wool stops fighting you and collapses like a tired, docile little darling under your hands. From there on out it felts willingly and beautifully — except for a funny little quirk it has toward the end of fulling. But that is only about having the last word, nothing that will cause you to love it any less. (You'll have to try it yourself, I can't tell *all* of its secrets!)

Tortilla Placemats

The idea for these fun placemats emerged during a workshop for studying different wools. I noticed that the color and surface of one of the mystery wools looked a lot like a tortilla. Missing my little adobe house in New Mexico and the tortillas I made there, I decided to recreate them — right down to the burned spots! After felting a few samples, I chose a Finn crossbreed from a local shepherd. After a trip to the home improvement store and a conversation with a very confused salesman ("You want to burn what?"), I came home with the perfect tool to make the spots: a plumber's torch.

Before and After

Template Size: your own, based on felting a sample

Finished Size: 15" diameter

Shrinkage Rate: varied based on fiber used (see Project Notes)

What You Need

- basic felting supplies (*see page* 20.)
- a plumber's torch
- 1.5 oz. of wool per tortilla

Project Notes

- You can use any wool you wish to make the placemats; just aim for a similar color (which means avoiding bleached white wool). Many types of wool will work, but you might try Finn, Romney, Corriedale, or natural Merino. Processed Merino roving doesn't give the right look for this project.

- Don't forget to stretch out the placemats during the fulling stage. Keep your hands working mostly out along the edges, as circular shapes are very prone to overfelting in the middle.

- Burning the spots is the trickiest part of this project, so make a couple of extra placemats on which to practice. Wool is not highly flammable, so it's actually difficult to get it to burn below the surface layer. Burn it too little and the spots will wash away. Burn too long and you'll get a hole. After a few tries, you'll get the hang of it.

- If you'd rather not work with a torch, you can either skip the burn spots or paint them on the surface with fabric paint. Or you might sandwich a bit of tan wool here and there in a middle layer of the cream fleece and it may bleed through enough to form spots.

What You Do

1. Felt a sample. With an unfamiliar wool, it's best to felt a sample to test its properties and determine the shrinkage rate. Create a plastic template based on your findings.

2. Organize your space. Lay down the bubble wrap (bubbles facing up) followed by a working sheet of plastic. Collect your supplies.

3. Lay out the wool. Divide the wool for each tortilla into three equal piles. If working with roving, lay out the wool as described for the Poppy Pillow, with the fibers placed horizontally in the first layer, vertically in the second layer, and radially in the third layer. (*See page* 85.) If working with batting, tear strips to fill the circle, with the first layer horizontal, the second vertical, and the last horizontal again.

template size is based on the shrinkage rate of the wool you use

Step 3

4. Wet, felt, and full. Felt and full the project. (*See pages* 74–76.) Rinse the finished placemats and leave them to dry. To preserve the bubbled surface texture, do not iron.

5. Burn the spots. When the placemats are dry, take them outdoors. Take sensible safety precautions and follow the manufacturer's instructions to light the torch. (*See* Caution *below.*) Hold the torch at an angle to burn a few spots on the wool and test how far away to hold the torch. After a few minutes, rub the spots deeper into the felt. The surface fibers will crumble; just blow them away. You should be left with a brownish stain. Let the finished placemats sit out overnight before hand washing them.

Step 5

CAUTION

When burning wool with a plumber's torch, wear a mask and goggles. Fumes from the singed wool are unpleasant smelling, so do the burning outdoors. You should, of course, work on a nonflammable surface, such as a driveway. A moment or two after you singe the wool, the smell will begin to fade. After airing out the tortilla overnight, there will be no residual odor.

Fulling Pointers

Because feltmaking is relatively new in the United States, many felters have not yet seen a lot of well-made felt from other parts of the world. With so many of us still new to the medium, degrees of fulling are often underestimated and our felt tends to be on the soft side. Whether felt should be soft or hard depends on its purpose, of course.

Hard, stiff felt is not necessarily good felt if you are making drapable clothing. But for shoes, boots, rugs, and upholstery fabric you must full your felt for a very long time to make it tight enough to stand up to longtime wear and abrasion. Many feltmakers are surprised to find that making such felt requires hours of fulling the fabric by hand.

Just as you can "felt" something, if you define that as patchy bits of fleece matting together, you can also "full" something, if you throw it around for a while and it shrinks a bit. It *has* fulled somewhat, but it has not been fulled very well or with any expertise — and shrinkage is likely to be uneven throughout the felt. You can learn to recognize this by stretching a finished piece to see if it pulls out too far, rebounds faster in some areas than others, or appears tighter in the middle than toward the edges. All of these factors

DESIGN TIPS

• *Scale.* Think about combining patterns of different sizes in your design. With yarns, use different thicknesses.

• *Texture.* Textures can give a design a very different surface energy. In general, rough surfaces absorb light, feel organic, and seem "warmer." Smooth surfaces reflect light, feel more formal, and seem "cooler."

• *Color.* Perhaps the aspect of design we notice first, color is personal and provides endless opportunity for expression. Experiment with a color wheel and try out combinations in your felt. Notice the difference between felting two wool colors side by side versus mixing them together before felting. Color complements are a safe bet if you are just learning how to combine colors in a design. But also work with value (dark versus light colors), saturation (rich versus subtle colors), and sections of the color wheel to experience different effects.

• *Continuity.* Distribute your design elements across the entire surface of your felt, not just in the center. Try repeating your pattern, even allowing portions of it to fall off the edge.

• *Embellishments.* Adding yarns, ribbons, beads, strips of fabric, and other items can really make your felt personal.

indicate an unevenness deep within the felt, usually due to incomplete fulling.

The thing to keep in mind is that your eyes are not the best judge of sufficient fulling. Master feltmakers show us that fulling is a matter of constantly moving the felt around while rolling it — folding it in half, opening it out again, working it upside down, working it diagonally, and so on. The feltmaker must learn to trust what the eyes *don't* see: that the wool fibers are operating on a much slower scale and need slow working over time to entangle evenly and completely.

Like many other feltmakers, I did not completely grasp these concepts at first. However, after I studied with master Turkish feltmaker Mehmet Girgic (*see page* 125), my feltmaking changed forever. Since then, I am more able to rely on what I feel and anticipate as I make felt, instead of what I see. It's like dancing with a partner and learning how *not* to lead. Instead of thinking of steps in my head, I learned to felt at the pace of the changing wool, letting my hands guide me and using my whole body in a fluid manner to work with the felt.

In the projects that follow, you can put your fulling skills to the test and make some beautiful, durable felt fabric.

Yardage of any thickness provides a great opportunity to cut loose and play with surface design. (*See* Design Tips *on page* 113.) These projects are meant to produce one large piece of upholstery felt, but you can choose instead to make a few small pieces and sew them together later for a patchwork effect. You may want to full each small piece by hand separately to finish it (after fulling it most of the way in a mat).

Carved Coaster Set

Imagine the custom gifts you can make with this project! Use someone's favorite colors to carve an animal, symbol, or abstract design — or the logo for your favorite sports team. Just be forewarned that the carving takes longer than you think, so don't plan on these for a last-minute gift.

Before and After

Template Size: 33" × 33"

Finished Size. 24.5" × 24.5"

Shrinkage Rate: 26% using suggested fiber

What You Need

- basic felting supplies (*see page* 20.)
- tailor's chalk
- ruler
- sharp, small-tipped scissors, spring-loaded if possible
- 2 oz. of C-1 or other wool for each color layer (aim for four or five color layers)
- ½–¾ oz. of Merino roving to match each color selected above

Project Notes

- In addition to carving, this project will give you the opportunity to mix wools. Once you know the characteristics of a wool, you can combine wools to get just the right mixture for the felt you want.

- This project uses Norwegian C-1 batts and Merino roving, which work together beautifully for everything from upholstery fabric to sculpture to sculpted hats. The C-1 contributes strength, sheen, durability, and structure (body). Merino not only adds a wide range of color choices, but also wets out faster and holds water better. Being a smaller, finer fiber, it can also fill in air pockets in the felt and tighten things down faster.

• The exact ratio of the C-1 to Merino is up to you. Play around to see what combination gives you a felt you like. As a starting point, use a 4:1 ratio (four parts C-1 to one part Merino), because carving requires a sturdy felt.

What You Do

1. Organize your space. Lay down your bubble wrap (bubbles facing up) followed by a working sheet of plastic. Collect your supplies.

2. Build the first layer. Draw a 32" square on your plastic for the template. Working in one color for the first layer, evenly lay down the C-1 batting.

3. Build the second layer. Cut the Merino roving that matches the C-1 layer into 3", lengths and spread the bits around randomly to make a layer on top of the C-1 layer. This is an example of breaking the rules — you don't usually cut

roving because uneven, overlapping fibers felt better. In this case, the little bits of Merino will serve as a glue. Shortened and free, they will dive down into the pile and fill in the spaces and gaps among the larger C-1 fibers.

4. Build the remaining color layers. For each color layer, repeat steps 2 and 3. When you're done, take a moment to study how high this pile of wool has become. All of that height (mostly air space trapped in the batting) is about to come crashing down onto the mat when you wet out the wool. Notice how big your square becomes when this happens. It doesn't matter much now, when making flat yardage. But it will be an important thing to know about later, when you learn about seams.

5. Wet, felt, and full. Cover the pile with tulle, then wet it out, felt, and full. (*See pages* 74–76.) Rinse out the soap and leave the felt out to dry.

6. Cut the coasters. When your felt has dried, it's time to cut it into coasters. Using tailor's chalk and a ruler, mark off a grid of 4" squares. Cut as many coasters

33"

33"

Step 2

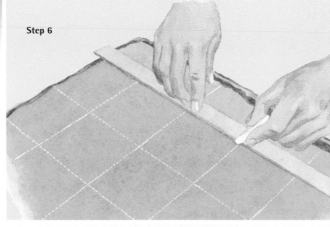

Step 6

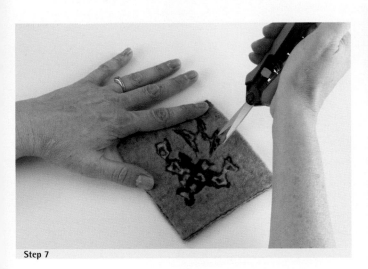

Step 7

as you wish. Any remaining yardage can be made into something else — for instance, a matching trivet or a handbag handle.

7. Carve the felt. Using sharp, pointed scissors, cut patterns into the layered felt to reveal the colors. Practice on a scrap piece first. You might prefer the back side of your felt, as the layers might look prettier. (*See* Carving Felt *below*.)

Feltmaker Karen Page of Pittsburgh, Pennsylvania, is known for her breathtaking carved felt artwork. This layered felt was very well fulled and carved over a long period of time (weeks or months).

CARVING FELT

Carved felt is beautiful, but it takes a long time to make. The key to creating a piece that lasts — and won't puff up into lint — is to use sturdy wools and felt that have been fulled very well. Making any cut into felt opens it up like a wound, providing a place for fibers to escape. If the fibers are really locked together, your design will stay as you intended, in the exact shape and size as the cut from your scissors. Follow these tips for creating your own great designs!

• Cut directly down (vertically) into the pile when first opening the top layer.

• Always cut very slowly. Even when you get the hang of it, it's easy to cut right through to a layer you didn't intend to expose. If you make a mistake, turn it into a design element. There are no mistakes in felt, right?

• Use the very tips of your scissors to cut into a layer sideways a little bit. This helps to better expose the color.

• Smaller round cuts are more stable than long gashes because round cuts are self-stabilizing. It's a good idea to break a broad pattern into smaller cuts, rather like making a design with mosaic tiles.

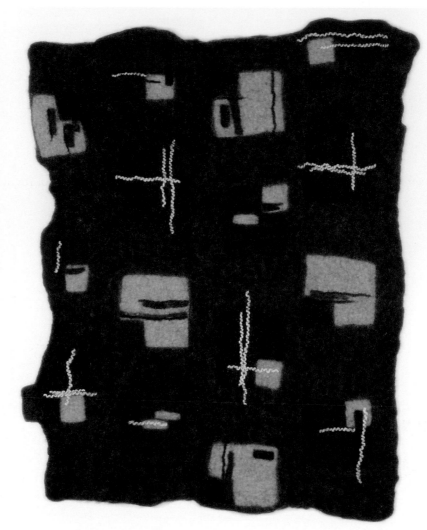

Upholstery Yardage

Sturdy felt yardage — for use in upholstery, floor pillows, book bags, and so on — is a lot of fun to make. Step right into the shoes of a textile designer! The key to very high-quality upholstery yardage is understanding just how long your felt should be fulled. But the most enjoyable part is working with shapes and colors!

Before and After

Template Size: 40" × 48"

Finished Size: varied based on fiber used

Shrinkage Rate: varied based on fiber used

What You Need

• basic felting supplies (*see page* 20.)

• a steam iron

• about 10 oz. of Norwegian C-1 or other wool (roving or batts) for the main color

• prefelts and yarns for surface decoration (we used red, yellow, and blue prefelts plus black and white yarn)

Project Notes

- For this project, use a bamboo mat, if you have one, instead of bubble wrap. With thicker felts, you are working a deeper pile of wool. A firm mat more evenly distributes the pressure you apply across the surface of the wool. This helps to felt and full the fibers more consistently.

- You can use any wool you like. Just felt a sample first to make sure it fulls down tightly enough to give you the look you desire.

- Norwegian C-1 is a great wool for upholstery because it wears well and has a nice reflective sheen. Longer-stapled Romney wool would make a good substitute, and Coopworth would also work.

- Your prefelt embellishments don't need to be made of the same wool as your yardage, but they will adhere much faster if they are. Since you won't be using the fast-felting Merino in your mix this time, keep in mind that the entire process will take a little longer. This is completely normal for most wools.

- Batts can be used instead of roving. (*See* Laying Out Batting *below*.)

What You Do

1. Organize your space. Lay down the bamboo mat followed by a working sheet of plastic. Collect your supplies.

2. Draw the template. With a black marker, draw a 40" by 48" rectangle directly on the 4 mil working sheet of plastic, roughly in the center. Unless you are determined to make a specifically sized yardage, it's fine to proceed without knowing your exact shrinkage rate. If you are using a wool that is coarser than

LAYING OUT BATTING

Batts are easy to lay out because the fibers are already fluffed up and slightly more randomized than the fibers in roving. If the batt is well prepared, you can peel off very sheer strips that are perfect for felting. Even so, a batt still has a dominant carding direction or grain that might show in the finished felt. Minimize this by alternating the direction of each layer of wool. Some pointers follow:

- Within each layer, tear the batt sheet into strips. The ragged edges provide good locking points for the fibers to grab onto one another. Divide batts along their grain, where they split apart easily and evenly.

- You don't need to overlap or shingle the strips as you do with roving — batted fibers stick very easily to one another. It's enough to just tease the seam between two strips with your fingers as you go.

Step 2

40"

48"

Merino for the first time, keep in mind that the shrinkage rate will probably be lower than you're used to. The C-1 wool has an approximate shrinkage rate of 25 to 30 percent, which varies a bit with the number of layers and how much prefelt is piled on the surface (more prefelt = slightly less shrinkage).

3. Lay out the wool. Divide your wool into piles and lay them out in the usual way, alternating the direction of the fibers each time. (*See pages* 107–108.)

4. Lay out your surface design. Play with prefelts and yarns of your choice until you have a design you're happy with.

5. Wet, felt, and full. Follow instructions for wetting, felting, and fulling (*see pages* 74–76). Here are some pointers:

- In the later stages of fulling, it's very important to stretch your yardage often

between rollings. For extra-durable yardage, stop occasionally to iron or steam it. The steam produced by the damp felt relaxes the fibers even more than pulling on it.

- When you go back to fulling after steaming, the felt becomes even harder. Full for as long as you think is necessary, in the mat or by hand or both. For very high quality, full a piece this size by hand for about three hours.

- Fulling by hand will give you a lot of information about how the felt is locking down that you can't feel when working through the mat. When you're satisfied that the piece is fulled, give it a couple of final rolls in a bamboo mat to smooth out the felt before final finishing.

6. Finish up. Rinse, iron, and dry as usual.

New England Boot Tray

If you live in a climate with snowy winters or a rainy season, you'll appreciate having this sturdy boot tray handy just inside your door. If you are lucky enough to live in a sunny, mild climate, the tray is a perfect place to drop your muddy gardening clogs. You can even hose it down to clean it — Karakul wool is very rugged! The colorful spots you see are made by shaving through the textured top layer to reveal the middle layer of wool.

Before and After

Template Size: 26" × 36"

Finished Size: varied based on fiber used

Shrinkage Rate: varied based on fiber used

What You Need

- basic felting supplies (*see page* 20.)

- one or two disposable razors or very sharp scissors, to shave and snip the finished surface

- coordinating thread, needle, and thimble to hand sew the sides of the tray or a sewing machine with a leather needle

- a steam iron (optional)

- 8–9 oz. of Karakul wool (whites, grays, and shades of brown from mocha to espresso are available)

- about 4 oz. of brightly colored down breed or Harrisville wool

Project Notes

• This project is a simple variation of the flat yardage projects. All of the steps are the same except for the last one of sewing strips of yardage to the sides to make the walls of the tray. However, I've included one new twist: You will deliberately use in the middle layer of the tray wool that doesn't full down tightly. Sandwiched between two layers of wool that felt extremely fast, the down wool will just sit there and become trapped inside by the fast-felting outer wool. This creates a nice, spongy cushion with a hard-wearing covering — a great concept for chair pads as well as boot trays.

• Karakul is an extremely coarse wool with kemp and long straight fibers. This wool is very unusual and quite different from more commonly used wool. It's very primitive and has a wonderful texture for home decor projects, such as rugs or outdoor sculpture. Although coarse, it felts as fast or faster than Merino and has an even higher shrinkage rate. Karakul means business!

• Choose any down breed like Suffolk, Dorset, or Hampshire for your middle layer. Try to find a dyed color to make the tray more interesting. I used Harrisville fleece, a mixture of mostly down breeds that comes in a gorgeous color palette. However, because Harrisville fleece is a very short-fibered wool mixture, it's prone to pilling. So, be careful in the last step, where you'll shave the top layer of the project to reveal the color of the wool inside. Just keep your shaved spots on the small side if you are using Harrisville wool.

26"

Step 2

36"

What You Do

1. *Organize your space.* Lay down your bubble wrap (bubbles facing up) followed by a working sheet of plastic. Collect your supplies.

2. *Draw the template.* Center and draw a 26" × 36" rectangle directly on your plastic with a black marker. Once again, you don't need to know an exact shrinkage rate since you're essentially making a large sample.

3. *Lay out the wool.* Divide your Karakul wool in half and set aside one half. Lay out the bottom layer with the first half. For the second layer, lay out the down breed wool or Harrisville wool. (We laid out regions of three different colors.) Use the other half of the Karakul wool for the third layer. *Note:* Since both wools I used are random batting, the direction of the layers was not an issue. If your top and bottom fiber is strongly directional, lay these layers at right angles to keep the shrinkage more even.

4. *Wet, felt, and full.* Cover your project with tulle, then wet it, felt it, and

Step 5

full it. This time the fulling will feel very different: Often the Karakul layers felt to themselves first and feel like silk paper. Full long enough for little bumps to form on the surface; this means the Karakul fibers are finally reaching down through the downy layer. If you don't full it long enough, down fleece will fluff out of any decorative cuts you make in the top layer. Make sure the bumps on the felt's surface are very small (about the size of the end of ballpoint pen) before you stop fulling, because they will be much easier to shave.

5. Shave the felt. When the felt is dry, use a disposable razor to make two passes across the top layer of the boot tray. In the first pass, remove all of the obvious loose hairs. In the second pass, shave away the highest parts of the bumps on the Karakul surface. Press hard and use a flicking motion with the razor, or use small, very sharp scissors to snip away tiny holes. This will reveal the colored down wool in the middle layer. It's very important to make only small dots ($\frac{1}{8}$" to $\frac{1}{4}$"), or the down fleece will puff out like big lint balls. Work slowly and stop frequently to look at your design to determine areas that need more revealed color.

6. Make the sides. For double-layered sides that are not only colorful but also strong enough to remain upright, do the following:

- Start by trimming off any uneven edges all around the tray, so that all edges are straight. Then, mark and cut a 1"-wide strip off all sides. Set them aside, to be used as reinforcing strips.

- Mark another 1"-wide strip on all sides. Cut out each of the four corners, then use an iron to steam and press the sides along the 1" fold lines until they are standing more or less upright.

- Trim the ends of the 1"-wide reinforcing strips as needed to fit the sides of the tray. With the most colorful side of each strip facing up, use a whip stitch to sew them to the folded sides of the tray (at the corners and along the fold line).

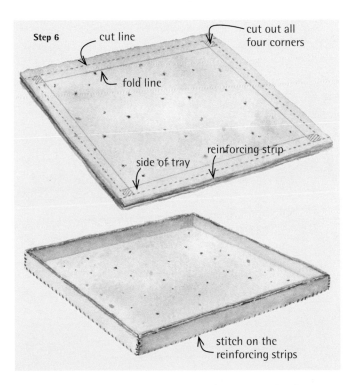

Step 6

cut line

cut out all four corners

fold line

reinforcing strip

side of tray

stitch on the reinforcing strips

Frequently Asked
Questions

Q. *I tried to make felt with my kids and we used some fleece donated by a local farm. It didn't stick together very well. What happened?*

A The most likely answer is that this was not a breed that was good for wet felting. Down breed sheep are very common, so it might have been this type of fleece. If you have any left, squeeze it in your hand to see if it's like a jack-in-the-box, compressing and then springing open quickly. If so, it may be down breed fleece. Try to find one of the breeds mentioned in this chapter. When working with children, Merino is a very good choice because it felts so easily. Karakul and Pelsull (Norwegian Götland) are also pretty fast, but they are more difficult to locate.

Q. *Is it possible to mix down breed fleece with good felting fleece to make it go further? Will this blend felt?*

A It depends, of course, on the amount of each in the mixture, but in general, yes. Since down breeds are so numerous in our country, they account for a large percentage of the wool pool. At least one popular mill that I am aware of uses down wool as part of its felting batts blend. Although the felt created with this wool has the distinctive "spongy" feel of down breed wool, it does felt fairly easily. However, because the fibers are very short and lintlike, they are prone to pilling. It all depends on the intended use of your felt.

Q. *You mention using felt samples outside — won't this ruin the felt?*

A Nope. It's okay when it's on the sheep and it's still okay when it's off the sheep. I do like to use felt where wind can help dry it out between rains, however. And it will definitely *change* the felt. But this is the most interesting part of creating outdoor art!

Q. *Can I felt my dog's or cat's hair?*

A Yes. It sometimes works better to lower the pH when felting these fibers; try felting them without any soap at all. If that doesn't work, add vinegar to the water. It's a good idea to mix dog or cat hair with wool for more predictable results. The fibers can be very slippery to work with, but it is possible to felt them. Dog or cat hair can also be applied as a final layer on a needle-felted project made of wool. Oregon artist Wendy Hallman makes unique, custom pet portraits with animal fibers. (*See* Resources.)

FEATURED ARTIST
Mehmet Girgic

Anyone interested in traditional feltmaking should know about Mehmet Girgic, the Turkish master feltmaker. Born into a feltmaking family, young Mehmet joined his grandfather, father, and uncle in their felting business, where they made kepeneks (shepherd cloaks) and felt rugs. (*See* Resources.)

In 1996, an English group of feltmakers came to Konya, Mehmet's hometown, to learn how to make felted rugs. Soon, Mehmet was contacted by interested people from many countries and began coming to the United States on a regular basis to teach special workshops. American feltmaker Theresa May O'Brien, one of Mehmet's apprentices, also teaches the Turkish feltmaking method. (*See some of her work on page* 287.)

After 25 years, the family business continues. Mehmet and his wife work together to keep traditional textile arts alive in the form of felt, natural dyeing processes, and research into traditional carpet design. Usually laughing with a twinkle in his eyes, Mehmet is always ready to talk about felt. Here are some of his comments for beginners:

Focus on your connection to the felt. When I watch people felting for the first time, I look for those who

become lost in the work, connect to the material, and stay focused on the felt. These are the people who make the best felters.

Making felt is always about relying on the energy of others. Even when you work alone, others have gone before you. When you work together in a group, there is an important thing that happens, an increased energy. This group energy feeds everyone, and I am always grateful to be able to say, 'We made the felt.'

3-D Seamless Felting

6

Many consider the *seamless*, or Scandinavian, technique to be the heart of wet feltmaking. Once you know the method, you can create almost anything that is three-dimensional, including felt clothing, hats, sculptural art, masks, footwear, handbags, and mittens. No wonder we recognize it as such a pivotal technique within the medium of felt.

Don't be confused by the term "seamless" — we do talk about the joining and construction of "seams," where two sides of a felt come together. However, no sewing is required, and a smoothly felted seam can truly appear seamless.

Essentially, seamless felting works as follows: Two flat, layered piles of wool are joined during the felting process to create a whole. The two flat halves are separated by a *resist* (a nonfelting material such as plastic) to keep the two sides from felting to each other. The fibers along the sides of the two halves are joined in a seam.

This creates a sealed package or sandwich made up of a layer of felt, the resist, and another layer of felt.

There are two options for seamless felting. One is the *closed resist method*, so called because the resist is completely enclosed on all sides by the wool seams. When the fulling stage is reached, a cut is made in the sealed package and the resist is removed from the middle. In the slightly different *open resist method*, the resist hangs freely out of at least one side of the project where no seam is needed. When it's time to full, the resist is simply pulled out and set aside. In both cases, the felt is initially flat, and later is fulled and custom-shaped into a three-dimensional object during fulling.

Frequently Asked
Questions

Q *What is the difference between the open and closed resists?*
A The difference is an important one, especially when it comes to understanding sculpting and shaping wool. It all has to do with fiber dynamics. The wool fibers full down differently when one side of the felt–resist–felt sandwich is left unjoined, because the stresses across the felt are different. Fibers near the open edge have an opportunity to migrate a little more freely than fibers in the interior regions of a felt where all edges are sealed into a flat but continuous pile. By and large, the closed resist method is the most commonly used seamless technique.

Q *If you're going to cut the sandwich open anyway, why make a completely sealed package in the first place?*
A To create an evenly fulled piece, it is preferable to keep the shrinkage stresses equal across the entire area of the felt. It's much more work to go back later to shape a partially hardened edge that was left open during felting. Better to completely enclose everything from the beginning and create the cut after the felt is stable. The exception is when using multiple resists for pockets, flaps, and secondary layers.

Q *Why does the wool felt differently along an open edge?*
A To fully understand the difference between open and closed resists, it helps to see it from the fibers' point of view. Let's look again at the sheep herding analogy. (*See* Corral Those Fibers *on page* 76.) In a closed resist method, you are closing off all escape routes, forcing the fibers to entangle inward toward other fibers. This is similar to stopping the herd in its tracks and tightly penning the animals into a circle — no escape. The result is a nicely even felt.

With an open resist, you are leaving one small area open — like a corral with an open rear gate to the trail. The sheep don't actually escape, but those near the gate can back up or move forward along the trail just a bit as the group is herded more tightly into the pen. It is this pressure release valve, this less-constrained area, that allows the feltmaker to full in customized ways and build a shape. We will discuss this more in the next chapter, but for now, let's move on to the elements of seamless felting.

More about Resists

Resists can be constructed from a number of materials. Many feltmakers in the United States use plastic, but some use cardboard, vinyl, thin craft foam, or cloth with a tight weave. Although the seamless technique was supposedly developed by Scandinavian feltmakers, a cotton fabric resist may have been used in the same manner by Persian felt hat makers several thousand years ago.

Cotton muslin was frequently used in experiments by American feltmakers in the 1970s and 1980s. Early felting techniques usually involved dunking the wool–resist package into hot and cold water to shock it. The washing machine was also commonly used to make felt.

Resists are like much of the rest of your felting equipment: The right choice of tools depends on the situation. For example, for very fine, one-layer Merino wool garments, use a 1 mil or 2 mil plastic resist. Because it's thin and flexible, this unobtrusive resist is perfect for gently protecting two delicate layers from each other.

If you are making a felt obelisk for an outdoor garden sculpture, you will be felting many layers of wool in a thick pile. For this project, you would need plastic vinyl or 6 mil plastic. However, if your wool pile is very thick, you need a resist that is thick enough for you to feel where its edges are so you'll know if it's slipping around inside. For this purpose, you could tape a couple of cardboard resists together. Cover them in duct tape if you intend to reuse the resist. If the wool you are working with is difficult to wet out, you could use both a resist and a mat that will let the water pass through.

Multiple Resists

Complex, three-dimensional shapes with pockets, flaps, or other attached appendages use multiple resists at the same time. Each resist functions to isolate a particular part of the shape from the main body of the piece. This technique allows you to create layers of felt that are attached at one point but flap freely from another, like overlapping fish scales or roof shingles. Multiple resists provide a fabulous way to unlock your creativity and make a design your own.

By using small resists that are completely buried within a larger wool pile, you can create wonderful windows and

RESIST TIPS
- When cutting out a resist, always round off the sharp tips of any corners. This will prevent them from poking through your delicate seams while felting is in process.

- When removing a resist, always make as tiny a cut as possible. Cuts can quite easily grow beyond their intended size. Take it slowly, one snip at a time, until you see how the felt behaves.

secret pockets that can later be stuffed with natural materials or any other objects that will fit inside. These little squares or regions of resist plastic are left in for the entire feltmaking process and then cut open at the end. Often, just locating them again becomes a fun little game; because the felt changes character so much, you don't recognize where they are and must find them by the sound of the crinkling plastic inside the felt. Using small, sharp scissors, you can cut down through the outer felt layers and strip them away or choose to leave them attached like the little windows on an Advent calendar.

Tackling Seams

Joining seams is always more difficult with combed top or commercial roving than it is with batting. This is because the straightened fibers of roving are linear and tend to move and felt in mostly one direction. The ends of the fibers (called rays) are where they first lock and attach. In batting, the randomized fibers have many attachment points sticking out in all directions. They are prone to stick to each other anyway, so they readily attach around the edges of two flat layers of wool that are being joined. Since commercial roving is so widely used, however, our instructions will be based on the use of this material. You can substitute batting without the need for additional instruction.

As you know by now, there are many ways to do the same things in feltmaking. We'll present some basics for making seams, but with time you may discover little tricks to customize your process. It's always useful to watch other felters make seamless felt for this reason, even if you're a pro at making flawless seams. Two primary options are:

- *Design Inside.* The two halves of the project are assembled with the design facing in, hidden inside the resist package. The piece is later turned inside out. The Road Trip Pillow Cover (*page* 133) is made using this method. One advantage is that seam construction, which is later turned to the inside of the project, does not show.

- *Design Outside.* When it's important to see the design as you work (for instance, when matching up stripes), you can build the layers with the design facing out. The Everybag (*page* 143) is made using this method.

FELTING IN THE WASHING MACHINE

A number of feltmakers prefer to use a washing machine to make their felt. The spanking action of the agitator results in *shock fulling*, where fibers immediately but unevenly lock together. A front-loading machine eliminates much of this distortion, but the felt is still being fulled without any controls along its borders. So, unprotected felt is likely to emerge overfelted in the center. This distortion is minimized with nuno felts since the fabric acts as a stabilizer.

While this approach is to be avoided when making fine-quality felts, it might be just the thing for the artist making free-form textures. It's also a nice way to create a bubbly textured felt that is meant to be somewhat unfinished inside, giving the felt a semiquilted feel. Homey chair pads can be made this way from a flat rectangle of thickly laid (about six or seven layers) prefelt.

For a more even result, wrap or enclose your wool in something. For instance, Norwegian felters carefully wrap their nuno felt in rolled towels and secure them with ties before fulling them in the dryer. Shapes with unequal dimensions are especially prone to shock fulling. For example, if you full a coat with sleeves and a hood, baste the coat closed or contain it in a dryer bag. Otherwise, the appendages flapping against the dryer drum will result in uneven shrinkage. This is less of a problem if you're fulling a flat rug, a ball, or any other project with a uniform shape.

Caution. Beware of clogging your appliances with fiber. For this reason alone, it's a good idea to wrap your felt in something before washing or drying it.

Tip. Someone once advised me to use the dryer to remove annoying guard hairs that were shedding from a fine felted scarf I made. I fluffed the scarf on "air" for two or three minutes, and it worked like a charm.

SHRINKAGE AND TEMPLATE SIZE

Although some felters initially avoid shrinkage calculation, it's simple enough once you know the formula. Truly accurate formulas for shrinkage rates should measure volume rather than area, so you would need to know the amount of wool spread over a specific space. But it's a good approximation for most flat felt to make a square sample, measure the change in length and width, and take an average. (*See page* 102.)

Use the worksheets below to figure out shrinkage rates or to calculate how large a template needs to be to reach a targeted size.

Calculation 1: Find the Shrinkage Rate

What you already know: The measurements of a sample piece, both before and after you felted it

What you want to know: The shrinkage rate for the wool used in that sample piece

Calculation 2: Find the Template Size

What you already know: The desired finished size/measurements of a piece and the shrinkage rate of the wool

What you want to know: How big to make the initial layout/template

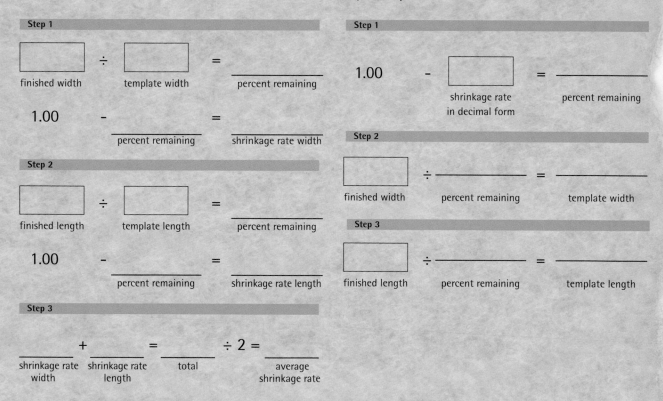

Note: When you felt something other than a square shape (which is most of the time), the shape itself will change the way the wool shrinks. Even simple rectangles will shrink differently in each direction. Averaging the length and width shrinkage is fine for square sample estimates; after all, you need to base your template size on something. Just know that as your shapes become more complex, shrinkage rates become more of a ballpark estimate than an exact science.

Road Trip Pillow Cover

Travel pillows are a terrific gift and dearly loved by all who receive them. This quick project can be a lot of fun when you want to mix some colors, try out a few new yarns, or simply practice making seams. You can make a cover to fit an existing travel pillow or fill the cover you make with pillow stuffing. Don't be surprised if you find yourself taking orders! As a bonus, this basic shape can be adapted to make any number of projects, including a handbag.

Before and After

Template Size: 24" × 32"

Finished Size: 15" × 20"

Shrinkage Rate: 37% using suggested fiber

What You Need

- basic felting supplies (*see page 20*)
- one extra sheet of 4 mil plastic, somewhat smaller than the bubble wrap
- 4 mil plastic for two copies of the template/resist
- soap glue (*see page 22*)
- small, sharp scissors
- a needle and thread
- a ready-made 15" × 20" travel pillow or loose polyester pillow stuffing
- prefelt, yarn, silk, or other embellishment
- about 3 oz. of Merino roving

Project Notes

- The steps below assume that you will be using commercial roving, which is fussier than batting and needs more detailed instructions. If you will be using batting instead, the basic steps are the same, but you needn't be concerned with the direction of the rays along the edges.

- Use a pool noodle as a rolling bar for this project.

- This pillow cover is made with the design inside/closed resist method.

Set It Up, Lay It Out: Side 1

1. Organize your space. Lay down your bubble wrap (bubbles facing up) followed by a sheet of working plastic. Collect your supplies.

2. Create the template and the resist. A typical travel pillow measures 15" by 20". If yours is that size, follow our calculations based on a 37 percent shrinkage rate. If you are making a cover to fit an existing pillow, measure its length and width from seam to seam and use the formula in this chapter to calculate the size of your template. (*See page* 132.) If you plan to stuff your cover, the exact dimensions aren't important. Trace two copies onto 4 mil plastic and cut them out. One will be your template and the other will be your resist. Round off the little corner tips.

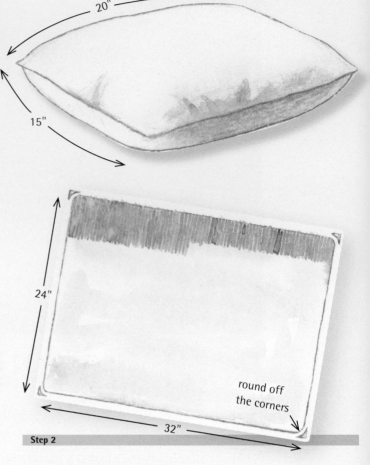

Step 2

3. Lay out the wool for Side 1 of the pillow. Divide the wool in half (one pile for each side of the pillow) and set one half aside. Divide the other half into three piles. Place the template on the working plastic and lay out three layers of Merino roving. Alternate the direction of the fibers for each layer and pay special attention along the seam edges. (*See* Working with Roving *on page* 65.)

4. *Embellish Side 1.* On top of the three layers, lay out prefelt, yarn, silk, or other embellishments. It's best to leave the ends of a few embellishments hanging out beyond your rays and template. These ends will later be wrapped around the resist seam and become felted onto Side 2, which makes the design appear uninterrupted and seamless.

Wet Out Side 1, Add the Resist

5. *Wet it out.* Lay the tulle over Side 1, then dribble some soap glue over any non-wool design elements to help them adhere. With wet, soapy hands, gently press down through the tulle to begin felting the design into the background wool. Vibrate the wool, don't move it. Be very careful not to shift the position of the fibers. Carefully add warm, soapy water to the middle of the pile and continue pressing until the design just begins to stick. (*See page* 67.)

6. *Roll briefly.* Use the pool noodle to roll up the bundle. Roll only for about two minutes or so to slightly begin felting Side 1. If you roll too long, the piece will begin to shrink and won't fit your resist.

7. *Add the resist.* With the tulle still in place, use a sponge to remove excess water from the felt. Then remove the tulle and center the resist on the top of Side 1. You will be looking through the plastic to the design. Now that the wool has been wetted, the rays of the roving should extend slightly beyond the edges of the resist on all sides.

Step 3

Step 4

Step 5

Step 6

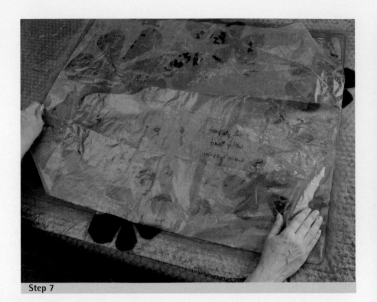

Step 7

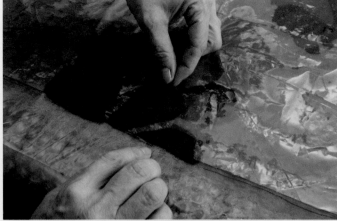

Step 8

ANATOMY OF A SEAM

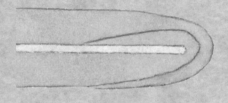

Seams are made by folding over the ends of the wetted wool, referred to as *rays*, along the edges of the resist. The rays from each side of the resist are "flipped" at different times, as described in the instructions. When you've finished all of the rays, the project will be constructed as shown, with the seams made of a 50:50 mix of rays from Sides 1 and 2.

Important: While flipping rays along an edge or corner, never allow rays from the same side to cross or overlap each other, or the seam is likely to fail there. Instead, anticipate tight corners by angling the rays as you approach, making room for all of them to lie flat in one layer.

Lay Out Side 2

8. *Lay out the design for Side 2.* This part takes some creative visualization because you build the design for Side 2 face down against the plastic — in other words, facing the design on the other side. (Remember, you turn the whole thing inside out later.) Smear the resist with slimy soap glue to adhere your design. Flip the trailing design yarns and shapes from Side 1 onto the top of the resist. Add new embellishments for the rest of the Side 2 design and pat them down onto the plastic. (Even if your soap glue has dried, the plastic will remain tacky.)

Step 9

Step 10

TROUBLESHOOTING

What if I have areas where there are no rays or too many rays?

- If there aren't enough rays, add a few fibers of roving in the bare spots, in 2" or 3" lengths that will felt in quickly. Wet the fibers and tuck the ends around to the other side.

- If you laid too much fiber along the template edges, wetting the wool can cause it to spread way beyond the template border. Welcome to the most common mistake made when learning seams! To avoid overly thick seams, trim off some of the rays. They will felt better if you snip into them as if you were making little fringes. Cut *into*, not *across*, the fibers.

9. Flip the rays from Side 1. Beginning in the middle of a side (not at a corner), lift up a line of rays, one small section at a time, and fold them over the edge of the resist. With your fingers, lightly comb each section flat and smooth, with all rays pointing straight toward the center. It's important not to let the rays overlap or they won't felt properly. When you go around a corner, this means angling the rays somewhat to compress them into a smaller space.

10. Lay out the wool for Side 2. Dry your hands and divide the remaining wool into three piles. Build all three layers the same way as for Side 1, using the resist as the template. Be careful not to extend the rays beyond the template lines — like the first side, the fibers will spread out when you wet them. *Reminder:* The first wool color you lay down on top of the surface design will be the dominant color on the finished pillow cover.

Wet Out Side 2, Felt It

11. Wet out Side 2. Cover the entire pile with tulle, carefully add warm, soapy water, and with wet, soapy hands, press down to begin felting. As mentioned in chapter 4, it helps to use a smaller square of plastic to spread the water. This time you will not be able to see your design, but imagine feeling the underlying bubbles on your bubble wrap as you apply deep pressure. Do this a few times around the entire project, then wrap it up and roll it for a couple of minutes.

12. Unroll it and turn it over. To do this, unroll the bundle and remove the tulle, then lay your second working sheet of plastic over the entire project. Press it down all over to seal the felt in between the two sheets of plastic as if it were inside a vacuum. Next, roll the encased felt up and reverse-roll it back out onto the table. Remove the original working sheet of plastic and the original template and set them aside. The back of Side 1 will face up now.

13. Flip the rays from Side 2. To complete the seams, fold over the rays as you did for Side 1. Now you will perform an extra step you didn't do on the other side. Using your tulle, create friction by rubbing in the direction of the rays all along each edge to felt them into the Side 1 felt. (*Note:* It's important not to rub *across* the rays or you will roll them into twisted threads that can't attach to anything.) You've already partially felted Side 1 rays when you rolled in step 11, so the Side 2 rays need a little help catching up. This step helps them to felt right in, making a strong seam. When you've felted all of the rays into the piece, you'll have a sealed "package" of felt with the surface design and the resist hidden away in the middle.

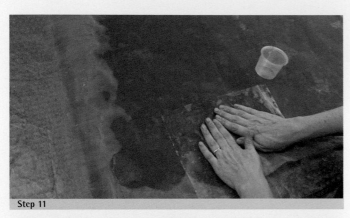

Step 11

Step 12

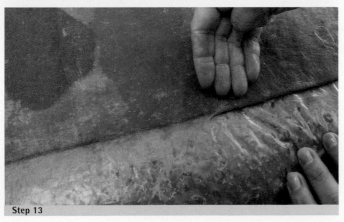

Step 13

Full It, Shape It

14. *Begin fulling.* Roll up the entire package in the tulle and gently roll out any excess cold water. Apply fresh hot water and soap, and roll the package in the net or bubble wrap for a few minutes. When you see the edges curling up slightly, this indicates that the felt is acting as one coherent piece and the seams have been proved. Stop rolling to prevent any further stress on the seams from the resist pushing against them from the inside.

15. *Cut the felt.* During this next step, keep the felt on the table and try not to lift it. The weight of the wet wool will pull on the seams if you pick it up off the table. For this pillow design, you will be cutting along one of the two shorter seam lines (to tuck in the pillow lengthwise), so check both ends, and cut along the weaker of the two. *Important:* Whenever you make a cut in your felt, work the edges immediately to restabilize them. (*See* Cutting and Sealing *below.*)

Step 14

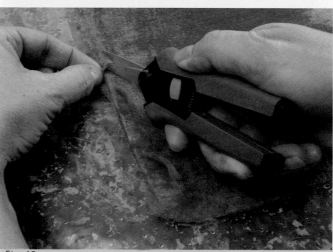

Step 15

CUTTING AND SEALING

Whenever you cut felt, you release some of the entangled fibers along the cut. Like the sheep in our analogy, these fibers are free to loosen and begin to separate from the group. (*See Corral Those Fibers, on page* 76.) A cut edge can grow quickly out of control and become too large if this happens. Always stop immediately after making a cut and *lightly* rub the seam parallel to the cut. This will seal the felt back together and stabilize it.

Step 16

Step 17

SHAPING AND FULLING

There is no exact sequence for shaping felt; the situation is unique for each project. However, the goal in each case is to set the memory of a shape into the wool. You start on this early, when the felt looks like a limp blob. The entanglement of the fibers is progressive — one fiber affects the next fiber, and working on one region affects fibers in other regions. You have a limited time frame for convincing the felt of its shape.

With all projects, shaping goes hand in hand with fulling, which means it begins when you cut the felt and remove the resist. Most people are surprised to learn that stretching the felt is an important part of this process. It helps to understand that the process is not linear but more of a dance — a push and pull to the end. Any number of different approaches can be effective.

Since the fiber scales are heat sensitive, sometimes you can adjust a set shape by submerging the felt in very hot water and starting over. But this may not work once the fibers are well entangled. In advanced shaping techniques, when the felt is being sculpted into complex shapes, feltmakers use steam and shaping tools to help them set a deep memory into the wool.

16. *Remove the resist.* Without lifting the felt off the table, reach in and gently pull out the plastic resist. To protect the fragile seam line, keep one hand on the seams as you pull.

17. *Continue fulling.* To strengthen the felt, *carefully* knead it in your hands on top of the bubble wrap. This motion quickly shrinks felt, so be careful not to use too much hand strength or do this for very long. After a minute or two, check to make sure nothing has felted together inside or along the edges. If it has, very gently separate the felt without putting any stress on the seams. By now your felt should have shrunk slightly and be strong enough to roll and shape.

18. *Begin shaping.* Since the pillow cover is essentially flat, shaping is less involved than for later projects. Focus primarily on making nicely rounded corners and even sides. With your hand flat against the seam *inside* the felt, gently rub the seam against the bubble wrap. Work the sharp seam line flat and make it disappear.

The goal is to erase all traces of the felt's memory of its former flat life. This includes how you let it sit on the table: Don't let it fall back into the flat position! At this early stage, you can very gently stretch the seam area as you move along the seam lines with your hands, rubbing them out. Work the felt slowly and gently at first until it becomes stronger.

19. *Shape and roll.* To create the final shape of the felt, alternate between rolling and shaping steps. How much of each depends on the project you're making.

Rolling. Lay down the felt — *not* in its original flat orientation. Roll it up in your bubble wrap or mat with the pool noodle in the center (leave the tulle on at first if you wish). Secure the bundle with ties and roll it on a flat, hard surface, using medium to strong pressure. Stop often to check and rotate the felt, so it will shrink evenly on all sides. If the piece gets cold, gently squeeze out the cold water and add hot, soapy water.

Shaping. When the piece has begun to shrink, open the roll, turn the cover inside out, and stretch the felt into the desired shape. Every time it's rolled, the felt returns to two dimensions, so stop frequently to work it back into your three-dimensional form. When you feel the time is right, stop rolling and shape the piece by hand. Measure the sides to check the shape. If one side is shrinking too much, stretch it out in that direction. Damp felt is very pliable and easy to manipulate by using some muscle. Don't be afraid to really pull on the felt, especially in misshapen areas — for instance, a corner that is shorter than the others.

20. Rinse and dry. When you are happy with the shape and size of the piece, rinse it well to remove all of the soap. Lay it flat to dry.

21. Finish the pillow. Slip the ready-made pillow into the cover or pack the cover with pillow stuffing. Then hand sew the opening.

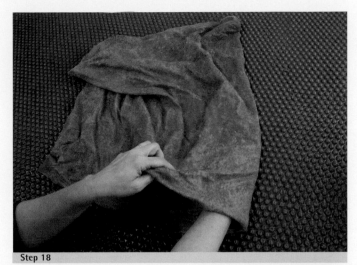

Step 18

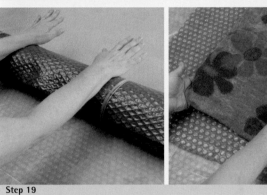

Step 19

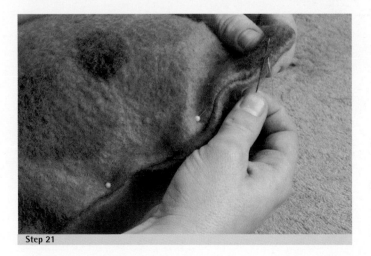

Step 21

Changing Gears

For the next project, the template shape is the same as for the travel pillow, but the process will follow the design outside method. The end result will be a simple handbag with attached cords and colored wool striping in the design. (By adding a small pocket, you will also be introduced to using multiple resists.) The steps are essentially the same as for the pillow, but with a different placement of the wool while making your seams.

There are good reasons for learning both the design inside and the design outside methods, so we recommend trying them both. The design outside method is good for attaching cording or other special features, monitoring how well the surface designs are sticking to the wool, applying fringe or spikes to the edges of the project, and lining up any colored striping patterns. It is possible to do all of these things using the design inside method, but it becomes more awkward.

The design outside method requires your seams to be impeccable, since they will show on the outside surface. If the seams are well made with evenly laid wool that is carefully placed around (not covering) key design elements, they will melt into place and become invisible — a perfect success. But if they are clunky and thick, they may create unsightly areas along the edges of your project or, worse, cover up parts of your design and ruin the seamless look you are trying to achieve.

THROUGH THICK AND THIN

It can be tricky, at first, to make seams of even thickness and strength. With practice, you will learn to create a smooth edge that appears seamless. Here's what to do if

- *your seams are too thin.* Unfortunately, once the piece is fulled, there isn't much you can do. This is a learned skill, and the more you try it, the better you'll do. However, some felters try padding the thin spots by needle felting some reinforcing wool along the seam. (*See* Just for Fun *on page* 16.)
- *your seam edges are too bulky and thick.* First, give thanks that you don't have holes (better to err on the side of thick seams rather than thin). Try thinning out the felt from inside by pushing with your thumb or finger across the seams. If a seam is truly fulled together, you can actually pull on the seam pretty hard to thin it out. Just go slowly until you are sure of the strength of the felt.

The Everybag

This pattern can be used as the basis for any number of handbags, pouches, or totes. Simply adjust the size, attachments, and number of resists to suit your own unique design. This one is made with a folded flap, an inner pocket, and a felted cord handle. (Directions for making the handle are on pages 51–53.) This is a great practice project for design outside construction. Make several, as gifts for your loved ones or as donations for a charity sale.

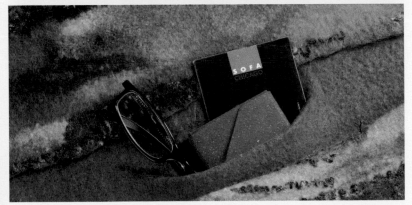

Before and After

Template Size: 30" x 40"

Finished Size: 20" x 26½"

Shrinkage Rate: 33%

What You Need:

- basic felting supplies (*see page* 20)
- one extra sheet of 4 mil plastic, somewhat smaller than the bubble wrap (optional)
- 4 mil plastic for two copies of the template/resist
- soap glue (*see page* 22)
- 2 mil plastic for the pocket resist
- 10 to 12 oz. of Merino roving in your choice of colors
- optional embellishments: colored gauze fabric, variegated yarn (I used Knitting Fever, Darling, 52% nylon/39% wool/9% acrylic, 69 yds/50 g, color 107)
- a felted cord handle

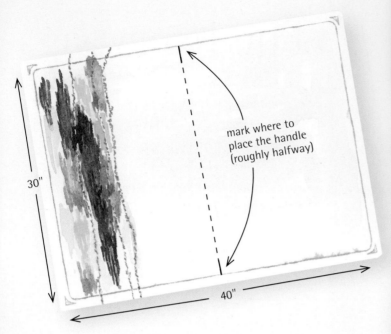

mark where to place the handle (roughly halfway)

30"

40"

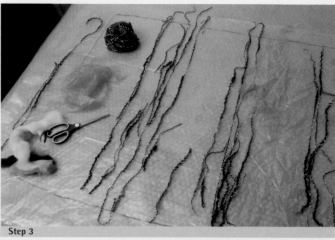

Step 3

Step 4

Project Notes

- Because of the way the bag is made and cut open, you will have a natural pouch on the inside of the flap. By adding a snap or other closure, you can create a second pocket within the flap itself for lightweight things such as receipts, notes, or coupons.

- As an option, this project also shows how to use an additional resist to create a pocket on the inside of the bag.

Set It Up, Lay Out Side 1

1. Organize your space. Lay down your bubble wrap (bubbles facing up) followed by a working sheet of plastic.

2. Create the template and the resists. Cut the template from the 4 mil plastic and trace a copy for laying out the first side — or just trace it right onto your working sheet. Mark on each side of the template where you will be placing the cord for the handle, about halfway down the length of the bag. From the 2 mil plastic, cut a resist that measures 9" by 12" for the pocket. A rectangular-shaped pocket placed vertically works best; a horizontal pocket may not be useful if it's too shallow after fulling.

Step 5

Step 7

Step 6

3. Lay out the design for Side 1. If you cut out a template, lay it down on the working plastic and then lay down the surface design. Divide your wool in half (one half for each side of the pillow) and set one half aside.

4. Lay out the first layer of wool for Side 1. Divide one pile of the wool into three piles; you will be laying out three layers of wool on each side, as before. If

you are layering different colors, keep in mind that the first layer will be the one that shows on the outside of the bag. Lay out the wool directly onto the template.

5. Build the next layer of Side 1. Lay out your second (middle) layer of wool, perpendicular to the first layer.

6. Place the pocket. Before you lay down the third (inside) layer of your bag, place the 2 mil pocket resist on the wool. It will be felted between the middle and inside layers; you will later cut the inside layer to open it up. Make sure the pocket is placed on what will be the bottom half of the purse, below where the corded handle will be.

7. Complete Side 1. Lay down the last layer of wool (again, perpendicular to the previous layer). It should completely cover the pocket resist, as if it were never there.

FREE POCKETS

The Everybag shows how to make a pocket within the wall of the felt. But what if you want to make a free-floating pocket that hangs like a flap or a little tongue? The easiest way is to make a mini-resist package within your big resist. And the time to do it is when all layers of Side 1 are laid out, wet, and lightly felted, just before you center and place your main resist. *Note:* These instructions are for a free pocket on the inside of the purse; outside pockets become a little more complicated when working with embellishments.

1. *Place a small sheet of working plastic* (with straight-cut sides) where you want the pocket to be. This allows you to work directly on Side 1 without disturbing anything. It also keeps the fiber for the pocket from felting onto the Side 1 fibers during the pocket construction.

2. *Cut a template in the shape* you want for the pocket. (For your first try, don't worry about an exact shrinkage rate, just start with a 8" to 10" pocket and let it shrink to whatever size it wants.) Position it on the small sheet of plastic as shown, lined up with the inside edge of the working sheet. Trace it directly onto the working plastic, then put it aside.

3. *Lay down new fibers directly* on the working plastic, following the outline of your traced shape. This is your Side 1 pocket layer. Build the layers as you would for any template, with one exception: On the pocket-opening side, allow the fibers to cross over onto the background felt (where they will attach). At the end of filling you'll cut a slit here to open the pocket.

4. *Wet the pocket* (with or without using tulle) and gently press the fibers with your hands to slightly felt it without disturbing the position of the rays. Then place the pocket template on top of the pocket fibers (lining it up with the pocket opening) and flip the rays.

5. *Lay down Side 2 fibers for the pocket*, building the layers as usual. Once again, allow the fibers at the pocket opening to overlap onto the background felt. (This step looks the same as step 3, but this time there is a layer beneath the fibers.) Wet the fibers and gently press to slightly felt them.

6. *Turn over the pocket* by gently lifting the small sheet of working plastic, pocket and all. Hold the pocket carefully against a flat palm so it won't wrinkle while you transfer the working plastic to the other side; then lay the pocket back down on top of it.

7. *Flip the rays from Side 2 of the pocket onto Side 1.* Felt them in a bit by covering them with tulle and rubbing in the direction of the fibers. Then felt the whole package for a couple of minutes. Leave the small working plastic in place so the pocket won't felt onto the main fibers of your bag.

8. *Center the main resist* for the bag and proceed with assembly of the project as if the pocket were not there. As you lay down the big resist, the pocket will be trapped between plastics and will remain free in the end except for where it was attached to the main fiber pile. Cut the pocket resist open toward the end of fulling the bag, and don't forget to stabilize the cut edge as usual.

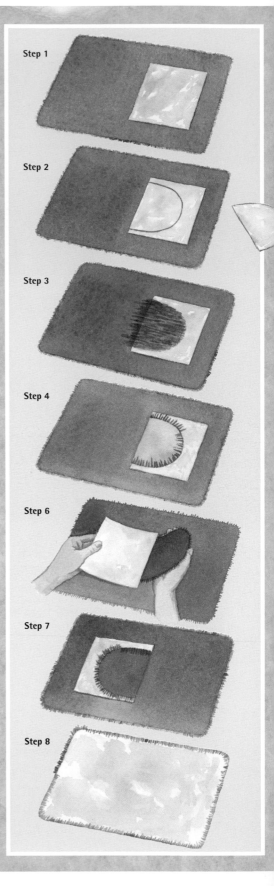

Step 1

Step 2

Step 3

Step 4

Step 6

Step 7

Step 8

Wet Out Side 1, Add the Resist

8. Wet out Side 1. Lay down the tulle and use warm, soapy water to wet out the wool. Using a pool noodle or other rolling bar, roll the felt only a short time so you don't begin to shrink it.

9. Add the resist. When you've created a light skin on the felt, remove the tulle and center the plastic resist for the handbag. Now that the wool has been wetted, the rays of the roving should extend beyond the edges of the resist on all sides.

10. Flip the rays from Side 1. Beginning in the middle of a side (not at a corner), lift up a line of rays, one small section at a time, and fold them over the edge of the resist. With your fingers, gently comb each section flat and smooth, with all rays pointing straight toward the center. It's important not to let the rays overlap or they won't felt properly. When you go around a corner, this means angling the rays somewhat to compress them into a smaller space.

11. Place the cord handle. Unwrap one end of the cording and fluff up the dry brush end fibers at that end.

a. Separate the brush end fibers into two halves. Refer to the marks for handle

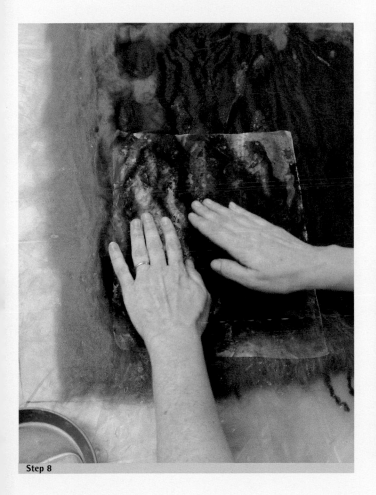

Step 8

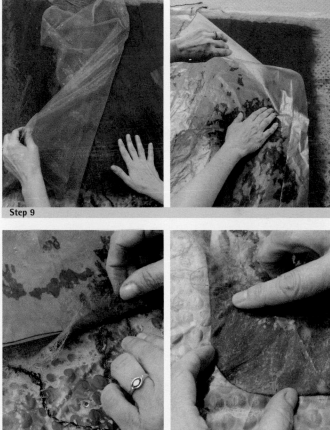

Step 9

Step 10

placement that you made earlier on the template, and lay half of the brush end fibers on either side of the felt/template.

b. With warm, soapy water, wet the ends and press them down straight, in alignment with the rays.

c. Bend the end of the cording and clip it. This will help you control the stiff cord handle so it doesn't disturb your seam.

d. Run the cording across the handbag and attach the other brush end to the marked location on the other side.

Lay Out Side 2

12. Lay out the wool for Side 2. The first layer will become the bag's other inside layer. Lay the wool evenly (in three perpendicular layers), but slightly less thick as you approach the edges (otherwise the wetted seams will expand and cover the design of Side 1). Work around the cord, gently moving it aside as needed.

13. Lay out the design for Side 2. On top of the third layer, lay out the surface design. Carefully lift the edges of the bag as needed to match up any special design elements (such as color stripes) on Side 1.

14. Separate the cord. Lay a strip of plastic between the cording and the top layer of wool, to keep the cord from disturbing the fibers.

15. Wet the fibers around the base of the cord. Add warm, soapy water to the fibers around the base of the handle and gently felt them. This will help stabilize the handle.

Wet Out Side 2, Felt It

16. Cover with tulle. Cover the entire pile with tulle netting, carefully removing the strip of plastic under the cording as you pull the tulle beneath it.

17. Wet out Side 2. Add warm, soapy water. To minimize disturbance of your design, it helps to pour the water onto your hand rather than directly onto the fibers. With wet, soapy hands, press down to begin felting. Press all around the entire project a few times.

Step A
Step B
Step C
Step D
Step 11

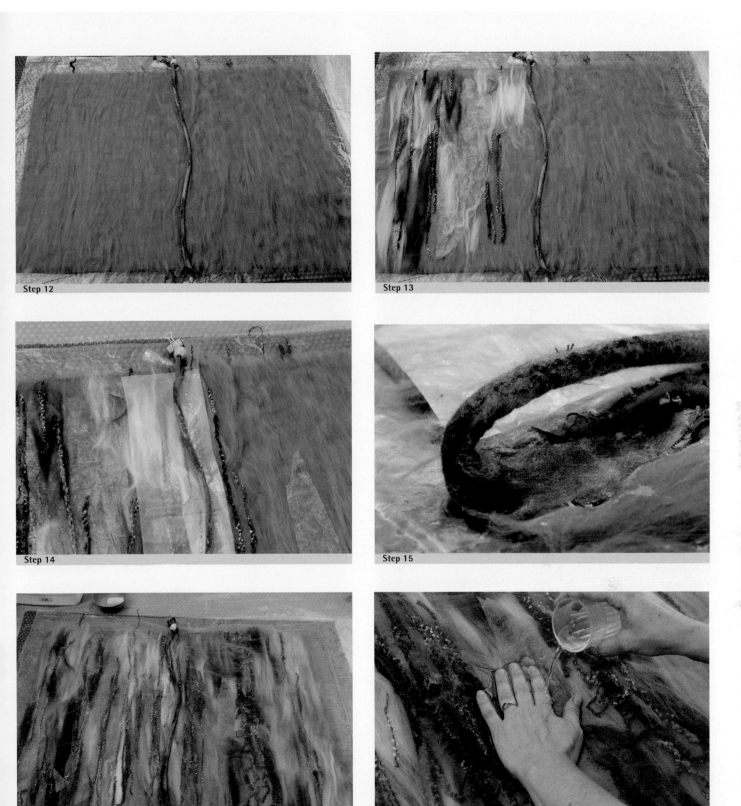

Step 12

Step 13

Step 14

Step 15

Step 16

Step 17

Step 18

Step 19

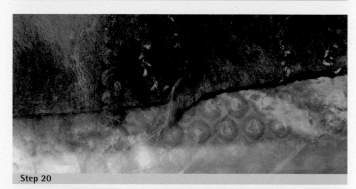

Step 20

Step 21

18. *Roll it.* Using a pool noodle or other rolling bar, wrap up the entire bundle and roll it for a couple of minutes.

19. *Unroll it and turn it over.* When a light skin has formed, remove the tulle and lay a second piece of working plastic over the bag to seal it in, then reverse-roll the project to turn it over. (*See step 12 on page* 138.) After turning, remove the first working sheet and template and set them aside.

20. *Flip the rays from Side 2.* To complete the seams, fold over the rays as you did for Side 1. Handle the rays carefully to be sure that they don't roll up or overlap each other. Wherever you can, comb them into place with your fingernail between the design elements.

21. *Felt the rays.* Replace the tulle and rub in the direction of the rays all along each edge to felt them into Side 1.

Full It, Shape It

22. *Start fulling.* Roll up the entire package in the tulle and gently roll out any excess cold water. Apply fresh hot water and soap, and roll the package in the tulle or bubble wrap for a few minutes. When you see the edges curling up slightly, stop rolling to prevent any further stress on the seams.

23. *Cut the felt.* Decide which side of your bag will be the front. You will be folding over the top portion of the bag (above the cording) as a flap in one direction or the other, so try it both ways. (*Note:* The flap will have two sides and an opening. A closure can be added later to make the flap functional.)

Lay the bag flat and cut from handle to handle horizontally across the *front* side of the bag. Take care not to cut into the base of the cord. Stabilize the cut edge immediately after cutting. (*See* Cutting and Sealing *on page* 139.)

Step 23

24. *Remove the resist.* Protect the seams with one hand while you gently remove the resist with the other hand.

25. *Continue fulling.* Work the felt some more before cutting out the pocket resist; otherwise the pocket might become too shallow during fulling. Although you may feel the 2 mil plastic wadding up a bit as the bag shrinks, just ignore it. To strengthen the felt, carefully knead it in your hands on top of the bubble wrap. After a minute or two, check to make sure nothing has felted together inside or along the edges. If it has, very gently separate the felt without putting any stress on the seams. Alternate between rolling and shaping (*see page* 141) as you full the handbag.

Step 24

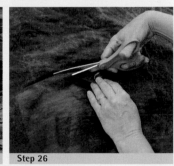
Step 26

26. *Cut out the pocket resist.* Wait until the final shaping to release the pocket resist. Turn the bag inside out and make one straight cut in the inside layer of felt, along one side of the resist. Stabilize the cut edge immediately after cutting.

Step 27

27. *Knead and stretch.* Turn the bag right-side out again and full by hand. Alternate between kneading and stretching the bag until the shape is set.

28. *Finish the bag.* For a smoother finish, roll the outside of the bag with a wooden dowel. Rinse out the soap and iron the bag a bit, then leave it to dry. Add a few snaps or a Velcro closure to the inside of the flap, if desired.

Step 28

THE SHAPE OF THINGS

It's fun to play around with folding a bag into different shapes. The time to do this is when the fulling is finished and the bag is still wet and pliable. Try a few folds, and when you decide on one, set the memory into the wool by ironing the creases you've made. Steam the creases as you iron and press down hard. You can clamp the folds in place while the bag dries, but be careful — if they're too tight, the clamps will leave marks on your bag.

A Brand-New Bag

Designing your own one-of-a-kind handbag can be both fun and challenging. It's natural to think first about creative shapes, but keep gravity and convenience in mind if you want the bag to be practical. Long, deep bags are attractive but can be dark and difficult when you have to search through the contents. Shallow, rectangular bags with exaggerated widths are very modern, but they don't always retain their shape.

Think of everyday uses and how a handbag will look and work with a body in motion. You can design multiple pockets for cell phones and keys or plan any number of attachments. Wide loops on the outside of a bag are great places to attach cords and handles. Or plant a short cord in the side of the purse for attaching a key ring.

To create double saddlebag totes or handbags with three or four lobes, practice using multiple resists between five or more layers of wool. For these designs, make your patterns large enough to account for the extra felt needed to create a folded, multicompartment bag. Experiment until you find the shrinkage

rate that works best for the number of layers and type of wool you are using.

As always, wools can be mixed to provide exactly the right materiality you're looking for. For example, try layering Merino wool (for color) with Romney or Shetland (for durability). A tote bag made from Icelandic wool is a beautiful thing to behold. It's not a good choice for a light summer bag, but for autumn or winter, this bag would be waterproof in the snow and tough enough to set down on an icy city sidewalk.

Remember that when mixing any two (or more) wools, they will need time to interact. The steps will proceed more slowly than with Merino roving, but the results can be well worth it. With your own wool blends, color choices, and custom design, you will be sure to make a fabulous handbag that is truly an artist's creation.

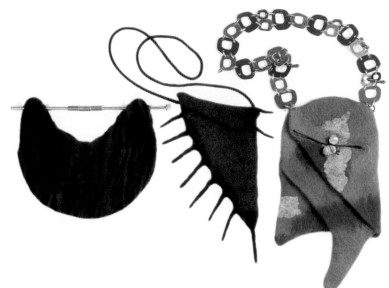

Creative Handles

Keep your eyes peeled for unusual materials that could serve as handbag straps and handles. Leather always seems to work with felt, and silver or aluminum provides a nice contrast to soft felted fabric. Knitted and fulled cords with eyelash and novelty yarns can provide a playful touch. And don't discount synthetic materials: They can provide a juxtaposition that highlights the handmade nature of the felt. Try adding a small bit of vinyl on the bottom of the handbag or using one or more brightly colored plastic ropes or cords as your handle. Unexpected design

elements can make the overall bag more sophisticated and exciting.

If you prefer to stick with natural fibers, you can try strong jute or sisal rope for texture. However, it's best to partially wrap them in coordinating felt to soften any scratchiness. Basket-making materials can also be a great source of inspiration. The possibilities are endless.

Working with students over the years, I've found that it helps to identify the intent of the maker. Some like to experiment to see what will stick, what will happen, what will blend or curl or fall apart. Usually people wish to express themselves by choosing favorite hues; but some like to accent texture and dampen color effects by working with shadows or limited color ranges. Especially when designing a line of handbags, consider the interplay of these variables. Narrowing things down will give you the consistent, fashionable look of a true collection.

Meanwhile, if you want some more guided practice, here's a new shape to try with some interesting twists and variations.

Sun Tote

If you don't mind being the center of attention, carry this bag-with-attitude! It's guaranteed to stop people in their tracks, so allow extra time in your day for explaining how you made this marvel all by yourself! We'll give you the basics, but there is plenty of room for your own creative innovations. This tote is made using the design outside method to enable you to place and felt the spikes on the outside.

Before and After

Template Size: 24" diameter

Finished Size: 16" diameter

Shrinkage Rate: 33%

What You Need

- basic felting supplies (*see page* 20)
- one extra sheet of 4 mil working plastic, somewhat smaller than the bubble wrap
- 4 mil plastic for two copies of the template/resist
- medallion-type decoration (this one is a belt buckle) or custom-felted disk
- 40" strip of foam core, cork, or other semirigid material to glue or sew along the rim of the bag to stabilize its shape
- magnetic clasp, available from handbag suppliers
- beads or small metal hardware for decoration on spikes and handle (optional)
- a steam iron (optional)
- 6–7 oz. total of red, orange, and yellow Merino wool
- about 0.5 oz. of deep red Merino wool for spikes
- 10 yd. *each* of red and tan suede leather thong cording for handle (*see* Resources)

Set It Up, Lay It Out

1. Organize your space. Lay down your bubble wrap (bubbles facing up) followed by a working sheet of plastic. Collect your supplies.

2. Create the template and the resist. Trace two circles that are 24" across and cut them out. One is for the Side 1 template; the other is for the resist.

3. Make the spikes. Make 12 to 14 spikes that are approximately 3" long. (*See* Attaching Cords and Spikes *on page* 47.) When creating spikes from Merino roving, sometimes the long fibers result in a brushy end that is too long and stringy. Trim the ends a bit by snipping off any extra-long tendrils, but avoid straight-across cuts that won't felt well. Aim for a fringed, uneven edge and leave enough fibers for the spike to attach securely.

4. Lay out the wool. Divide each of the wool colors into two equal amounts (for Sides 1 and 2). Set the Side 2 wool aside and divide each of the Side 1 colors into thirds (for three layers). On top of the template, lay out the first layer of wool in a radial pattern, starting at the center. Blend the colors from yellow in the center to orange to red along the edges. (Use the finished purse as a guide.) Test the pile's thickness often. The tendency is to make the middle much thicker than the edges, so try to keep the thickness even across the circle. Lay out the second and third layer in the same way as the first.

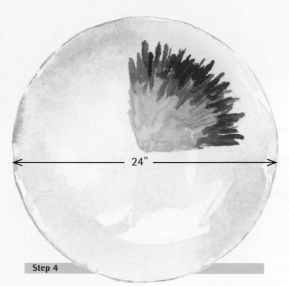

24"

Step 4

Wet Out Side 1, Lay Out Side 2

5. Wet out Side 1. Lay down your tulle and wet out the wool. Roll the felt only for a short time so you don't begin to shrink it.

6. Add the resist. When you've created a light skin on the felt, remove the tulle and center the plastic resist over the wool. Now that the wool has been wetted, the rays of the roving should extend beyond the edges of the resist on all sides.

7. Flip the rays from Side 1. Lift up a line of rays, one small section at a time, and fold them over the edge of the resist. With your fingers, comb the rays toward the center, taking care that the rays don't overlap.

8. Lay out the wool for Side 2. Lay out three even layers of wool in a radial pattern on top of the resist, in the same way as for Side 1.

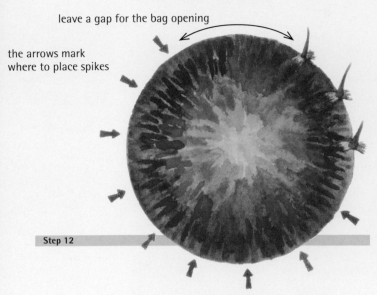

leave a gap for the bag opening

the arrows mark where to place spikes

Step 12

Wet Out Side 2, Felt It

9. Wet out Side 2. Cover the entire pile with tulle, add warm, soapy water, and with wet, soapy hands press down to begin felting. Do this a few times around the entire project, then wrap it up and roll it for a couple of minutes.

10. Unroll it and turn it over. When a light skin has formed, remove the tulle and lay a second piece of working plastic over the bag to seal it in, then turn the project over. Remove the first working sheet of plastic and the template and set them aside.

11. Flip the rays. To complete the seams, fold over the rays as you did for Side 1. Ordinarily you would now replace the tulle and rub parallel to the rays to felt them into Side 1. However, skip that for now and go to the next step.

12. Place the spikes. Start placing spikes around the perimeter of the circle, as shown. Leave a section with no spikes where the opening of the bag will be. For each spike, divide the brush end in half and position half of it on the felt and the other half to the outside of the template. Use the tulle and your finger to felt the first half of the brush end into Side 1, right along with rays of Side 2. Try not to get the dry half of the brush end very wet, or at the very least don't let the fibers twist and tangle. (*See* Attaching Cords and Spikes *on page 47.*)

13. Turn it over again. To attach the other half of the brush ends, lay a sheet of working plastic over the felt to seal it in, then turn the project over. Side 2 will now face up again. Remove the sheet of working plastic now on top. Position the other half of each brush end, cover it with tulle, and felt the fibers into Side 2. The bag is now a colorful package with spikes along the edge and the resist inside.

AS YOU WISH

Practice your seams on small bags to find a style that pleases you. Any shapes with equal dimensions — squares, circles, and rectangles — are fairly straightforward. If you venture into irregular, free-form shapes, it helps to know that felt fulls a little differently in a shape that isn't the same on all sides. Some areas pull in a little faster than others, depending on the length of the sides and the angles involved. When using roving, flipping over the wool rays gets a little trickier when you're working in tight angles. It's all doable, and your skills will improve with practice.

DRESS IT UP

Attach any type of handles or embellishments that you wish. Here are some finishing ideas for the Sun Tote.

- For the handle (left), we made slits in the felt on either side of the bag opening, reinforced them with leather patches, and threaded long strips of leather cords back and forth.

- If the bag won't be holding heavy items, you can simplify the handle by cutting a number of colored cords to the desired length, gathering them together, and sewing them firmly to the bag.

- We added metal hardware "beads" to the cords and spikes. Three or four different cords were strung at once through some beads to keep them grouped together.

- We wrapped and sewed a strip of red leather (right) around a portion of the cords to keep them together. Another option would be to felt bands of wool to gather up sections of the cording.

- As an option for keeping the bag closed, buy a magnetic closure and follow the manufacturer's instructions.

Full It, Shape It

14. *Begin fulling.* Roll up the entire package in the tulle and gently roll out any excess cold water. Apply fresh hot water and soap, and roll the package in the tulle or bubble wrap for a few minutes. When you see the edges curling up slightly, stop rolling to prevent any further stress on the seams.

15. *Cut the felt to remove the resist.* Cut along the seam where the opening of the bag will be and seal the cuts. (*See page* 139.) Protect the seams with one hand while you gently remove the resist with the other hand.

16. *Continue fulling.* To strengthen the felt, carefully knead it in your hands on top of the bubble wrap. After a minute or two, check to make sure nothing has felted together inside or along the edges. If it has, very gently separate the felt without putting any stress on the seams.

17. *Shape and roll.* Alternate between rolling and shaping (*see page* 141) as you

Step 18

full the handbag. Begin shaping the sides of the purse early on to set a firm 2" to 3" edge along the outer rim. Alternate between pinching and pressing the felt out with your hand.

18. *Finish the bag.* After setting the bag's final shape, rinse it and iron it a bit while the felt is still damp. When it is completely dry, sew or glue in a stabilizing strip, if desired. Add a handle and other attachments as desired. (*See* Dress It Up, *above*.)

Slippers and Boots

The malleable nature of felt works to your advantage when you want to custom-shape exact sizes and contours, for instance, when making slippers. Making a template for seamless footwear is less precise than for other projects to allow for shaping around the ankle. It's unfortunately quite easy to underestimate the space needed for the top of the foot and to end up with a slipper that is the right size for the bottom of your foot but won't fit over your ankle. We compensate by creating extra room in the ankle area that can later be fulled to fit.

This is especially important when making felted boots that will extend up the legs. Narrow shapes around legs and ankles shrink in a complex way compared to predictable pieces of felt that are more equal in dimensions. It's helpful to fudge a little extra room when tracing your foot onto the plastic. Don't be discouraged if your first pair of slippers doesn't fit quite right. Well-shaped footwear takes a little practice.

MAKING A SLIPPER TEMPLATE

To make two identical slippers, lay out both in one U-shaped template and felt them at the same time. The shape is cut in half later when you take out the resist.

1. *Lightly trace* the shape of your foot onto a white sheet of paper. Draw an outline about 1" to 2" all around the foot tracing, but don't include details like toes and arches. Although you started with a tracing of the *bottom* of your foot, the outline will serve as a guide for the *sides* of the slippers.

2. *Slip the paper* under one end of a 3' by 4' sheet of plastic and trace the outermost outline (ignore the original foot shape). Bisect the center of this shape with two lines, extending the horizontal line beyond the edge of the shape as shown. Extend it about as far as the shape is wide or a few inches longer if you want to have cuffs on your slippers. Draw a second horizontal line from the bottom heel area out the same distance, and connect the two horizontal lines with a vertical line as shown.

3. *Complete the template* by sketching in a smooth, shallow curve from the top of the foot shape down to the ankle area.

4. *Fold the plastic* along the cuff line and trace the outline you have drawn. When you open the plastic, you should have a shape that looks like a wide-bottomed letter "U". *Note:* To make a holiday stocking or a pair of boots, the primary difference will be height, so add to the distance on either side of the cuff line.

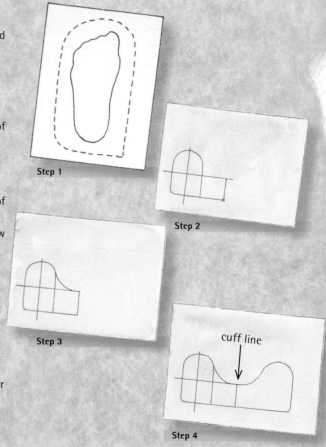

Step 1

Step 2

Step 3

Step 4

cuff line

Double Happiness Slippers

Felt and slippers just seem to be a perfect match — and when you can custom-design your patterns and colors, even better. This project offers a unisex design that is very practical. These slippers are handsome on their own, but feel free to add your own special touches with creative trims or stitches. We'll be using the design outside method, so you can easily add prefelt or yarn embellishments. Since felt can be slippery on wood or vinyl floors, you may want to take the project a step further by painting or sewing nonskid strips on the soles or trying out a suede soling kit.

What You Need

- basic felting supplies (*see page* 20)
- one extra sheet of 4 mil plastic, somewhat smaller than the bubble wrap
- 4 mil plastic for two copies of the template/resist
- ruler or metal tape measure
- 4 oz. of taupe C-1 Norwegian batt wool
- 2 oz. of brick red Merino roving
- two black Chinese frog closures and four black buttons (optional)

Project Notes

- Boots, slippers, and mittens are often created with one resist that is later cut in half. This not only saves repeating the steps but also helps ensure that the fiber layout, amount of rolling, and so forth are all the same for each member of the pair.

- We used a combination of C-1 Norwegian wool for durability and Merino roving for softness and color. If you use two colors, expect them to blend; if you want one of the colors to be dominant, use more layers of that color and less of the other. Many combinations of C-1 and Merino will work for this project, so don't worry about the ratio of the two. We did not embellish the surface with yarns, but if you choose to do so, remember that you are making the slippers with the design outside method, so the yarns will be placed against the outside color.

- Whatever wool you use, the exact shrinkage rate with slippers is difficult to determine, and not particularly useful when making a template. Instead of calculating with percentages, we will use a time-tested formula (*see* Making a Slipper Template *on page* 158) that might seem counterintuitive, but it works.

- The slipper template often looks huge to beginners, but slippers full down a lot more than you think, especially in length and around the ankle. Slippers also tend to shrink in unpredictable ways, partly because of their asymmetrical shape. Nine times out of ten, first-time felt slippers end up too small rather than too big, so check the size often as you full. You can always full them down further if they're too large.

Step 3

Set It Up, Lay Out Side 1

1. *Organize your space.* Lay down your bubble wrap (bubbles facing up) followed by a working sheet of plastic. Collect your supplies.

2. *Create the template/resist.* Make a template. Cut two copies, or draw one directly on the working plastic.

3. *Lay out the wool for Side 1.* Whatever ratio of C-1 and Merino you are using, divide that total amount in half for the two sides (you'll be laying out the whole U shape at once). Lay down the outside wool color first, followed by the inside color. We used three layers of Merino followed by three layers of C-1. (If you want embellishment, lay it down first, *before* the outside color.)

Wet Out Side 1, Lay Out Side 2

4. *Wet out Side 1.* Lay down the tulle and wet out the wool. Press your hand down a few times in a plunging motion to thoroughly wet out the wools. Gently

press the pile to felt it slightly. Expect the wools to reject each other at first. Break the surface tension on the coarser C-1 wool fibers and speed the process by using more soap than you would for Merino alone.

5. *Add the resist.* When the wet wool expands, the slipper shape may become slightly distorted, so don't felt the wool too long at this point or let it shift around. Center the resist as best you can, and if there are any areas with no wool at all along an edge, add some to fill in.

6. *Flip the rays from Side 1.* (*See* page 137.)

7. *Lay out Side 2.* This time start with the three layers of C-1, followed by three layers of Merino. Add embellishments, if desired.

Wet It, Felt It

8. *Wet out Side 2.* Cover the entire pile with tulle, add warm, soapy water, and with wet, soapy hands, press down to begin felting. Press around the project a few times, then wrap it up and roll it for a couple of minutes.

9. *Unroll it and turn it over.* When a light skin has formed, remove the tulle and lay a second piece of working plastic over the felt to seal it in. Roll the entire thing up and reverse-roll it back out onto the table. (*See page* 138.) After turning, remove the working sheet of plastic and the template.

10. *Flip the rays from Side 2.* (*See* page 138.) Replace the tulle and rub in the direction of the rays along each edge to felt them into Side 1.

Full It, Shape It

11. *Begin fulling.* Roll up the entire package in the tulle and gently roll out any excess cold water. Apply fresh hot water and soap, and roll the package in the tulle or bubble wrap for a few minutes until the edges curl up slightly.

12. *Cut the felt to remove the resist.* Cut the felt in half where the opening of the slippers will be and seal the cuts. (*See* page 139.) Gently remove the resist from each half. From here on, work on one slipper at a time, or alternate working them both down together.

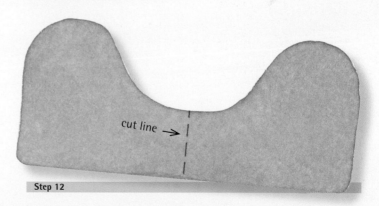

cut line →

Step 12

13. *Full it and shape it.* (*See pages* 140–141.) Here are a few pointers relevant to making felted slippers:

- Use your own intuition to full the slippers into shape. Try them on frequently if you're making them for yourself. Nothing helps more than looking and feeling how they sit on your feet. Some felters even like to wear them around damp after fulling to set a custom shape.

- You'll be surprised how quickly a slipper can shrink end to end. Keep stretching out the slipper lengthwise and along its front, even while shrinking down the sides. You want to set the memory for a size that will fit!

- Slippers are meant to be on the comfy side, so most people don't worry too much about precise shaping. But if you do want to make a more formal slipper with nice lines, shaping is best done on a pair of shoe forms, or *lasts.* (See Resources.) Slip one inside a partially fulled slipper and spot-full by rubbing against certain areas (like a wide ankle) to shrink the felt. Styrofoam lasts are available but tend to be quite wide in the ankle. You might need to finish that

part of the slipper by hand. The Styrofoam lasts, however, are useful for felting slippers and booties in the washing machine.

- To try on the slippers while fulling, you can snip a slight opening in the top rim, but don't make any deep cuts until you've stabilized the felt by fulling a while. The final cuts to shape the top of the slipper are better made after the felt is completely fulled or even dry.

- Allow yourself to deviate from the pattern and customize the design a bit. Do you want a rolled-over cuff for extra warmth or a more elegant outline for lounging slippers? Are you leaving enough room for additions like needle felting, ribbons, embroidery, or needlepoint? Will the slippers have closures and if so, what will you use?

14. *Finish up.* When you've achieved a desired shape that fits, let the slippers air-dry. You may want to leave a generous ankle opening for ease of fit. We sewed two buttons on either side of the ankle to hold a frog closure in place on each slipper.

Journal Cover

Making a cover for your journal, photo album, or scrapbook is a great opportunity to learn about open resists. Personalize your cover with your favorite symbols, motifs, or initials. This is where felt really shines. It's so forgiving that you can coax it into fitting even if your measurements were a little bit off! We used the design inside method for this project. The template and finished size will depend on the book you wish to cover, but we've given our measurements as a point of reference.

Before and After
Template Size: 16½" x 23" (open)

Finished Size: 11" x 15½" (open)

Shrinkage Rate: 33%

What You Need
- basic felting supplies (*see page* 20)
- 4 mil plastic for two copies of the template/resist
- soap glue (*see page* 22)
- a steam iron (optional)
- 3–6 oz. of Merino roving in your choice of colors
- yarns, silks, prefelts, or other embellishments

Project Note

If the finished cover is too tight or short, gently steam it with an iron and pull it evenly outward. If it's too large, steam it and full it further by rolling the surface with a hard dowel or rolling the piece in a wooden mat.

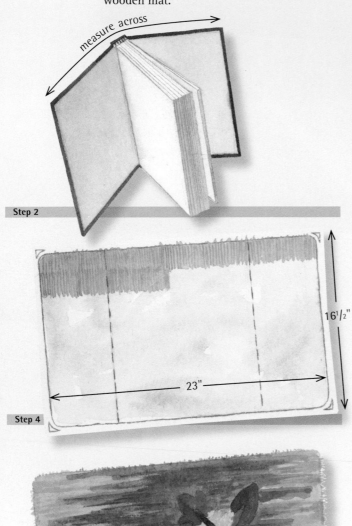

measure across

Step 2

Step 4

23"

16¹/₂"

Set It Up, Lay Out Side 1

1. Organize your space. Lay down your bubble wrap (bubbles facing up) followed by a working sheet of plastic. Collect your supplies.

2. Measure the book you wish to cover. Take the width measurement across the entire back with the book partially open. Add 1" to both the length and the width to make sure the edges of the book will be covered.

3. Create the template and the resist. If you're working with Merino, use 33 percent as your shrinkage rate and calculate the template size. (*See page* 132.) Draw the template outline, then mark where the flaps will end — about a quarter of the way in on each side, as shown. Mark and cut out two copies of the template, with flap lines marked, and round off the corners. One copy will be used as the resist.

4. Lay out the wool for Side 1. Divide your wool into thirds. Two thirds will be used for Side 1 (the length of the entire book cover), and one third will be used for Side 2 (the inside flaps). Set aside one third and use the other two thirds to build two layers on Side 1.

5. Embellish Side 1. On top of the layers, lay out the design you want to appear on the cover. Keep in mind that the elements might shift in unexpected ways when you're fitting the finished cover, so don't get too attached to an exact design placement.

Step 5

Wet Out Side 1, Add the Resist

6. Wet it out. Lay the tulle over Side 1, then dribble some soap glue onto any nonwool design elements to help them adhere. With wet, soapy hands, gently press down through the tulle to begin felting the design into the background. Add warm, soapy water to the middle of the pile and press until the design just begins to stick, then roll up the bundle. Roll for about two minutes or so, to slightly begin felting Side 1.

7. Add the resist. With the tulle still in place, use a sponge to remove excess water from the felt. Then remove the tulle and center the resist on the top of Side 1. You will be looking through the plastic to the design. The rays of the wet roving should extend beyond the edges of the resist on all sides.

Lay Out Side 2

8. Lay out the design for Side 2. If you want a design on the flaps, start by smearing a little soap glue on the flap areas of the resist. Flip over any trailing design yarns or shapes from Side 1, then lay out other design elements on the flap areas.

9. Flip the rays from Side 1. Along the edges of *the flap area only*, lift up a line of rays, one small section at a time, and fold them over the edge of the resist. Press the rays toward the center without overlapping them. Do not flip any rays along the middle portion (top or bottom) between the flaps; these rays will felt into a line on their own.

10. Lay out the wool for Side 2 of the flaps. Take the remaining pile of wool you set aside and divide it in half (one for each flap). Divide each half into two or three layers, to match the thickness of Side 1. Lay out the wool in each flap region, using the line on the template as your guide. Leave the center portion uncovered (the plastic resist will be showing).

Wet Out Side 2, Felt and Full

11. Wet it out. Cover the pile with tulle, add water to the flaps, and roll the fibers a bit.

12. Unroll it and turn it over. Using a second working sheet of plastic to seal in the felt, flip the project over. Remove the original working sheet and the tulle, and set them aside.

13. Flip the rays from Side 2. Carefully fold over the Side 2 rays, cover them with tulle, and rub through the tulle enough to start felting them into Side 1.

14. Start fulling. Roll the package as usual, but this time the felted seams won't curl up because the plastic resist is not completely enclosed. The resist will start buckling up in the middle instead. When this starts to happen, check to make sure your designs are adhering, then remove the resist. Carefully turn the book cover inside out, keeping it flat on the table while you do so to prevent the heavy wet felt from pulling apart at the seams.

15. Full and shape the felt. Work the felt in the same way as the Road Trip

Pillow Cover. (*See pages* 139–141.) Use a kneading motion to strengthen it before warming it up and rolling it. Check the size against the book from time to time to see how the shrinkage is progressing.

16. Finish up. Rinse out the soap and let the felt dry a bit. While it's still damp, slip the cover onto your book to check the size. Remove the cover and iron it to put a nice finish on it, then leave it flat to dry.

Variation
Magazine Stool Cover

This is an adorable project for any room and can be customized for any decor. We used a sleek, modern, bentwood stool purchased at a local home store chain, but you can cover any number of flat-topped stools to get different looks. Or expand the length of the seat cover to make something like a table runner with pockets to lay across an old trunk. Here are a few pointers:

• Use the design outside method so you can see the design as you lay out the wool. It helps when lines are meant to follow the slight flare of the stool's legs.

• Try using two smaller resists for the pockets (one on each side) instead of one large one as we did with the book cover. Either will work, but you may like one better. The point is to think first about what you want to create and then decide how you'll do it. Avoid the temptation to get too attached to a particular set of instructions!

• When measuring your stool, obtain the following measurements:

A = _____ = total length

B = _____ = width across the top of the stool

C = _____ = length of desired pocket

D = _____ = width across the bottom of the leg (if different from B)

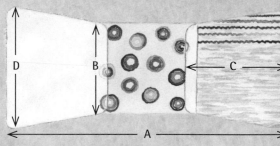

Calculate the size of your template based on your shrinkage rate. (*See page 132.*)

• We left the edges natural, but for a more finished look, attach trim along the open edges of the pockets. Use Velcro or nonskid matting to keep the felt from slipping off the stool.

Nicole Chazaud Telaar

Imagine finding a way to make felt for a living! Nicole Chazaud Telaar's solution was to launch Festive Fibers. Having worked for years as a professional designer of home furnishing fabrics, Nicole recognized the opportunity feltmaking provided. Combining her passion for wool and color with a focused business strategy, she succeeded in developing a highly visible product for a niche market. (*See* Resources.)

Her Flappers Chair shows an imaginative use of multiple resists. Layers of plastic isolate distinct sections of wool, allowing the wool to felt on either side of each resist but never onto the layers above or below it. Once these free flaps have formed a skin, they will no longer try to felt to each other. Then the resists are removed and the flaps are fulled along with main body of the project.

I am inspired by the idea that feltmaking can be a vehicle for me to make patterned fabrics. The ease of creating felt fabrics that don't involve screens and printing make the medium most spontaneous. As feltmakers, we can experiment with technique, color mixtures, and pattern layout all with small investments in time, money, space, and materials. If it doesn't work, wipe off your table and you're ready to try again!

Nicole, who now partners Festive Fibers with her husband, Tom, makes upholstery fabric for the textile trade and licenses her popular designs. They have helped to raise the public's awareness of felt through their striking color palettes and warm, friendly designs.

For this carefully planned piece, Nicole's goal was "not to have any flaps cut off by the upholsterer, so each component was an exact fit!" *Flappers Chair*, proprietary blend of wool hand-dyed with acid dyes, 33" wide x 33" deep x 27" high.

7

Shaping
Hats

Felt has been used to make hats for many centuries — and no wonder, because felt and hats are a perfect match. Distinctive and protective wool hats have been worn by warriors, members of craftsmen's guilds, government officials, and ordinary people just trying to stay warm, all testament to the timelessness of this medium. Feltmaking history is forever entwined with the hat-making industry, which offers an important window into earlier feltmaking methods.

Hat workshops are among the most common classes offered by feltmaking instructors. Hats in their many forms provide the felter with an opportunity to take skills to a new level, usually by exploring shaping. Shaping and sculpting wool is a skill that develops with time, and making hats is perhaps the most common way to develop that skill; however, the techniques covered in this chapter can also be applied to vessels and other forms of sculpture.

The softness, structure, and stiffness of a wool are, like all other material characteristics, somewhat subjective. Consider blending fine wools for softness inside your hat with other wools that might provide texture or structure. Use what works for your intended purpose, and be open to trying new wools, fibers, and mixes.

Of the many methods for making hats, we present two in detail in this chapter. The first uses the flat or closed resist method already introduced in chapter 6. Hats constructed by this method are made with seams on all sides and later cut open at an appropriate place and worked into three dimensions.

The second uses the open resist double hood method developed by Zoltán Mihalkó (*see the box at left*) and Beth Beede (*see page* 205). In this method, which is ideal for broad-brimmed hats, two partially seamed cones are assembled inside one another to make one complete, durable hat with a double layer of wool.

As we move into the projects involving more advanced shaping concepts, let's pause and clarify a few things. Felting with an open resist is a different process than working with a closed resist because the stresses on the felt are less predictable. The open end of the felt serves as an "open gate" for the fibers in a sense. This means that the overall size and shape of the felt can change more radically as you move through the feltmaking process compared to the relatively stable shape of a closed resist.

COWBOY HAT LEGACY

Feltmaker Beth Beede first heard about Old World hatmaker Zoltán Mihalkó in 1984 when attending an international felt conference in Hungary. Having seen him conduct a felting demonstration, Beede wrote:

"We were all mesmerized watching him turn, in a very short time, a small pile of wool into a very solid finished hat. He was truly a master, wasting no motions and checking each step. We were told that most of his professional life was spent making hats for the Hungarian cowboys and shepherds, and selling them at nearby markets. Later in his career, he was also commissioned to make some hats for museums.

"The method I have taught is an adaptation of what he did. For example, I would certainly not recommend dipping one's hands into near boiling water with a high concentration of sulfuric acid, as he did in the fulling process. Nor would very many people be able to bow-card loose wool and direct it into piles the exact shape needed to form parts of the hood."

Luckily, Beth's adaptations of the method allow a simple way to create this very versatile shape. For many years, Beth has taught this technique in her "Broad-Brimmed Felted Hat" workshop, enjoyed by hundreds of people of all ages. By sharing this technique, she is passing on a very old tradition and helping to keep the technique alive for modern feltmakers. (*See pages* 192–195.)

Although this is challenging, it also allows the feltmaker the freedom to work with a hat or vessel in a whole new way. Much like working with clay, the shape develops with time. You begin with a general shape (such as the bell shape in the double hood method) and work specific areas first to set various features. It helps to think about the shaping process as a finite journey with the wool. Every fulling motion matters because it will "harden" the felt a little more in that area. Advanced shaping is basically about moving forward in a logical progression to create the desired shape.

With felting, there are many ways to approach the same thing, but some ways are more direct or better suited than others. As you enter into collaboration with the wool of your choice, your wish is to create a particular shape from your imagination. The wool's response is to do the best it can to comply within the limits of its materiality, but you must help it along by making the job as easy as possible. The cardinal rule of agreement on this point is to begin as close to the intended shape as possible. The felt will reward you with fabulous shapes built of deeply ingrained, structural memory that will last through time.

" Happy Accidents

While teaching beginners to felt, I learned to monitor the common mistake of laying out rays that were too long and stringy to make a neat seam. I owe the Flame Beret design (*see page 172*) to a young student who strayed down this erring path while my attention was elsewhere. Her rays had become so excessively long that I saw a new design possibility. Together we guided the temporarily lost and failing beret to its rightful path of destiny.

The Flame Beret

Although it's usually one of the first projects taught to beginning feltmakers, the beret is sometimes maligned as pretentious or simply "not my style." Don't be fooled! The beret shape is a great starting point for customizing many simple hat shapes. Not only that, it makes a fairly effortless transformation into a vessel or bag just by turning it upside down while you full it. This beret is straightforward, simple, and fast with a dash of unique surface design. We used the closed resist and design outside methods so you can easily keep track of the flames.

Before and After

Template Size: 15" diameter

Finished Size: 10" diameter

Shrinkage Rate: 33% using suggested fiber

What You Need

- basic felting supplies (*see page* 20)
- 4 mil plastic for two copies of the template/resist
- one extra sheet of 4 mil plastic, somewhat smaller than the bubble wrap
- a plastic lid or plate that is about 5" in diameter
- soap glue (*see page* 22)
- a wooden dowel
- small, sharp scissors
- a steam iron
- 2 oz. each of Merino roving of two contrasting colors
- bias tape, ultrasuede, microfiber, or leather to trim the rim of the beret (optional)

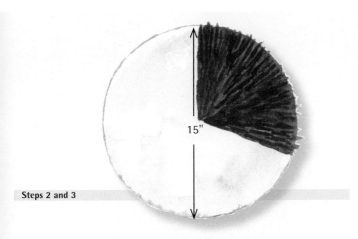

Steps 2 and 3

15"

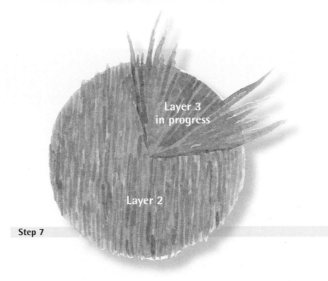

Step 7

Layer 3 in progress

Layer 2

Set It Up, Lay Out Side 1

1. Organize your space. Lay down your bubble wrap, followed by a working sheet of plastic. Collect your supplies.

2. Create the template and the resist. Draw a 15"-diameter circle on the 4 mil plastic and cut it out. This will be the resist. Trace another, if desired, or trace the circle directly onto your working plastic for the template.

3. Lay out the wool for Side 1. Decide which color will be the flames (Side 2) and set it aside. Divide the Side 1 wool into thirds. Lay out the first layer (which will show on the outside) in a radial pattern on your template. Lay out the second and third layers horizontally and vertically.

Wet Out Side 1, Lay Out Side 2

4. Wet it out. Lay the tulle over Side 1 and wet out the wool. Roll it up and felt it for a couple of minutes until you've created a light skin on the felt.

5. Add the resist. Sponge away excess water, remove the tulle, and center the resist on the top of Side 1. The rays of the wet roving should extend beyond the edges of the resist on all sides.

6. Flip the rays from Side 1. Lift up a line of rays, one section at a time, and fold them over the edge of the resist. Point the rays toward the center without allowing them to twist or overlap.

7. Lay out the wool for Side 2. Dry your hands and divide the second color of wool into three piles. Build the first layer for Side 2 horizontally and the second layer vertically. Lay out the third layer (which will show on the outside) in a radial pattern. Lay out some of the rays like long flames, as shown.

Wet Out Side 2, Felt It

8. Wet out Side 2. Cover the whole pile with tulle and carefully add warm, soapy water. Press around the entire project several times, then wrap it up and roll it for a couple of minutes.

9. Unroll it and turn it over. Use a second working sheet of plastic to turn over the project. (*See* If You Dare, *below.*) Remove the original working sheet and the original template, and set them aside. If the project is very wet, replace the tulle for a moment and sponge out any excess water. The "flame" fibers will attach more easily to damp fleece than they will to soaking-wet fibers.

10. Flip the rays from Side 2. Fold over the long flames and rays onto the Side 1 background. Take extra care not to let the fibers roll onto themselves as you flip them over. Separate and divide some of them to create a burning effect, but

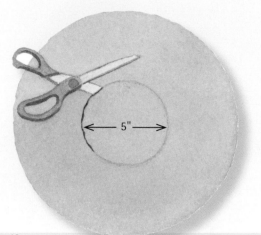

Step 12

keep them flat as you do this and touch them as little as possible. Cover the rays with tulle and *slowly* felt them in as usual, but don't be too vigorous or press too hard too fast. Follow the line of the flames as you press. Dribbling on a bit of soap glue may help felt them in.

Full It, Shape It

11. Begin fulling. Roll up the entire package in tulle and gently roll out any excess cold water. Apply fresh hot water and soap, and roll the package in tulle or bubble wrap for a few minutes. When the edges curl up slightly, stop rolling.

Shocking Information

Students have asked, "Can I toss the beret to full it?" Well, you can and many do. But tossing the beret around, scrunching it up, and throwing it in the sink will *shock full* the beret. This causes it to overfelt and pucker in the middle. Circular designs made with roving laid in a radial pattern are especially prone to overfelting, since the fibers will naturally travel toward the center of the circle. To achieve the most even consistency and highest quality, I prefer to roll my felt, for berets and otherwise. Nuno felt, however, is a different matter. Shock fulling works well with nuno, as puckering is unlikely with a stabilizing fabric.

IF YOU DARE

When turning the project over to flip the rays, it's usually best to use a second working sheet of plastic to seal it down. For a small project like this, though, you can skip the second working sheet if you're careful. Here are some pointers:

- Avoid touching the rays and edge areas when you pick up the project.
- Treat the felt like a newborn infant — don't raise it higher into the air than is necessary and handle it gently.
- Turn over the projects with confidence and in one smooth motion, but avoid "The Splat" — dropping the felt quickly as if you can't wait to be rid of it. The Splat results in hopelessly shifted, smeared rays and a resist that is no longer correctly centered.

Possible color combinations

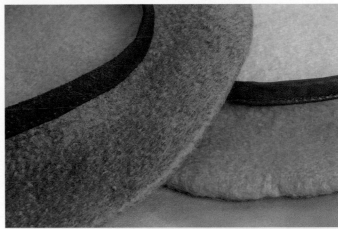

Step 15

12. *Remove the resist.* Cut the head hole by centering the 5" plastic lid or plate in the exact center of Side 2 (the side without the flames showing). By rotating the circle in place a few times, you'll leave an indentation on the felt showing where to cut the hole. Use small, sharp scissors to snip a hole vertically straight down into the felt, stopping at the plastic resist. Slip the scissors into the hole and cut around the circle to remove it. (Save the felt circle to use later as prefelt.) Protect the seam edges with one hand while you reach inside to remove the resist. Immediately seal the cut (*see page* 139); otherwise the head opening for your beret will quickly grow too big.

13. *Continue fulling.* Knead the felt in your hands on top of the bubble wrap until it begins to shrink.

14. *Shape and roll.* Final shaping is up to the artist. Some prefer to keep a pancakelike beret shape, but most people prefer a softer edge that can be manipulated a bit by the wearer. Alternate between rolling and shaping (*see page* 141) as you full the beret.

15. *Finish up.* Finish up by hand rolling the surface of the felt with a wooden dowel. Rinse out the soap and lay the felt flat to dry; then iron it while it's still damp for a nice, professional finish. Finish the opening with trim, if desired.

" *Mais Oui!*

Beret variations are endless. This one has no color distinction between the top and bottom layers, and the seams have been worked until they are invisible. Randomly coiled black wool yarn has been felted in, and the head opening has been left as natural, untrimmed felt (very soft against the hair).

Variation

Watermelon Hat

The basic beret can be easily adapted into the Watermelon Hat — the perfect bit of silliness for a Fourth of July picnic or a kid's summer camp. The shape of this hat was inspired by the now-famous Queen Beret designed by American feltmaker Chad Alice Hagen. (*See page* 87.) The shape-shift from a perfectly round beret certainly came as a surprise to me when I first saw Chad's hat years ago. It also forced my formal introduction to and respect for an iron, which I'd successfully avoided for most of my adult life until I became a feltmaker.

Both versions of the Watermelon Hat — seeds on the top or seeds on the bottom — are made the same way. The only difference is which side you cut for the head opening. Follow the same steps as for the Flame Beret, but with these additional notes:

- The basic supplies are the same, except that a 17" circle template is advised for a slightly wider hat. For wool, we used 1.8 ounces of Merino roving in a couple of shades of green (with a bit of white) for the rind and 1.2 ounces of pink for the watermelon. Cut ¹/₂" to ³/₄" seeds from a small piece of dark brown or black prefelt.

- The trickiest part is keeping track of the design, so stick with the design outside method. It pays to make sure that the seeds are in the right place, since they are the star of the show! *Note:* If you're planning to have the seeds on the bottom, make sure they are placed far enough toward the outside that you won't lose them when you cut the hole.

- When laying out the wool, card or mix the green wools together and save the white to mix in with the greens for the outermost visible layer. Leave the colors only partly carded, not well blended, since you want the rind to have streaks. Be sure to keep the blended wool combed out straight; don't let it tangle in on itself.

- Plan for the green "rind" wool to be Side 2. That way the short green rays will be wrapped around last and become the ones that are visible. Keeping the green rays uniform (not threadlike) makes a more realistic rind than letting the pink rays stray into the green layer.

- To make the rind even more realistic, blend in a sheer layer of chopped-up white Merino fleece between the green rays and the pink fleece of Side 1 (not shown in our example).

- Shaping the fruit slice involves pulling repeatedly during fulling to translate the circle into an arc. It's a challenge to perfect the shape because you'll find that there will be small areas of extra felt that you must spot full to get a good fit. When you have it just the way you want it, iron the hat to set the shape.

Plum Derby

The adaptable derby works well for many occasions. Make it in pale pastels with a peony pin for a spring wedding; black and tan with a velvet ribbon for a charity fashion show; or purple and red for ladies of a certain age and attitude. And, of course, make up one in your favorite colors for everyday wear. This project uses the closed resist method with the design inside, which allows you to create a continuous pattern of yarns and other embellishments around the crown with no visible seam.

Before and After

Template Size: 16" wide x 15" tall (flat)

Finished Size: 22" around x 10" high

Shrinkage Rate: about 33%

What You Need

- basic felting supplies (*see page* 20)
- one extra sheet of 4 mil plastic, somewhat smaller than the bubble wrap
- 4 mil plastic for two copies of the template/resist

- a derby-shaped hat block of appropriate size (*see* Resources)
- a needle and thread, if needed for attaching any trims or brim material
- soap glue (*see page* 22)
- small, sharp scissors
- a steam iron or a wooden dowel
- 3 oz. of plum Merino roving
- coordinating yarn or embellishments (I used yarn and about ¹/₂ oz. of dyed Lincoln locks)

Project Notes

- Fine derby hats with well-set domes are usually finished by fulling on a hat block. Inexpensive options are widely available. The hat forms pictured on page 182 are patented by Hat Shapers. (*See* Resources.) Or you can use a bowl, ball, or any other shape around the house that will suit your purpose.

- Have fun customizing your hat with yarns, trims, flowers, ribbons, or something more unusual such as shells or baubles.

Set It Up, Lay Out Side 1

1. Organize your space. Lay down your bubble wrap, followed by a working sheet of plastic. Collect your supplies.

2. Create the template/resist. (*See* Making a Hat Template *on the opposite page*.) You'll need two copies.

3. Lay out the wool for Side 1. Divide your wool in half and set one half aside. Divide the other half into thirds and lay out three layers of wool, with each layer perpendicular to the one before it.

4. Embellish Side 1. Lay out any yarns or decorations as desired. For a seamless wraparound look, leave some of the ends trailing over the edges of the template (to be folded over later).

Wet Out Side 1, Lay Out Side 2

5. Wet it out. Lay the tulle over Side 1. Wet out the wool, then roll it up and felt it for a couple of minutes.

Step 4

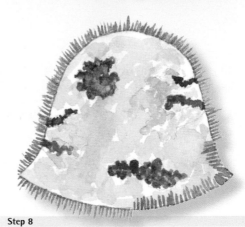
Step 8

6. Add the resist. Sponge away excess water, remove the tulle, and center the resist on the top of Side 1. You will be looking through the plastic to the design. The rays of the wet roving should extend beyond the edges of the resist on all sides.

7. Lay out the design for Side 2. Smear the resist with soap glue and flip over any trailing yarns and shapes from Side 1. Lay out the design for Side 2, face down.

8. Flip the rays from Side 1. Lift up a line of rays, one small section at a time, and fold them over the edge of the resist. Press the rays toward the center without overlapping them.

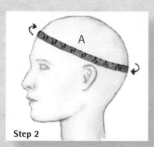

Step 2

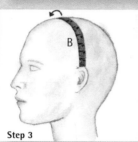

Step 3

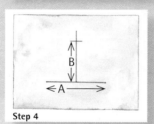

Step 4

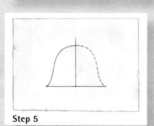

Step 5

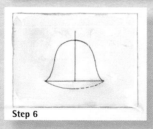

Step 6

MAKING A HAT TEMPLATE

To make a simple hat template, measure the distance around your head at the widest point and the distance from ear to ear across the top of your head. Since the template is a flat piece of plastic with two sides, you will divide each number by two for the right fit. Don't worry about an exact measurement for a brim. We'll add 2" to the height of the hat as an approximation. With practice, you will get a better feel for how the brim shrinks as you work a hat.

1. *Measure your head around the widest point* and divide that number in half.

> A = circumference of head _____ ÷ 2 = _____

2. *Measure from ear to ear across the top of your head* and divide that number in half.

> B = over top of head _____ ÷ 2 = _____

3. *To get the correct template size,* upsize the A and B measurements to allow for shrinkage. It's fine to round up any fractions to the next whole number. The formula below applies if you're using Merino or another wool with a shrinkage rate of about 33%. (*Otherwise, see* Shrinkage and Template Size *on page* 132.)

> 1.00 minus .33 (percent shrinkage rate) = .67
> A = _____ ÷ .67 = _____ (template width)
>
> B + 2" (for the brim) = _____ ÷ .67 = _____ (template height)

4. *Use the two new A and B measurements* to plot an upside-down "T" on a sheet of 4 mil plastic.

5. *Drawing the shape* for the hat template requires a bit of guessing, but don't worry. Felt is such a forgiving fabric; you can adjust the shape quite a bit as you full it. Sketch a curved line on one side, of the template, then flip the plastic to trace the identical curve onto the other side.

6. *To account for the curvature* of the brim, draw a curved line along the bottom as shown. Once again, draw the line on one side, then flip the plastic to match the curve on the other side. If the brim turns out to be too wide, you can always trim some away later.

Step 12

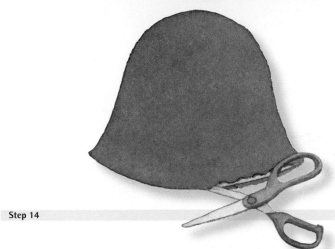

Step 14

the original sheet of plastic and the original template, and set them aside. The back of Side 1 will now face up.

12. *Flip the rays from Side 2.* Fold over the rays and replace the tulle. Rub in the direction of the rays to felt them into Side 1.

Full It, Shape It

13. *Begin fulling.* Roll up the entire package in the tulle and gently roll out any excess cold water. Apply fresh hot water and soap, and roll the package in the tulle or bubble wrap for a few minutes. When you see the edges curling up slightly, stop rolling.

14. *Remove the resist.* With the felt flat on the table, cut the felt as shown and gently remove the resist. Seal the cut.

15. *Continue fulling.* Knead the felt in your hands on top of the bubble wrap. Be sure to rotate the hat in all directions while rolling it, and try not to lay it back down on your mat in its original flat orientation. Instead, open it up and lay it down with the original seam line in the middle.

9. *Lay out the wool for Side 2.* Dry your hands and divide the remaining wool into three piles. Build all three layers the same way as for Side 1, using the resist as the template.

Wet Out Side 2, Felt It

10. *Wet out Side 2.* Cover the entire pile with tulle, carefully add warm, soapy water, and press down with wet, soapy hands to begin felting. Press around the entire project several times, then wrap it up and roll it for a couple of minutes.

11. *Unroll it and turn it over.* Use a second working sheet of plastic to seal in the felt and turn over the project. Remove

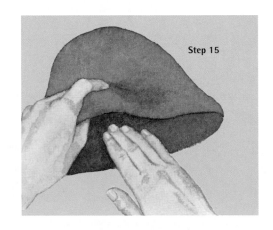

Step 15

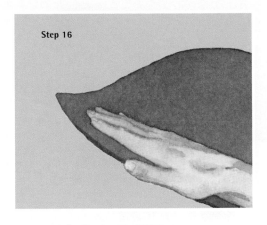

Step 16

16. Begin shaping. After smoothing out the obvious two-dimensional seams, the first step in the shaping of a hat is to stabilize the base of the crown by fulling it inward. This will start setting the wool's first general memory of the shape it will become. The Plum Derby is some-

what forgiving, since you are not creating a tight custom fit. But it is still helpful to spot full the crown a bit (wherever the bend occurs) right from the beginning.

17. Shape and roll. As soon as you are able, sponge away some of the water and try on the hat. Although you may experience a drip or two of water down your neck, you will better understand how the hat is shrinking and what you need to do for a better fit. Repeat this once or twice during the fulling process. When you're getting close to the size you want, rinse out the soap and finish the final shaping on a hat block of the appropriate size. (*See* Using a Hat Block *below.*)

USING A HAT BLOCK

We will cover formal shaping on a hat block later in the chapter. (*See page* 202.) But the Plum Derby is a simple hat, so if you just want to set the basic shape and be done with it, follow these tips:

- Hat blocks are meant to be final shapers. Don't put the hat on the form until you can stretch it over the form to get it on; otherwise, you have more fulling to do that is more efficiently accomplished on the table.

- Hat blocks vary in their construction, but if the shape you're making has a defined crown, it's useful to tie a tight string or use a jumbo rubber band to secure the felt hat at the base of the crown. Some blocks have a carved groove at the crown base especially for this reason. Other blocks are meant to accept pins to help stabilize the hats.

- Assuming that you have already rinsed the felt before stretching it on the block, smooth it out with an iron or a wooden handle of some sort. (Avoid ironing any embellishments that won't tolerate the heat.) With many hat blocks, you can iron a hat while it is on its block, but check first to make sure the hat block (many of which are plastic) won't melt.

- Steaming the felt excessively while it is on a hat block is a common mistake. The steam adds water, and too much moisture relaxes the fibers. Fulling is the way to set the shape. (See Using Steam *on page* 200.)

Hat Sizes

If you decide to purchase a hat block, use this chart as a general guideline for how your measurements translate into a hat size.

Hat Size		Head Circumference	
X-small	6 $^1/_2$	20$^1/_4$ inches	52 cm
	6 $^5/_8$	20$^3/_4$ inches	53 cm
small	6 $^3/_4$	21$^1/_8$ inches	54 cm
	6 $^7/_8$	21$^1/_2$ inches	55 cm
medium	7	21$^7/_8$ inches	56 cm
	7 $^1/_8$	22$^1/_4$ inches	57 cm
large	7 $^1/_4$	22$^5/_8$ inches	58 cm
	7 $^3/_8$	23 inches	59 cm
X-large	7 $^1/_2$	23$^1/_2$ inches	60 cm
	7 $^5/_8$	23$^7/_8$ inches	61 cm
XX-large	7 $^3/_4$	24$^1/_4$ inches	62 cm
	7 $^7/_8$	24$^5/_8$ inches	63 cm
	8	25 inches	64 cm

Variation
The Cutting-Edge Hat

This great variation of the Plum Derby is based on the idea of a
paper mobile. The directions for making the hat are the same except
you increase the width of the brim by at least 3" for some leeway.
The variation happens at the end of the process, when you make a
spiral cut into the hat and then sew it back together in an altered
way. Vary the design by making different types of cuts, as shown
(looking down on the top of the hat). For the most unique and beautiful designs, put it all on the line! Sharpen your scissors and go
forth bravely with confidence! (For you chickens, try this on a hat
you are less than happy with — it might be an improvement!)

seen from above

seen from above

seen from above

Mushrooms and Roses

I considered the design for this hat for a number of years. Because I've always been amazed at the amount of wool required to sculpt ridges, I wanted to fully explore this by creating a surface entirely made of convolutions. I originally dubbed it the Mushroom Hat, which describes both its prefelted shape (as a fresh mushroom) and its final form (a shriveled mushroom). But no one liked the idea of a mushroom on their head, so the elegant Rose Hat evolved. This project is made with the closed resist and design inside methods and does not require a hat block.

Before and After

Template Size: 36" wide x 20" high (including brim)

Finished Size: about 24" wide x 8" tall with a 5" brim (before adding the creases)

Shrinkage Rate: 33% using suggested fiber

What You Need

- basic felting supplies (*see page* 20)
- one extra sheet of 4 mil plastic, somewhat smaller than the bubble wrap
- 4 mil plastic for two copies of the template/resist
- clamps (*see at right*) of various sizes, including lots of small ones (about 30 clamps)
- scraps of heavy plastic or fabric to slip under the clamps to prevent marks

- small, sharp scissors
- a covered pot for boiling hat (optional)
- about 4½–6 oz. of Merino roving for the main color (depending on the shape you make), plus 0.5 oz. of a contrasting color
- ribbon for brim (optional)

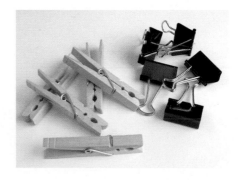

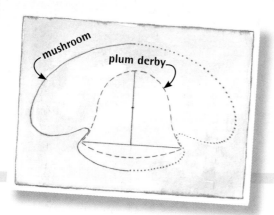

Set It Up,
Lay Out Side 1

1. Organize your space. Lay down your bubble wrap, followed by a working sheet of plastic. Collect your supplies.

2. Create the template/resist. Follow the directions for making a hat template. (*See page* 179.) Or, if you've already made the Plum Derby, use the same template as a starting point. Leave plenty of room around the template outline to expand the shape. Depending on the shape you choose, add an extra third to half of the hat's height and/or width to make the enlarged shape of your choice. Fold the template in half vertically to make sure the two halves of the hat match. Make two copies of the finished template, or draw one directly on the working plastic. *Note:* When making this pattern for the first time, avoid increasing the height and the width by large amounts. The shaping will take a long time and the hat will get quite heavy.

3. Lay out the wool for Side 1. Divide the main and contrasting colors of wool in half. Set aside one half of the main color and both halves of the contrasting color for a moment. Divide the remaining

CHOOSING YOUR SHAPE

The steps for the Mushroom and Rose hats are the same, but the template/resist is not set in stone. Using the Plum Derby template as a starting point, draw the template shape freehand, increasing the width and height as you wish. What are your preferences? Tall but tight? Wide with soft shaping? How much brim? Here are two template options to consider:

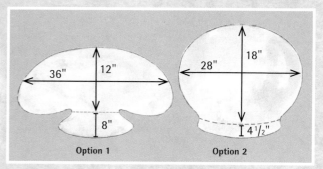

Option 1 — 36", 12", 8"

Option 2 — 28", 18", 4½"

Option 1. The brown and pink project hats (on page 184) were both made with a wide, saddlebag mushroom shape. A flare was added at the bottom for the brim.

Option 2. The red rose hat (pictured above) was made essentially the same way, but it is a smaller hat with a close-fitting brim. In this case, you start with a mushroom shape that is not as wide and a little taller. Very little is added at the bottom for a brim.

By all means, experiment with your own shape! There's only one rule: Always calculate the base of the hat (at the dotted line) by the circumference of your head divided by two and upsized to allow for shrinkage. Otherwise the hat will be too tight to fit over your head or so big that it will flop over your eyes. Every other factor can be variable.

THE FJORD SYNDROME

If you're making a hat with a wide brim, you may encounter a problem area in the template. If the brim and the body of the hat are close together, they may form a shape rather like a fjord (a narrow coastal inlet). Take care when laying out wool along those edges. When wet, the rays have a tendency to spread out and merge, making it difficult to flip them over and make a seam. Following these suggestions will help control this syndrome:

- Anticipate the problem by angling the farthest rays backward. This allows maximum space for the unfortunate rays that find themselves on top of each other in the crook of the hairpin curve.

- Roving fibers that are too long and wispy have a tendency to migrate right on across the gap when wet. You can minimize this by cutting bits of roving into 2" pieces to lay thinly along the problem edges as short rays.

- Most of all, slow down and take your time while in the fjord — just as you would if you were really there. Just sit back, wrapped in a fabulous cable-knit sweater, and enjoy the view, in no rush at all.

main color in thirds. Lay three layers of wool, with each layer perpendicular to the one before it. If you are making a brim, beware of the Fjord Syndrome. (*See the box at left.*)

4. Embellish Side 1. For the variegated or mottled effect of this hat, you'll be linking up little roving strips in the contrasting color. To do this, split the contrasting color for Side 1 in half down its length. Repeat this until you end up with a number of thin strips. These strips will melt right into the background fleece much more easily than thick roving. (*See* Roving as Embellishment *on the facing page.*) Lay each of the strips in a pattern of one continuous line all over the top of Side 1, but not on any part of the brim. Leave a few of your lines and loops laid out beyond the pattern so you can flip them over for continuity on Side 2.

Wet Out Side 1, Lay Out Side 2

5. Wet it out. Lay the tulle over Side 1. As you wet out the wool, make sure the roving strips are well attached to the background felt before you start rolling the felt. Add a little soap glue, if necessary. You don't want the roving to shift inside the closed resist package later on.

6. Add the resist. Sponge away excess water, remove the tulle, and center the resist on the top of Side 1.

7. Lay out the design for Side 2. Smear the resist with soap glue to help the Side 2 roving stay put, and flip over any trailing yarns and shapes from Side 1. Lay out the roving strips for Side 2 directly on the plastic, and tease up some fibers from the Side 1 strips wherever you attach new roving.

8. Flip the rays from Side 1. Lift up a line of rays, one small section at a time, and fold them over the edge of the resist. Press the rays toward the center without overlapping them.

9. Lay out the wool for Side 2. Dry your hands and divide the remaining wool into three piles. Build all three layers the same way as for Side 1, using the resist as the template.

Wet Out Side 2, Felt It

10. Wet out Side 2. Cover the entire pile with tulle, carefully add warm, soapy water, and with wet, soapy hands press down to begin felting. Press around the entire project several times, then wrap it up and roll it for a couple of minutes.

11. Unroll it and turn it over. Use a second working sheet of plastic to turn over the project. Remove the original working sheet of plastic and the original template, and set them aside. The back of Side 1 will now face up.

12. Flip the rays from Side 2. Fold over the rays and replace the tulle. Rub in the direction of the rays to felt them into Side 1.

Full It, Shape It

13. Begin fulling. Roll up the entire package in the tulle and gently roll out any excess cold water. Apply fresh hot water and soap, and roll the package in the tulle or bubble wrap for a few minutes. When you see the edges curling up slightly, stop rolling.

ROVING AS EMBELLISHMENT

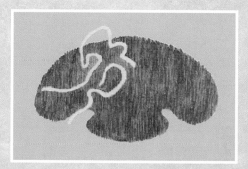

Roving has a hard time attaching along its length, especially if it's in a thick rope. The fibers tend to stay confined within the rope rather than migrating and blending with the background rays. When you thin the roving down, the fibers are much more exposed and available to attach.

We are compounding the roving challenge with the twists and turns required for this design. So, we help the roving stay put and lay flat by drawing it out a bit. "Drawing" simply means pulling the fibers farther apart, but not going so far as to break the roving apart. This technique is especially helpful when bending the roving around a curve.

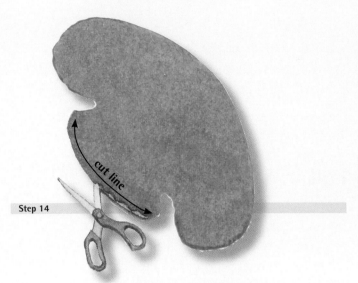

Step 14

cut line

14. Remove the resist. With the felt flat on the table, cut the felt as shown and gently remove the resist. Seal the cut. (*See page* 139.)

15. Continue fulling. Knead the felt in your hands on top of the bubble wrap. Be sure to rotate the hat in all directions while rolling it, and try not to lay it back down on your mat in its original flat orientation. Instead, open it up and lay it down with the original seam line in the middle.

16. Begin shaping. After smoothing out the obvious two-dimensional seams, it's time to start setting folds. Work with the design right-side out. Scrunch up areas of the hat's crown in your hands to make ridges that follow (in a very general way) the curved lines of the contrasting roving. Follow this by hand rolling. (Yes, you'll lose the ridges temporarily, but the wool has already started to remember.) Repeat scrunching and rolling until some dominant folds begin to appear. These

will guide the placement of the remaining folds on the crown. Before you start the final shaping, rinse the soap out of the felt.

17. Set the shape. Shaping can be done in two ways for this project: create the ridges completely by hand or set them by clamping and then boiling the felt. The second way is much faster and sets a more defined shape (*see the brown version of this hat on page* 184). However, hand shaping gives the hat a softer, old-fashioned feel (*see the salmon pink version of this hat on page* 184).

- **For soft folds:** Continue hand shaping until you become tired, then clamp the ridges you've made so far. Slip bits of heavy plastic under the clamps to protect the hat from marks that can otherwise appear from the clamps. Allow the hat to dry.

- **For sharply defined folds:** Clamp the folds securely with different-sized metal clips, placing strips of heavy fabric between the felt and the clamp. Use fabric instead of plastic, as you will boil the hat in a covered pot for about 10 to 15 minutes (which may melt the plastic). Remove the hat with tongs and drain off the water. Set the hat aside to cool, leaving the clamps on until it has dried.

18. Finish Up. Add a ribbon around the brim if desired.

Origami Hat

This colorful hat is totally unique each time and coveted by everyone who sees it. We're not going to tell you exactly how to fold it — that would spoil all the fun! The idea is to make it up as you go along rather than figuring it out ahead of time. Dabbling with prefelt shapes and yarn geometries further adds to the wonderful complexity of this design experiment. And best of all, after using all of that brain power, you can slip it on and proudly walk out the door. Brains and beauty — always a winning combination!

Project Notes

- To showcase the hat's unique geometry, it helps to limit yourself to three or four colors with different values.

- This hat is best made using the design outside, closed resist method so you can better see how the geometric shapes from the two sides come together. Sometimes they may join across the seam like a stripe; other times you might want to abruptly change the design on the other side just to see what happens when the hat is folded.

- I used less wool than usual to make thinner felt. This increases the shrinkage rate even though we're using Merino (less wool = more shrinkage).

- As with paper, the thinner the felt, the more easily it will accept a sharp, ironed crease — and the more times you can fold it. In chapters 9 and 10, we practice laying very thin layers of wool, which results in beautiful, even felts that have a lot of drape. The Origami Hat is a good project to revisit once you've perfected these skills. Meanwhile, there's a first time for everything, so take your best shot at laying out the fleece evenly and as thinly as you dare.

Set It Up, Lay Out Side 1

1. Organize your space. Lay down your bubble wrap, followed by a working sheet of plastic. Collect your supplies.

2. Create the template/resist. Make two copies of the template, or draw one directly on the working sheet of plastic.

3. Lay out the surface design. Divide each of the wool colors in half, and set half aside. Working on one of your templates or directly on the working sheet, smear a little soap glue around and lay down your surface design. It's interesting to make a few straight lines with yarn and then watch how they bend around later as they are folded. Leave a few design lines extending beyond the pattern border.

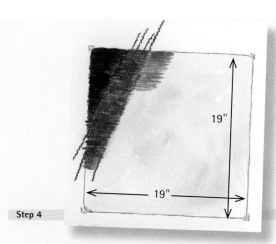

Step 4

19"

19"

4. Lay out the wool for Side 1. Divide the wool for this side in half. Use each half to lay out a layer, keeping each as thin as you can while still maintaining even coverage. Each layer should be nearly see-through. (You might be able to see your yarn design right through the layers after you wet out the wool.)

Wet Out Side 1, Lay Out Side 2

5. Wet out Side 1. Lay down the tulle and wet out the wool until it starts to hold together slightly. Roll the felt for a couple of minutes.

6. Add the resist and flip the rays. Remove the tulle and center the plastic resist over the wool. Fold over the rays without flipping the long yarn ends. Since we are using the design outside method, leave the yarn ends alone for now while you lay out the background fleece for Side 2.

7. Lay out the wool for Side 2. Lay out two thin, even layers of wool in the same way as for Side 1. Carefully flip the yarns from Side 1. As you add the rest of your design, you can match up Side 2 yarn to the flipped rays to make the design appear continuous.

Wet Out Side 2, Felt It

8. Wet out Side 2. Cover the entire pile with tulle and dribble soap glue on the design yarns. Gently press the soap glue onto the embellishments, then wet out the rest of Side 2. With wet, soapy hands, press down to begin felting. Do this a few times around the entire project, then wrap it up and roll it for a couple of minutes.

9. Unroll it and turn it over. When a light skin has formed, remove the tulle and lay a second piece of working plastic over the bag to seal in the project, then turn it over. After turning, remove the original working sheet and the template and set them aside.

10. Flip the rays. Carefully flip over the Side 2 rays by laying them between the design yarns. If you keep these ultrathin rays relatively straight and handle them gently, they will melt right into Side 1. It's okay to angle them up between yarns while completing the seam. Replace the tulle and rub parallel to the rays to felt them in.

Full It, Shape It

11. Start fulling. Roll up the felt in the tulle and gently roll out any excess cold water. Apply fresh hot water and soap, and roll the package for a few minutes.

12. Remove the resist. When the edges start to curl, cut an opening along one of the sides or wherever else you wish. Make the cut about 5" to 6" to begin with, and stabilize the cut felt. (*See page* 139.) You can enlarge the cut later, if needed. If you want to be really surprised, place the head hole somewhere unexpected — at an angle

Step 10

Step 12

in the bottom left, for example. Support your seams as you pull out the resist.

13. Roll and shape. Here's where you start making up your own design. Smooth out the seam line as usual, or incorporate it into your folding geometry. Roll the felt just enough to shrink it down some, then start working on the final folding and ironing. Set creases and iron them down very firmly while monitoring the overall fit and guiding the size and shape of the head opening. Thoroughly rinse the felt before beginning the final shaping. Fold and iron very firmly as many times as it takes to make the hat almost fold up on itself.

14. Finish up. To dry the hat, leave it flat or stretch the opening over a shallow hat block or other object that will hold it upright without disturbing the folded shape. Finish with trim around the opening, if desired.

The Double Hood

The Mihalkó-Beede Double Hood technique is a clever variation on a traditional, ancient felting method. By assembling two partially seamed cones inside one another, the method creates a very durable hat with a double layer of wool. The hat is broad-brimmed by nature because of its initial cone shape, but later shaping or even trimming can lead to unique designs. Attachments can also be added.

The sloping bell shape of the double hood is what produces the broad brim or high crown or both — that and the dynamics of the open resist method. Because the bottom of the hood is open, the fibers are not held as tightly as and are free to move more than the fibers in the top of the crown or along the sides. This becomes a great advantage when setting a shape in felt. It allows you to shape the more restricted (top) areas first and then move on down the hat, shaping as you go. The flexible brim region has some give and can accommodate the changing stresses on the felt.

Think of the brim as being very alive, changing dramatically throughout the process. This is why you never cut or shape the brim until the very end of fulling. When all else is shaped, you can give the hardworking, generous brim a rest and finally set its permanent shape.

The double hood hat is a good choice if you want to make a hat that requires lots of felt for shaping in the crown area. A good example is a cowboy hat, which not only has a brim but also requires folds to be set into the crown. Beginning with a broad bell allows you to use all of that felt to shape into folds. With experience you will discover many hat shapes and determine your favorite method. Felted hats and other shaped felt, like vessels and masks, require skill and experience.

Understanding the shape of your pattern is the key. Be aware that there are boundaries to what you can do within one pattern, and try to make your shaping decisions early on so you can move toward fulling in that shape in a logical way. If you want to make a pillbox hat, for instance, the double hood method is not a good choice because right off the bat you will be fighting the pattern into a straight-sided shape. You have a limited time to touch and shape the wool, so begin with something that is close to the finished shape you desire.

It's helpful to understand that different wools will affect your hat's shrinkage. Most people first make this hat with short-fiber Merino batts, and the standard pattern size developed by Beth Beede is intended for this wool. But you needn't be limited to Merino. Try a blend of alpaca fiber or fibers from other local farm animals. And if the hat is meant to endure long hours in the elements, consider using a hardier, more water-repellent wool. Two popular options to consider are:

- a blend of Norwegian C-1 and Merino
- a batt from Norway that contains a 50/50 mix of Norwegian C-1 and Pelsull, which contributes a beautiful heather look. *Note:* These batts are sometimes called Götland because Norwegian Pelsull behaves like Swedish Götland wool (which is a little better known).

WHY NORWEGIAN WOOL?

You may be wondering: Why use wool from Norway when we have plenty of sheep in the United States? The countries of Scandinavia have been producing felting wool for a long time, and the mills there have a good understanding of feltmaking. They offer large quantities of consistent, quality-controlled wool that is evenly dyed and available in batt form — all things that are currently unavailable on a large scale in the United States.

Most of our commercial felting wool comes from overseas. Australia produces most of the Merino wool sold worldwide. Götland wool (from Sweden) and the similar Pelsull (a crossbreed of the Götland sheep developed in Norway) are prized by feltmakers throughout the world for being extremely fast felting. Nonetheless, many feltmakers prefer to prepare and dye fibers found at local small farms and sheep fairs. The choice is yours — why not try them all?

Merino rams are known for their curled horns, which can grow into long spirals.

MAKING A DOUBLE HOOD TEMPLATE

Essentially this technique involves making two separate flat sides (the hoods) and then wrapping them in opposite directions around a narrower resist. For this technique, you will be using the same size template regardless of your head size. This works because the felt package is open at the bottom, allowing the hat to change in size and shape much more freely than with a closed resist pattern.

 The double hood templates come from Beth Beede's classes. To make your own, trace the template drawings and enlarge them on a copier until they are the designated size. (It helps to fold each tracing in half and enlarge just the halves onto 11" x 17" sheets of paper that will need to be taped together.) This takes a bit of fussing, but once you have it, you can use the template indefinitely. Trace both outlines onto plastic, including the three arrows at the top of each cone. Cut two copies of the hood template and one copy of the resist.

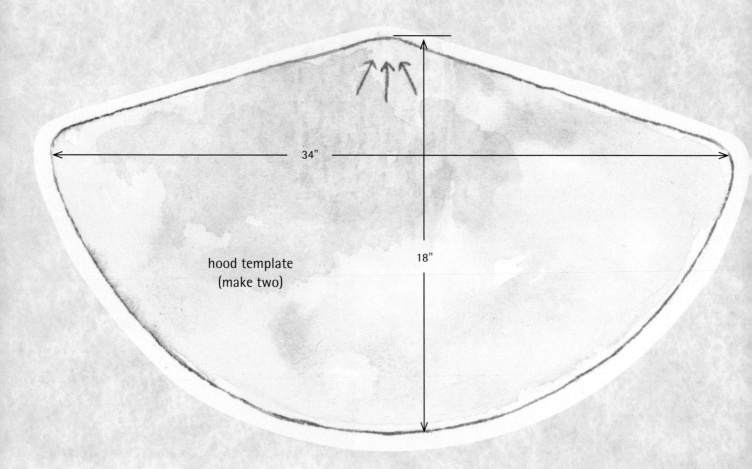

34"

18"

hood template
(make two)

Notes

- The dimensions given here are calculated for a shrinkage rate of 30 percent. If you make the hat in a wool with a different shrinkage rate, adjust the size of the template accordingly.

- When using short-fiber Merino (with a shrinkage rate of 40 to 45 percent), you need to increase the size of the templates. The hoods should be 22" high by 40" wide, and the inside resist should be 23" high by 28" wide.

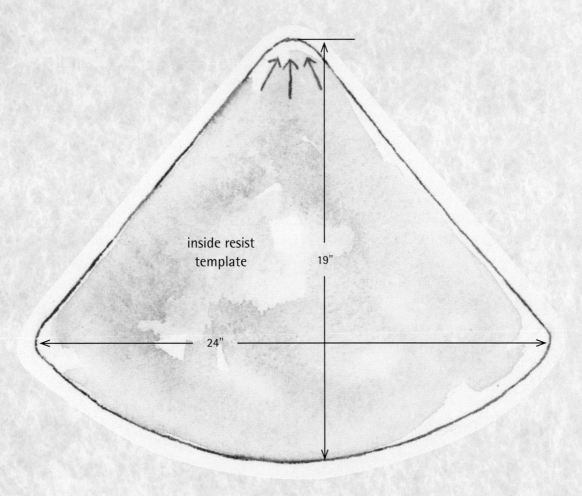

inside resist
template

19"

24"

The Glacier Bay Hat

This hat's name was inspired by its colors, reminiscent of turquoise-blue glacier waters. As the white C-1 fibers and the blue-green Merino fibers migrated and blended with one another, they created the impression of a fine, icy mist. This lovely broad-brimmed cloche is a favorite of women and men alike — with a trimmed oval brim, it easily becomes the ultimate cool-weather fishing hat. A wider brim can accommodate pinned decoration or show off some of your felted cording projects from chapter 3. This project uses the double hood method, and the round dome of the hat is finished on a hat block.

Before and After

Template Size: 18" x 34"

Finished Size: variable; full to fit

Shrinkage Rate: 30% using suggested fiber

What You Need

- basic felting supplies (*see page* 20)
- one extra sheet of 4 mil plastic, somewhat smaller than the bubble wrap
- 4 mil plastic for two copies of the template/resist
- soap glue (*see page* 22)
- a hat block of the appropriate size, preferably cloche style
- a small roller, dowel, hairbrush handle, or other smooth fulling tool (*see photo at right*)
- a steamer or steam iron
- a disposable razor
- 5.5 oz. of white Norwegian C-1 wool batt, plus a little extra
- 1 oz. of Merino/silk roving, plus a little extra
- blue-green dyed silk hankies and mint green mohair yarn, or embellishments of your choice
- finishing decoration (we used a wired ribbon with blue dupioni silk)

Set It Up, Lay It Out

1. Organize your space. Lay down your bubble wrap (bubbles facing up) followed by a working sheet of plastic. Collect your supplies.

2. Create the templates and the resist. Follow the instructions for making a double hood template. (*See pages* 194–195.) Label one copy of the hood "Hood A" and the other copy "Hood B." Label the last piece "Inside Resist."

3. Lay out the C-1 wool for Hood A. Lay the Hood A template on the working sheet of plastic. Tear off a large handful of the C-1 batt and set it aside (for patching seams later in the process). Weigh the rest of the C-1, divide it in half, and set half aside. Split the C-1 batt into long, transparent strips and fill in the Hood A template. Continue building up even layers until you've used up this half of the C-1.

4. Lay out the Merino roving for Hood A. This next layer will be the inside surface of the hat. Reserve a small handful of the Merino roving (for patching seams later), then lay out all of the roving in even layers on top of the C-1 batting. Using the working plastic as a tray, set this template and wool aside.

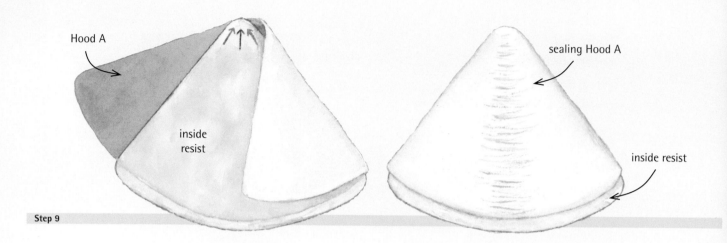

Hood A

inside resist

sealing Hood A

inside resist

Step 9

5. Lay out the embellishments. Lay the Hood B template on a clean working sheet of plastic. Hood B will be the top layer of the hat, and the first layer you build will show on the outer surface of your hat. Smear a layer of soap glue on the template and lay out your surface design. If you are using a silk hankie, make a few small slits in it to help the wool penetrate and felt it in; otherwise it might later peel off like paper. Add yarn in whatever pattern you like. Embellishments placed near the bottom of the cone will show on the brim, and those at the top will show on the crown.

6. Lay out the C-1 wool for Hood B. Split the remaining C-1 wool batt into long, transparent strips and fill in the Hood B template. Continue building up even layers until you've used up this half of the C-1. Set this template aside.

Wet It Out, Felt It

7. Felt Hood A. Lay the tulle on top of the Hood A wool pile. Add hot, soapy water, saturate the pile, and roll the whole thing in the bubble wrap for 5 to 7 minutes using medium pressure. Open the roll and check the felt. If the fibers are beginning to lock down into a skin, go on

NOTES ON SHAPING

- In a simple cloche style, the crown and brim remain in basically the same proportions as they began. You need only to refine the shape by fulling at the crown base and then finishing the hat on a block to set its form.

- For a fedora, cowboy hat, or any hat with an indented crown, you will need extra height to form the indentation. (See page 201.) This requires a lot of pulling on the crown portion of the cone to form a taller shape.

- For a sombrero or hat with a very wide brim, you don't need such a high crown. In this case, focus more on pulling out the bottom of the cone.

- As you roll the felt to shrink it down and then open it up to stretch it out into a shape, it will seem like these two things are working against each other. However, it is this push and pull that slowly hardens and trains the wool into the shape you want.

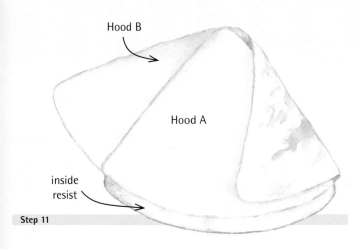

Hood B

Hood A

inside resist

Step 11

to the next step. If they're still loose and hairy, roll a little more. *Note:* Merino felts faster than coarser C-1 wool, so you may have to give them a little time to come together, but don't roll so long that you begin to shrink the cone.

8. *Add the resist.* Unroll the Hood A felt and center the smaller, cone-shaped resist on it. Match the top of the resist cone to the top of the hood. Here's where the three arrows at the top of the cone become important: They confirm which end is the top. The felt can spread and shift quite a bit during rolling, so its shape can be misleading.

9. *Wrap Hood A.* Fold up the sides of Hood A to make a cone shape around the resist. Move the resist around a bit to find the optimum position. Try to make the sides match perfectly without overlap. (*Note:* The resist should stick out of the bottom a bit; this keeps the two sides from felting together along the opening.) If the sides don't meet, use the reserve wool as needed to join the two sides. Make

sure there is no hole at the top of your hat; if you see one, patch it closed without folding the top of the cone over on itself; otherwise you'll create a bump in the top of your hat. When you've completed this step, lift the working plastic and put Hood A and its template aside.

10. *Felt Hood B.* Lay the tulle on top of the Hood B wool pile. Add hot, soapy water, saturate the pile, and roll the whole package in bubble wrap for 5 to 7 minutes using medium pressure. Keep rolling until the embellishments adhere to the wool.

11. *Wrap Hood B.* Unroll the Hood B felt. Carefully turn over the wrapped Hood A and center it, seam side down, on Hood B. Set the Side A template aside. Fold the sides of Hood B around Hood A. Pat in a bit of extra soap along the seam to help it felt together. Make sure the wool is still wet and that you still have a closed point at the top of your cone. You can add a bit of wool as needed to keep the thickness even.

USING A WASHBOARD

Glass washboards can be useful in feltmaking, but beware: Scrubbing felt with a washboard is a form of shock fulling that is best used with thick felts, not with delicate nuno or cobweb. It's most appropriate for the later stages of fulling thick boots, a double hood hat, or a heavy vest. The glass lines of the board are deceptively sharp, so be careful. Not only will they abrade the surface of the felt, they will also cut knuckles in a flash.

When using a washboard, try your best to *roll* the felt along the ridges. Things change very fast on a washboard, so unroll the felt and look at it after a couple of passes. Because felt can become permanently hard, causing you to lose control of your shape, use a washboard only at the end of the process and never directly on an embellished design.

Note: Expert felter Pat Spark uses a net-covered glass washboard on her nuno felts. Gently rubbing the surface flat-handed, perpendicular to the ridges, she says, puts "a great skin on the felt."

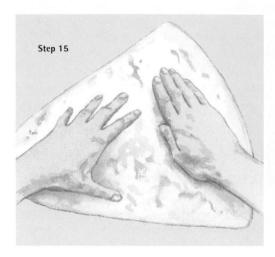

Step 15

12. Continue felting. Use the working plastic under the felt to move the felt off the bubble wrap. Turn the bubble wrap over (bubble side down). Move the working plastic and the cone together back to the bubble wrap. Turn the cone over so it is seam side down on the bubble wrap. Using a pool noodle or other rolling bar, roll the whole package in the bubble wrap

for about 5 to 8 minutes, then unroll the cone and turn it over. Add more hot, soapy water if needed. Roll the cone again for 5 to 8 more minutes. When the layers have fused and the felt has formed a good skin, you are ready to full the hat.

Full It, Shape It

13. Start fulling. Check for any visible trace of the seams; gently press, pull, and smooth them with your fingers as needed to erase them. Pull on the felt to stretch it out in all directions, and then, working on the bubble side of the wrap, roll it by hand for a minute or so. Open up the felt, turn it 90 degrees, and roll it again from the other side.

14. Remove the resist. Gently reach inside and pull out the resist without lifting the felt off the table. The felt will be heavy, so fold the cone in half or thirds so you can pick it up to press out the cold water. Resaturate the felt until it's sitting in a puddle of hot, soapy water. Begin to very gently knead it without lifting it off the table — all that water plus gravity can put too much stress on the seams. When it feels less fragile, you can lift it as you knead it and use a stronger hand motion. Knead it for 3 to 4 minutes.

15. Start shaping. When the felt begins to shrink, it's important to start setting the shape of the hat as you continue to roll and shrink it. By setting a memory in the wool early on, you won't have to fight the hat into a new shape after it begins to harden. Unless you want an umbrella-shaped hat, now is the time to start training the base of the crown inward

USING STEAM

The idea that steaming will set a shape in felt is often misunderstood. Steam is a powerful way to help shape your felt, but it doesn't work alone. Steaming loosens and relaxes the felt, but it's the fulling that you do immediately after the steam that tightens the felt. The combination of these two steps, performed over and over, causes the felt to harden.

Don't fall into the trap of using too much steam on your hat while it's on the block. Every time you steam, you must follow up by retightening that same area. The best course of action is to steam an area well, work it for a while, and then move to another area. Steaming the whole hat at once repeatedly isn't helpful because you'll create a new challenge for the wool: gravity. Too much steam introduces too much water back into your shape and will interfere with setting the wool's memory. Go easy with the steam!

THE CLASSIC FEDORA

Once you've learned the double hood technique, there are any number of shapes you can create, using essentially the same steps. One is the classic fedora shape. This man's hat was made using short-fiber Merino batting and required a larger template to account for the higher shrinkage rate. With a few hours of devoted shaping and finishing on a professional hat block, you can create a family heirloom that will last a very long time.

Fedoras aren't just for men! This lovely feminine version was felted with kiwi green Norwegian C-1 wool and then dip-dyed in a turquoise blue that altered the color to teal green. Clothespins clipped along the hat's brim acted as resists to the blue dye, preserving strips of the original kiwi color.

(where a hatband would be located). To do this, roll up the felt in your hands and spot full the base of the crown. Position your hands above that exact area when you roll it up, and apply a lot of pressure when you roll. You can spot full directly on the felt by working it firmly in that precise place, pinching and scrunching the wool.

16. Check the fit often. When the hat approaches the right size, wring out the water and try it on. It should be a little tight on your head so it will stretch snugly over the hat block. If it isn't, focus on the areas that are too large and full it some more. When you're satisfied that it's snug enough, rinse out the soap and water. Dry it as much as possible by wrapping the felt in a dry towel and stepping on it (the gravity of water still in the felt will fight your shaping efforts).

17. Use the hat block. Pull the felt onto the hat block and secure the base (hatband area) with a strong, tight rubber band. Rub any kind of tool that isn't too abrasive on the felt's surface to continue to tighten its shape on the hat block. I've used spoons, ribbed Tupperware lids, the handle end of paintbrushes, the back of a hairbrush — be creative! Just be sure you're not ripping up the nice smooth surface of your felt.

18. Finish up. When the hat looks finished and fits your head snugly, use the smooth end of a brush to polish the surface or iron it while it's on the hat block. Let the hat dry on the hat block. Attach any trim, cording, or embellishments as desired. To reduce areas where too many white fibers have overpowered the Merino color, or to make the hat less hairy, shave the surface of the felt with a razor. (*See page* 123.) Felters commonly shave the surface of their felt, but you should do so carefully. You can easily ruin embellishments!

Midnight Swirl

This pretty hat is an extreme variation of the double hood method. The hat is very stylish from the back, and the swirl leaves a wake of whispers when it passes. The heathered cobalt Norwegian C-1 and Pelsull blend is very fast felting. The brim was heavily trimmed, and the fit of the swirl as it sits on the head is made possible by the tiers that create small rings inside the hat; otherwise the sides would be too wide and the hat would slip down over the eyes. The Midnight Swirl is a work of art that pushes the limits of the double hood shape!

Project Notes

Shaping a hat like this is always a very fluid, very personal process. But follow these tips to help you find your own way.

- Use the same hat pattern and internal resist piece as for the Glacier Bay Hat.

- If you want to make a set of nested tiers, stretch some extra height into the crown during the beginning of shaping.

- Work the ridges of the walls over and over again, overemphasizing their height, since they will sink down a bit.

- Begin at the top of the crown when

USING STIFFENERS

One of the most common questions intermediate feltmakers ask is how to stiffen felt. Most any type of wool will stiffen in the fulling process, although some will stiffen more readily and better than others. For example, it is possible to alternately full, steam, and stretch Merino to make a very stiff hat with a rigid brim, but on the whole, the internal structure of the felt will still be softer when compared to a coarser wool of the same thickness.

So what do you do when you want a piece of felt to be very rigid? You might choose to apply a stiffener. Shellac, gelatin size, and diluted glues of various sorts are all stiffening agents. Most stiffeners should be applied when the felt is wet or damp to allow full penetration. Experiment to see what works best.

Be aware that some stiffeners will yellow the fiber with time, some leave a residue, and some are toxic. Always test your choice thoroughly to ensure that it's the best option for your project. And one more note: Don't confuse stiffness with strength. A spider web is very strong but not stiff; the same goes for well-made felt.

making tiers and work downward. This allows the bottom portion of your felt to act as a buffer zone of give-and-take with respect to the fulling action in the top part of the hat. The outer edges are always shaped last. Trim the brim as needed at the end.

- Set the final swirls with metal clips if you wish, but remember to put a plastic scrap underneath each clamp so you don't leave marks on your felt.

THE JESTER HAT

This wonderful hat, created by Catherine Rogers, can absolutely cast a spell and seems to do just that to everyone who sees it. And it makes you very, very happy when you wear it on your head! There are dozens of ways to embellish such a hat:

- Add quilting stitching or beads to the balls on the spikes.

- Add sparkle and glistening accents such as novelty yarns or Angelina fiber to the top layer of wool while you're laying out your hat.

- Add prefelt designs or silk roving to the surface for a more dramatic look.

FEATURED ARTIST
Beth Beede

American feltmaker Beth Beede is known throughout the world as a profoundly influential artist and teacher. Recently retired after working with fibers for over 40 years, she is revered in the United States as the "mother of American felt-making." Characteristically uncomfortable with the title, though, Beth prefers to keep the spotlight on the material itself and the magic that results when knowledge is openly shared.

Widely traveled, Beth explored, learned, and taught feltmaking in Hungary on a Fulbright Scholarship in 1985–86. As part of a small group of invited artists, Beth visited feltmaking nomads in Mongolia in 1991. In 1992, she recorded the methods of a Whirling Dervishes hat maker in Turkey and later the techniques of two of the last old hat makers in Oaxaca, Mexico. Her work has helped to connect many feltmakers throughout the world and helps us all to remember that feltmaking is a process based on traditions much older than our own.

Beth also created the felt-on-a-ball approach to making hats and vessels, now widely known as the Beede Ball technique. Essentially, wool is wrapped around a collapsible ball, held on by pantyhose nylons, and felted in soapy water. The ball is then

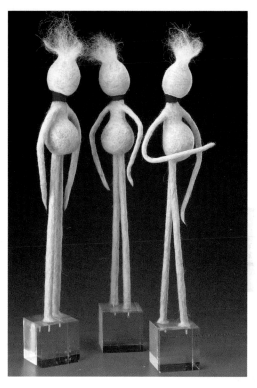

For this whimsical sculpture, Beth felted wool over a wire armature. *Red Necks*, Merino and Karakul fleece, 24" x 3 1/2" x 3 1/2".

removed and the felt shaped as desired. As is often true, other feltmakers arrived at the same idea independently. However, the elegantly simple Beede Ball is the method known to most people today and is passed around on the Internet, taught by many, and even sold in kits. Most felters who teach or make vessels have used this technique.

Nuno Felting

Aside from needle felting, nuno felting is the fastest growing technique in modern feltmaking — and with good reason. Nuno felt is not only lightweight, visually appealing, and fun to wear, it's also fast and easy to make. What's not to like?

To create nuno felt, very small amounts of wool are layered on a pre-existing fabric, usually silk or cotton. During the felting process, the wool fibers migrate through the weave of the cloth and entangle, pulling the cloth along with them as they shrink. The result is a fully integrated and highly textural fabric that resembles *ruching* (tightly gathered pleats). Nuno differs from ruching, however, in that it gathers in all directions rather than just one, making the fabric appear bubbled.

Nuno is Japanese for fabric or cloth. The word became associated with this technique during the collaborative effort of Polly Stirling and her Japanese assistant, Sachiko Kotaka. (*See page* 231.) Together, they created nuno felt garments in Australia in the mid-1990s. Today they are widely credited with popularizing the technique, although northern Europeans developed a similar technique about a decade earlier. Their term "laminated felting" is preferred by some feltmakers, since Nuno is also the name of a textile design company in Japan. Laminated felting certainly describes the technique well. But in recent years, the term "nuno-filt" has become so widespread in Europe, it seems the term is here to stay.

The nuno technique reveals the true power and elegance of wool and is a perfect example of the diversity of feltmaking. Nuno felting strips things down to the bare bones, making use of wool's alchemic power even when using so very few fibers. When we experience the total transformation of so few bits of wool on cloth, somehow the power of the process is more starkly revealed to us. This appreciation only deepens as we move from using sheer silk gauze and chiffon to working with denser and tighter weaves.

This experimentation in textural effects is interesting and useful from an artist's point of view, but nuno felt is also very practical as a wearable fabric. It is incredibly lightweight and drapes the body beautifully. Not only is it gorgeous, but it also completely takes people off guard when they learn how it's created. *"This* is felt?"

In the broad view of things, nuno is still a relatively new technique, and it's only in the past year or two that European books have introduced the subject. American trends in feltmaking follow European ones, and this introduction of ideas is accelerated by the increase in European teachers traveling to the United States and vice versa. Nuno leads the way in attracting new artists to feltmaking, and in America, the technique is spreading like wildfire in all areas of the country. Artists in California, the Southwest, and the Southeast are embracing this light and airy felt that can be worn year-round in any climate.

This chapter contains some introductory projects to show you the technique. Most nuno felters make clothing, which ultimately involves clothing construction — something beyond the scope of this book. However, felters also commonly create free-form clothing styles with nuno felt yardage. A wide shawl or wrap can double as an artistic wraparound skirt, for example. It all depends on personal style.

What's Different?

Nuno feltmaking relies on slightly different skills than traditional, or wet, feltmaking. The principles are the same, as are many of the basic steps. However, creating a fusion of wool fiber and fabric is different from creating a piece of solid felt. Let's take a closer look at how these two processes vary.

Using Cloth

The biggest difference in nuno felt compared to regular felt is the presence of a preexisting fabric. No matter what cloth is used, it will always have a stabilizing effect on the felt. Felt rug makers have used this concept for years by incorporating a thin layer of cotton muslin or similar fabric inside the pile of wool to give it strength. When cloth and wool are layered and felted together, the crossing warp and weft lines of the cloth provide stability to areas of fiber that may otherwise be sparse or uneven.

Equipment

Usually the plastics and mats appropriate for nuno are softer and gentler than those used for traditional feltmaking. This is a new kind of journey with the wool — working with thin layers of fibers that need to be coaxed through the fabric's weave. The fibers must be given time to find their way through the cloth and worked gently so they don't end up felting to each other first. Vigorous rubbing and hot water will cause the wool to felt too quickly.

Very fine tulle can sometimes be used as a covering, but even that will sometimes be too rough for the delicate

Nuno vs. Wet Felting

Step	Nuno Felting	Traditional Felting
Setup	• loose-weave cloth and wool fibers • 1 mil or 2 mil working plastic • sheer polyester curtain	• wool fibers only • 4 mil working plastic • tulle or other coarser netting
Wetting out	• lightly dribbled or sprayed water	• water poured from a cup
Felting	• bubble wrap or rug mat	• bamboo or other options
Fulling	• lighter, more random touch	• even, steady pressure

nuno surface. More commonly, a sheer polyester curtain is used as a covering. Although less transparent, it's smoother and less likely to snag any surface design.

Using a 1 mil or 2 mil working sheet of plastic instead of 4 mil will allow you to feel what's happening through the plastic.

The rigid bamboo mat that works so well for fulling a large pile of wool is inappropriate here. For rolling, bubble wrap or a nonskid rug mat works best. The bubbles act as tiny trampolines, providing a vertical felting motion that helps the fibers find their way up and down through the weave. Nonslip rug mats provide some vertical give and are a good choice for large nuno work. The water runs through these porous mats more easily than through bubble wrap.

Technique

The primary differences in nuno felting and traditional felting techniques revolve around the need for a lighter touch. For example, when wetting out the cloth and fiber layers through a sheer polyester curtain, it's vital to avoid disrupting the thin layer of fiber. Even pouring a tiny stream of water directly from a cup is too much of a disturbance. From the fibers' point of view, this might as well be a tsunami! Instead, in nuno felting, either spray the water from above like a mist (*see page 255*) or apply water by pouring it onto the back of your hand and letting it trickle onto the curtain. Your goal is to saturate the fiber and cloth without moving the fibers.

In nuno felting, instead of vibrating the felt with your hands to begin the felting (as you do in traditional methods), roll the covered project right from the beginning. Your hands are too strong for that thin layer of fiber. If you work it directly, the separate fibers would felt too quickly into a skin and never migrate down through the weave of the cloth. Rolling gets the fibers moving a little bit and helps them migrate toward openings in the fabric in a more subtle way.

BASIC NUNO SUPPLIES
Because nuno felting differs from traditional felting, the supplies you'll need are different as well. Assemble this list of items before you begin any nuno felting project.

- a piece of bubble wrap large enough to accommodate your project
- a working sheet of 1 mil or 2 mil plastic, somewhat smaller than the bubble wrap
- a piece of sheer polyester curtain the same size as the working plastic
- a nonskid rug mat for fulling (optional)
- a pool noodle to use as a dowel for rolling
- elastic ties cut from spandex fabric
- a small bucket or tub of soapy water
- a few small sponges
- a towel
- a black waterproof marker
- a measuring tape

Once the fibers are through the weave, the fulling begins. In the traditional felting projects in the earlier chapters, you guided the fibers so they felted and fulled evenly across the project. In nuno felting, this becomes less important because the fabric now dictates much of the felt's internal structure. Although you can certainly block in the corners and edges of the nuno with your palm, many people prefer to allow the fibers to move wherever they will, which results in highly scalloped edges and what I call butterfly corners. (*See page* 217.) As you work with nuno over time, you might prefer to control your yardage by stabilizing the edges and corners, and to experiment with a more deliberate placement of textures within the piece.

Another key difference between nuno versus traditional felt is in the way that you full it. Shock fulling doesn't hurt nuno felt; in fact, it's recommended. But why? The answer lies in fiber dynamics. When felt is tossed, there is a shock to the fibers when it lands — think of it as fiber whiplash! In traditional felt, this causes a leapfrog motion inside the fiber pile, where adjacent fibers jump past each other to attach to those farther out. This creates uneven air pockets in the felt and results in overfelting. But in nuno felt, you are working with only a very thin layer of wool, not a three-dimensional pile of fiber. Also, the fabric weave structure strongly restricts fiber movement.

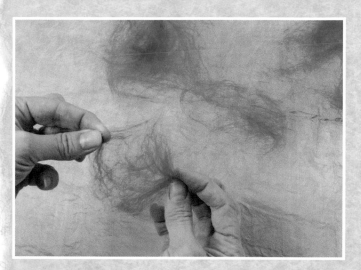

NUNO TEST RUN

To get a feel for how nuno felting works, try this experiment:

1. Lay out two layers of wool in a 12" by 12" square.

2. Cut two strips of silk chiffon, cotton gauze, or doubled cheesecloth about 3" to 4" wide and 12" long.

3. Lay one strip along one edge of your wool pile and the other on the opposite edge. The wool in the middle of your sample should have no cloth. On one of the cloth strips, add small tufts of fibers by fluffing them open in your hand and letting them fall onto the cloth. With this technique, called *clouding*, these few little fibers will act like glue to help felt the fabric.

4. Lay a polyester curtain over the pile, and then wet out the pile. Roll it all up around a pool noodle in bubble wrap and felt the pile. Check the tulle or curtain often to prevent it from sticking to the felt. When it does, slowly peel it off, then lay it back down on the felt.

5. When the fabric begins to pucker, finish fulling the sample by kneading it in your hands and tossing it a little bit. Add fresh hot water and repeat this step to finish fulling it.

6. Now spread it out. You should see a difference in the shrinkage rate across the sample. Try to pull on the sample in different directions to see what happens. Notice the difference in width across the sample. It should be apparent that fabric stabilizes the fibers and traps them in its structure, whereas fibers that are left alone lock down tightly and shrink more.

Dramatic Textures

So much of the beauty of nuno lies in the lovely textural effects that happen when the wool grabs the fabric and makes it pucker. Three factors in particular affect how this texture develops:

- the amount of wool
- the density or openness of the fabric's weave
- the size (diameter) of the wool fibers

With experience you can learn to alter these factors to create subtle variations in your nuno felt.

Amount of Wool

As mentioned, one primary difference in nuno felting is the amount of wool being used. In theory, nuno felting involves felting a single plane of fiber onto a plane of cloth. In reality, the plane of wool you lay down when making nuno is thicker than one fiber, but it's still thin when compared to the pile of wool you laid down for traditional felt.

Density of the Fabric

As you might imagine, fibers can most easily penetrate fabrics with an open weave, resulting in a texture closest to a complete fusion. For instance, chiffons and gauzes are easy to felt because the fibers migrate through the cloth almost as if it weren't there. A denser weave allows the fewest number of fibers through, but some will usually penetrate and the process will proceed. For example, using a dense weave such as 8 mm silk habotai (a kind of shiny China silk) results in a very interesting texture with larger bubbles than those produced using 5 mm habotai. This dramatic texture might be used for only a portion of a garment, for example, for a lapel instead of an entire jacket.

Size of Fibers

If you were to use the same 8 mm silk habotai as above but with wool fibers that are smaller in diameter, the effect would be the same as if you were using a more open weave. This is because the smaller wool fibers find their way more easily through the fabric. The Merino roving we typically use in feltmaking is generally available as 22 micron, or 64s. (*See* Felting Wools Chart *on pages* 94–96.) But finer Merino — most typically 17–19 micron, the lower range of which is commonly called *superfine Merino* — is available to feltmakers as well. This Merino has been used primarily by European nuno feltmakers, although it is now becoming more widely available in the United States. It is still more difficult to find than the standard 22 micron.

Choosing the Fabric

The lightest-weight nuno is created with the finest fibers and an open-weave fabric. Silks are by far the most commonly used cloth. Silk is measured in *momme* (abbreviated as *mm*), which refers to its density of weave (or thread count). The higher the momme, the heavier the fabric. Types of silk commonly used for nuno include gauze, chiffon, organza, and habotai.

Many weights of cottons can also be used with good results. Polyester blends are also an option, but the results are more unpredictable due in part to the slippery nature of the synthetic fibers. One theory is that fibers that travel through the polyester weave can slip back out again. Also, synthetic weaves are often more rigid than natural fibers. This quality discourages individual fibers that may be trying to migrate through the weave in slightly different directions.

When you are evaluating fabrics for nuno felting, apply "the breath test." Blow sharply through the weave to see if you can feel air moving through the cloth onto your fingers. If so, the weave is open and will probably work as a nuno fabric.

It's also a good idea to test your cloth of choice before investing time in a full-blown project. If you intend to make clothing, use the natural drape of the fabric as a guide as to whether or not it will drape after felting. Although drape is also affected by how much wool is used, if the fabric doesn't drape before you felt it, it will only become stiffer after felting.

" *Extreme Nuno Options*

When first learning nuno, I couldn't wait to experiment on a variety of fabrics. I wondered: If I felt slowly over time, can I coax fibers through a fabric that seems impossible to penetrate? I decided to try it on a piece of cotton duck canvas I had lying around the studio. I laid out the wool, lined up my favorite music CDs, and went to work. After eight hours, I'd succeeded. I worked for another two hours stabilizing the fabric and learning how to make perfectly square corners.

I won't be repeating this anytime soon, but the result was some of the firmest and most evenly textured nuno I've ever created (*pictured right*). I use it as a hot pad on a long kitchen table, but the weight of it would also work well for a durable rug. Feltmakers Mehmet Girgic (*see page* 125) and Theresa May O'Brien have developed something similar for their Osman rug technique (*see page* 287), although they use a lighter-weight muslin instead of cotton duck.

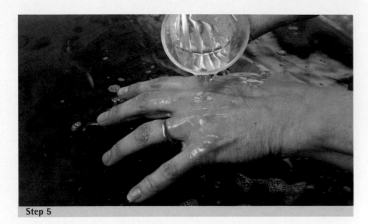

Step 5

Step 7

letting it trickle onto the curtain. Do this until the wool and fiber are saturated.

6. Roll it up. Roll up the project with a pool noodle or other rolling tool. Secure the roll with ties and roll it for about 200 rolls (or 4 to 5 minutes). Unroll the bundle and reverse directions by rolling up the noodle from the opposite side. Roll from this direction the same amount of rolls (or the same amount of time).

7. Remove the polyester curtain. After this step, it's a good idea to lift back the curtain to make sure it hasn't felted into your project. Curl it back slowly, rolling as you go. Keep your hand directly behind the curtain on the felt's surface to prevent ripping up the design as you roll back the

curtain. Once you've checked the curtain, put it back in place. You will need it for a while yet — you just don't want it to become part of the scarf!

8. Check the felt. Check the back side of the fabric to see if the fibers have migrated through the weave. To do this, press out some of the water at one of the corners and turn the nuno onto the back of your hand. Search across the fabric surface for the nearly invisible fiber hairs. (*See* What to Look For *below.*)

9. Keep rolling. It takes some experience to know exactly when to stop rolling and begin fulling. Usually it takes around 800 rolls in each direction before the fibers come through well enough on a scarf.

WHAT TO LOOK FOR

Checking the back of fabric for fiber migration can be tricky. Be sure to press out the water first, or the fibers you're looking for will remain flat against the fabric. Even when dry, the fibers are nearly invisible. To detect them, look across the top of the fabric, not directly at it. Imagine you are standing at the edge of a wheat field at sunset, looking across the wheat (your cloth) as you gaze toward the horizon. Suddenly you notice little clouds of insects flying right above the wheat (the fibers that have made it through the weave). Some felters compare these fibers to the fine hairs on goosebumps on human skin.

Full It

The exact series of fulling steps will vary greatly from feltmaker to feltmaker. The important thing is to first briefly stabilize your edges to make sure the fibers have come through the fabric and will not peel away. After that, it's simply a matter of working the piece in different ways to agitate the fibers and shrink the piece. Here's one way to go about it:

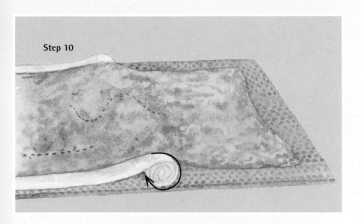

Step 10

the bubble wrap like a gentle washboard. Full the scarf with your palms until the nuno texture (on the fabric side) appears even and the fiber side of the scarf looks similar to your usual finished felt. Keep going until it won't shrink anymore.

14. *Finish it.* Rinse the scarf thoroughly, and lay it flat to dry.

15. *Measure the scarf.* If you plan to make nuno clothing, it's important to record the measurements of every piece of nuno you make. Write down the exact amount of wool you used, the direction in which you laid the wool, the prefelted size, and the finished size. With time and experience, you will be able to more accurately predict the interplay of shrinkage variables.

10. *Begin fulling.* Remove the curtain and set it aside. Also remove the underlying working sheet of plastic by reverse-rolling the plastic underneath the scarf. With the scarf against the bubble wrap, stabilize the edges by lightly rubbing parallel to the sides without moving the scarf around.

11. *Work the center.* With wet, slightly soapy hands, lightly full from one end of the fabric to the other. Use your flat palm to gently rub the nuno fabric against the bubbles on the bubble wrap.

12. *Keep going.* Repeat steps 10 and 11 until you reach the end of the scarf. The scarf should appear slightly wrinkled as it begins to shrink. Don't spend too much time working the scarf on this initial pass. The point is to make sure the nuno is behaving as one coherent piece of felt. Working the wool too vigorously will only felt the top layer of wool to itself.

13. *Add hot water.* When the piece is hanging together, press out all of the cold water. Leave the scarf in a little pile and pour on some hot, soapy water. From here on out, keep the water very hot to speed the process. Some felters like to work in the sink for this step, but I continue to use

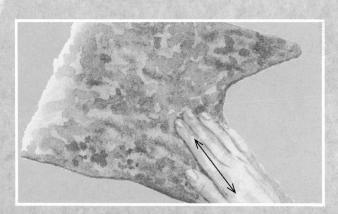

BUTTERFLIES, YES OR NO?

Butterfly corners happen naturally at both ends of a scarf as you felt it. If you're going for a scalloped, wavy look, you might be quite happy to let them be as they are. However, if you want a straighter edge, it's easy enough to shape the corners. With wet, soapy hands, rub the wet felt in the direction that you want it to shrink (on the diagonal).

RUFFLES, ANYONE?

The scarf you see here may look complicated, but it is a simple variation of the scarf we've given instructions for. Instead of laying fiber on a single flat layer of fabric, fold over the edges as shown (right) so the raw edges are trapped in the center by the wool. We used a 30"-wide piece of silk folded to 15" and laid a band of wool about 5" to 6" wide down the center. As long as you felt over the center where the fabric meets, you can adjust these dimensions as you wish to show more silk or more felt.

Variation
Open Collage

Instead of one separate piece of silk, you can lay down a number of pieces; however, keep them within the same overall outline of the original scarf (15" by 96"). Lay down wool in any pattern you wish, but remember that fabric won't felt to fabric. Be sure to lay wool between adjacent pieces of silk. The wool acts like a glue to hold things together.

This technique variation was used to create the Keyhole Scarf, a nuno wrap that can be worn on the body in numerous ways. So many options in one single accessory.

Variation
Stained Glass

Either loosely baste together or carefully lay out different colors of silk in a collage pattern. Lay the wool around the windows like the framework of stained glass. This variation takes a little more skill than the others, since you must watch carefully in the beginning to make sure the design doesn't shift. Basting the fabric windows together helps, and the loose threads can be pulled out later with little problem.

Lake Wyola Vest

You can have a lot of fun recycling old felt projects. As the scarves began to pile up in my studio, I realized that it was time for some of them to start a new life. With help from my apprentice and friend Rory Valentine, a new, easy-to-construct vest pattern was born. Its fresh, geometric design can be dressed up or down and is surprisingly versatile. The bluish greens and muddy browns in the vest inspired us to name it after Lake Wyola, Massachusetts, with its clear waters that allow you to see right down to the bottom.

What You Need

- three to five coordinating nuno scarves (we dyed three scarves in the same dye pot to coordinate the colors)
- a sewing machine, or needle and thread for sewing by hand
- long quilting pins
- a steamer or steam iron

Project Note

The project assumes you already have three to five finished nuno scarves to use. Pin them together to see if you will have enough length for the pattern you like, and if not, make another scarf in a coordinating color.

Monet Shawl

This beautiful shawl, inspired by Monet's famous water lily paintings, was envisioned as part of an ensemble designed entirely of felted works. (See page 271.) The shawl was also designed to take advantage of the fact that different fibers and blends have different shrinkage rates. Merino/Tencel blend and Merino/silk blend rovings are used in addition to regular Merino roving. You can add minor additional layers by using other fibers if you wish. Just make sure they are soft fibers that felt well. Angora rabbit and Cashmere blends would be two appropriate choices.

Before and After

Template Size: 5' x 9'

Finished Size: variable depending on cloth and wool used

Shrinkage Rate: variable, approximately 33–45%

What You Need

- basic nuno supplies (*see page* 210.)
- one extra sheet of 2 mil plastic
- soap glue (*see page* 22)
- 5.5 oz. of Merino wool
- 5.5 oz. of Merino/Tencel roving (50/50 blend in dusty green)
- 2 oz. of Merino/silk roving (50/50 blend, undyed white)
- small skeins of coordinating yarns with high wool or mohair content
- long strips of coordinated hand-dyed silk fabric (I used pieces of 5 mm silk habotai about ½ yd. wide and 2–3 yd. long, and 3 mm silk gauze.)

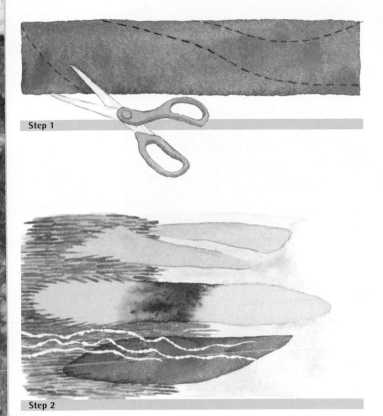

Step 1

Step 2

Project Notes

- The colored silks used for this project are hand dyed and therefore unique. No doubt you will choose a palette with coordinating yarns and fabrics that works for you. The Merino/Tencel roving is available from a number of suppliers, but always in a more limited color range than Merino roving. If you're open to using white in your shawl, you can worry less about how your colors will blend.

- If you are a dyer, you can create your own palette by using the same dye pot for different fibers. Each fabric will take the dye differently, but combined they will result in a unified family of related shades.

Set It Up, Lay It Out

1. Prepare the fabric. Cut the silks into longish strips. Taper the ends into points as shown.

2. Build the first layer. Lay down some very thin background wool, some yarns, and one or two of the fabric pieces. You might want to work in broad stripes so your shawl will have an underlying order beneath all of the wild texture – or not! It's also perfectly fine to have open areas (with no yarn, wool, or fabric) in this first layer.

3. Lay out a second layer. Where you have first laid wool, you can lay anything you wish (remember, wool is the glue). Where you've laid only fabric strips, you must next lay down wool before more fabric. The wool can be laid in any direction as long as you randomize it a bit. Hairy yarn like mohair will behave much the same as a wool layer if you lay down a lot of it.

4. Optional: Make a third layer. If you add a third and final layer, the shawl will shrink a little less than with two layers.

MULTI-STAGE WETTING

Try slightly under-wetting the project at first and then adding a little more water where it's needed after the first roll. This neat little trick allows all of the various materials time to absorb the water. Since we have many different things in the collage and each has its own surface tension, adding a little water at first and then more on a second pass prevents flooding the whole project at once.

Merino Coat Scarf

What a fast, easy way to brighten someone's spirits — felt them a fancy coat scarf. This elegant black scarf (with just a touch of color) goes well with just about anything. Or use a bright, warm color to spruce up a dark winter coat. (See page 243.) If you live in a warmer climate, make an extra-long, lightweight scarf for an artistic flair, or wear it as a belt. Although these scarves are not sheer, they are lightweight and include fun holes in the design. Consider this a quick project for warming up to the more challenging cobweb projects.

Before and After

Suggested Template Size: 12" x 78"

Finished Size: variable depending on the kind of fiber, amounts used, and layout

What You Need

- basic nuno supplies (*see page* 210)
- one 80"-long, continuous piece of black Merino roving, approximately 1.5 oz.
- about 0.25–0.5 oz. of dyed silk for embellishment

Project Notes

- If you prefer to see your design as you work, you can substitute very fine tulle netting for the polyester curtain.

- Since this scarf will be next to the delicate skin around the neck, Merino works well, even though it is not typically the fiber of choice for a cobweb project.

- Make plenty of holes in the scarf, since they are functional as well as decorative. With a large enough hole in the right place, you can pull one end of the scarf right through it (as the black scarf is shown on the model at left). You might be surprised at how much the holes close up during fulling, so don't worry about overdoing it.

Set It Up, Lay It Out

1. Set it up. Lay out bubble wrap with the bubble side facing up. Cover it with 2 mil plastic and draw a 12" by 78" rectangle directly on the plastic for the template. (The illustration shows just one end of the scarf.)

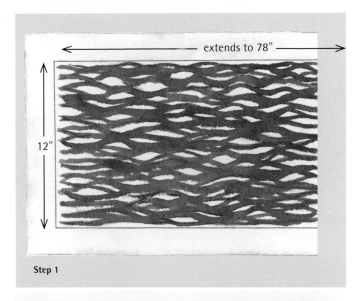

extends to 78"

12"

Step 1

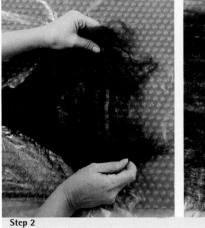

Step 2

2. Lay out the wool. Lay the roving across the plastic in one long strip. It's important to completely untwist the roving so that the fibers are straight. Spread the roving apart as wide as you can without tearing it. You should have large sheer areas where you can see right through the very thin wool. You may want to split the roving lengthwise if you feel you can open it up more easily this way. If so, simply lay the two long strips beside each other.

Step 3

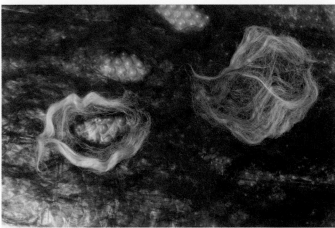
Step 4

should be no smaller than a quarter and no bigger than about 3" to 4" in diameter. Holes that are too small will shrink closed, and too many large holes cause the felt to shrink unevenly. You may have to split the silk a bit as you make the holes — just consider it as part of the wool. Try not to disturb the rest of your layout. If you like, create some larger holes through which you can pull one end of the scarf.

Wet It, Felt It, Full It

5. Get it wet. Lay the polyester curtain over the roving and gently wet it out, following these tips:

- Use a little more soap than you normally would. This helps to speed up the process and ensures that the curtain will peel off easily.

- Slowly and carefully dribble very soapy water through the curtain. Use as little water as possible to get the fibers completely wet. Too much water can very easily flood and displace the sparse fibers.

- Since the layer is so thin, the fibers will get cold very fast. Usually the friction from rolling is enough to heat the felt up again, but if you're working in a very cold room, you can warm it in a microwave before laying it down again.

6. Roll it. Gently roll the bundle on a pool noodle and felt it for about 3 or 4 minutes. When you roll back the curtain

3. Embellish. Lay down the silk embellishment, spreading it apart a little so the wool fibers can easily surround it and felt it into the scarf.

4. Make holes. Tease the fibers apart with your fingers to make a variety of holes in the roving. These

to check progress, keep your hand on the felt's surface directly behind the curtain to avoid ripping up the silk design. Check the felt often by laying your hand across it. Are the fibers starting to behave like a sheer sheet instead of individual hairs? If not, roll a little more.

7. Press with your hands. When a delicate skin has formed, sponge away any excess cold water. Remove the curtain and lay your warm, soapy palms down on the felt. Gently palm the felt — press deeply in slow, small circles without actually moving your hand across the surface of the felt. Try to feel the bubble wrap under your hands as you work. This pressure will help the scarf to full by keeping it warm while the fibers begin to entangle.

8. Finish fulling. To achieve the open cobweb effect, it's important to keep the felt from closing up and sticking to itself. The fibers are on the move, and because there are so few of them, they will try to grasp onto any fiber they touch. Control this by working the scarf only when it's spread flat, either in a roll or on your bubble wrap. Proceed with fulling by alternating between the following:

- Roll the scarf by hand on a wet towel (instead of on the bubble wrap), but leave the tulle or curtain in place at first so the felt doesn't stick to itself.

- Lay the scarf flat with the design facing up, and rub it against the bubble wrap with flattened palms.

Although it looks quite different, this orange scarf was basically made the same way as the black one on page 238. The primary difference lies in the fringed ends. These were made by laying loose strands of novelty yarn right into the wool pile during the layout.

Tip: To achieve the neat, professional look of this scarf, aim for straight edges and corners that are as evenly fulled as the center. Control wavering butterfly edges early on by blocking the boundaries of the scarf with the side of your hand. (*See* Corral Those Fibers *on page* 76.)

9. *Finish up.* Thoroughly rinse the scarf and remove excess water by pressing it with a towel. Put on the scarf and check the placement of the holes for pulling the scarf through. Use your fingers to open up these holes a little more, if needed. You can also gently pull on some wool at the ends and roll it in your fingers to make fringe. Cover the scarf with cloth to protect any embellishments and iron it flat while the fibers are damp. Leave it flat to air-dry.

Step 9

STRINGS AND THINGS

String scarves, made with lots of yarn, are popular and easy to make. They drape well over most anything. This variation can be made by following the felting and fulling directions for the Merino Coat Scarf. Here are some pointers:

- Make the scarves any length you wish, but we suggest a minimum prefelted length of 84" if you want to be able to wrap them at least once around and have a little drape.

- For best results, use loosely spun wool yarn for your base. Add prefelts, open-weave fabric swatches, and other embellishments to the surface of the grid. Invisible bits of cut-up roving act as wool glue to secure nonwool embellishments that won't felt.

- Be very generous with your yarn by spacing the strands closely and adding extra length for a more "expensive" look. Too little yarn results in a stringy scarf that catches on everything and doesn't drape well.

- As you move from felting to fulling, gently check the joining intersections of the roving or yarns and the fibers. Don't pull on them or they will surely come apart; just check that they are lightly attached. As long as you don't full it too roughly too soon, these joins will strengthen as you full the scarf.

Sheer Cobweb Scarf

It's such a treat to make a gorgeous, featherweight piece of cobweb. This one was made with a 50/50 alpaca/silk blend, but you can substitute other luxury fibers such as llama, Cashmere, or Angora. These fibers are often available blended with silk, which will give the scarf an added sheen. Each fiber will felt slightly differently, so it's best to make a smaller sample square first. This is a special project, so take care in choosing the fiber. If you're using alpaca or llama, check that the fibers have little or no guard hairs.

Before and After

Suggested Template Size: 15" x 108" (9')

Finished Size: highly variable depending on the kind of fiber and amounts used

What You Need

- basic nuno supplies (*see page* 210), except substitute very fine tulle for the polyester curtain

- one extra sheet of 2 mil plastic (for sanding only)

- 0.75–1 oz. of 50/50 fawn-colored alpaca-tussah silk blend luxury fiber

- small amount of embellishment (I used dyed silk thrower's waste.)

- a finishing sander with GFCI and safety equipment (optional)

Project Notes

- Beautiful, sheer, consistently even cobweb takes practice. If your first few attempts aren't as even as you'd like, be patient. After making your first scarf, you will be much more aware of how thinly laid fibers behave. Don't worry, every attempt to make fine cobweb is a fabulous journey into luxury for your hands.

- When using such small amounts of wool, the shrinkage rate varies dramatically. For instance, using 1 ounce versus ¾ ounce can alter the shrinkage rate by as much as 20 percent!

- Very fine tulle is the best choice for making cobweb felt. Coarse tulle, with its larger holes, is too rough. Polyester curtain is sometimes too soft. As a bonus, tulle allows you to see your design as you work.

What You Do

1. Set it up. Draw your desired template size on the 2 mil plastic. Place this on top of the bubble wrap.

2. Lay it out. Lay one sheer layer of the 50/50 alpaca-tussah blend in the long direction of your scarf. Slight variations are desirable in cobweb, so it's good if you leave a few bare spots. Add embellishment, if any.

3. Wet it out. Cover with tulle and wet out in the same way as the Merino Coat Scarf. (*See page* 240.) When the fiber is thoroughly saturated, sponge out all excess water and very carefully lift the tulle or curtain and set it aside for later.

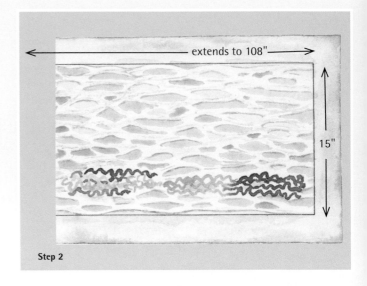

extends to 108"

15"

Step 2

Note: If you're using a sander, proceed to step 4; if you're felting by hand, skip to step 6.

4. Lay down plastic. Lay the second piece of 2 mil plastic on top of the scarf and seal it to the first working sheet of plastic. You want to create a vacuum with the scarf trapped in between so the fibers won't shift around when you sand.

5. Sand the surface. Following the safety tips on pages 236–237, sand evenly across the entire surface of the scarf. Work from one end to the other so you can be certain you've sanded all areas evenly. Stop frequently if you wish and lift the plastic to see how the fibers are coming together. When a skin has formed, you're ready to lightly full. Skip ahead to step 7.

6. Felt with your hands. Soap your hands well and felt across the scarf very slowly and carefully, using mostly palm pressure instead of a lot of movement. If desired, you can do this step with the tulle or curtain still on the scarf. Just be sure to avoid moving your hands too quickly across the surface, which will bring up fibers too fast and cause pilling. When a skin has formed, you're ready to move on to fulling.

7. Full and finish. The remaining steps are essentially the same as for the black Merino Coat Scarf. (*See pages* 240–241.) However, be even more careful not to let the scarf stick to itself or you will have a mess on your hands. Keep your scarf flat while fulling, no matter what method of fulling you use. Work the scarf damp, instead of wet, which will keep it lighter.

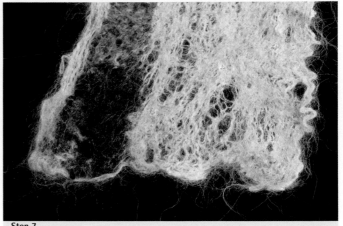
Step 7

LESS FIBER = MORE SHRINKAGE

When working with lightweight felts, it's critical to understand the relationship between fiber and shrinkage. Less fiber always means more shrinkage because the fibers must travel farther to find each other and entangle. If your fiber layer is extremely sheer, the scarf will shrink much more than if you used more fiber laid out at the same size.

To create felt with an extremely fine drape, plan for this effect by estimating a higher shrinkage rate. For example, if the usual three-layer shrinkage rate of your fiber is 40 percent, try calculating it at 50 to 60 percent shrinkage. This is something you must play around with and learn for yourself, because each situation will be a little different.

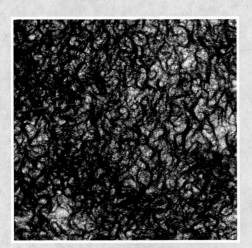

Cobweb and thin felts are more advanced techniques that require skill, practice, and a little intuition. If you simply want to make a stunning scarf without worrying about the exact shrinkage, just make it extra long and extra wide and see what happens! Its delicate softness will reward you, no matter what.

This close-up of a scarf made with a 50/50 Merino/Tencel blend reveals the fine, porous texture of cobweb felt.

Before and After

Template Size: 55" x 55"

Finished Size: 36" x 36"

Shrinkage Rate: 35%

What You Need

- basic nuno supplies (*see page* 210), except substitute very fine tulle for the polyester curtain

- a 6' x 6' piece of bubble wrap

- two 5' x 5' sheets of 2 mil plastic

- a package of 6–10 curtain clips

- a small café curtain tension rod to fit a standard window

- a steam iron and ironing cloth

- about 0.5 oz. of dyed silk

- 2–2.5 oz. of Wensleydale solid-color or hand-dyed roving

Wensleydale Café Curtains

Make these curtains not only for their gorgeous cobweb texture but also for the ever-changing patterns they cast on your walls as the light passes through. They're also a great solution for rooms where you need both light and privacy – a bathroom window, for example, or side porch. The project below is for café-style curtains (about 36" square without clips) and meant to be hung on a tension rod in the bottom half of a standard-sized window, but you could make a longer version for French doors.

Project Notes

- Although larger, this project is similar to the cobweb scarf in terms of steps. However, working with a completely different wool makes a big difference. It's wise to make a sample first, if you don't already have one in your notebook. Wensleydale wool speaks in a unique way and abruptly locks down tight at a certain point, creating a distinctive but subtle surface texture.

- Very fine tulle is the best choice here for making cobweb felt. Coarse tulle, with its larger holes, is too rough. Polyester curtain is sometimes too soft. As a bonus, tulle allows you to see your design as you work.

- Customize your own design at the top of the curtains using silk, locks, or other fibers. If you're looking for a dramatic texture, a fun choice is Ingeo, a shiny fiber made from corn plants (*see below*). Although the fibers have no curl of their own, they mimic the wool's texture in an interesting way as they felt into the curtain.

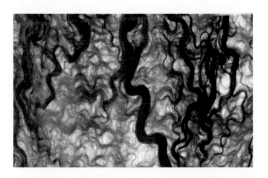

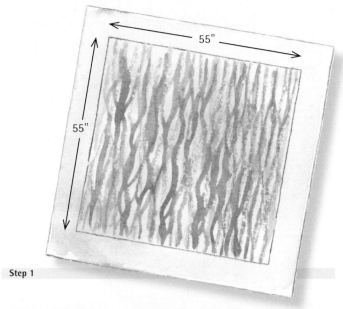

Step 1

Step 2

What You Do

1. Set it up. Draw a 55" by 55" square on the 2 mil plastic. Place this on top of the bubble wrap.

2. Lay it out. Divide the roving in half for two layers, and set one half aside. Split the roving into strands 58" to 60" long. As you spread out these strand widthwise, they will shorten slightly and should fit into your template. Lay out two layers (one horizontal, one vertical), allowing for some open areas.

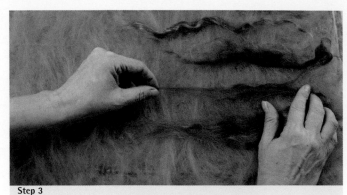

Step 3

Step 5

3. *Embellish*. Slightly spread apart the silk fibers, enough for the wool fibers to come through and felt them in. However, keep the silk strands as thick as possible to maintain their high sheen.

4. *Wet it, felt it, full it*. Cover the fibers with tulle and follow the same steps as for the Merino Coat Scarf. (*See pages* 240–241.) The curtain will take longer to felt than the scarf, of course. Follow the rules for fulling by hand and take your time so the felt will remain stable.

5. *Finish*. Thoroughly rinse the scarf and remove excess water by pressing it with a towel. Open up some of the holes a bit, if desired. Cover the scarf with cloth to protect the silk and iron it flat while the fibers are damp. Leave it flat until it is completely dry. Space the curtain clips evenly along the top edge of the curtain and thread them onto the tension rod. Gorgeous!

FEATHERWEIGHT FELTS

The term "featherweight" refers to felt weight between cobweb and the more traditional three- or four-layer Merino felts. The categories have blurred boundaries, though. The common thread is the materiality and behavior of the wool fiber.

Making very thin, fine felts is a skill feltmakers develop with practice. The idea is to use as little wool as possible to create extreme drape but still produce a fine coherent surface with no weak spots. Very lovely and luxurious felts can be made from a variety of luxury fibers and mixes — and the pieces become even better when they are properly fulled so they won't change shape with time. You could also opt to use a finer-diameter fiber, such as superfine or ultrafine Merino wool.

You can create sophisticated pieces by honing your fine felt technique and opting for neutral classic colors like taupe, gray, black, and white. Or you might prefer lots of color or embellishment.

Note: From a collector's standpoint, cobweb and featherweight felts made completely by hand are considered more valuable than those made using a sander. It's much more difficult and requires a master touch to coax along so few fibers without disturbing them.

FEATURED ARTIST
Lori Flood

Have you ever wondered what it would be like to have your own felting business? Is it possible to make a living selling felt? These are questions Lori Flood began asking herself as she fell deeper and deeper under the spell of felt. While working as a medical research technician, Lori began taking workshops and exploring the world of feltmaking. In May of 2004, she decided to make the transition to full-time artist and now maintains a successful wholesale line as well as a retail fiber outlet.

Lori describes the process as a series of learning curves, but she is always happy to share advice with other artists. Some things she has tackled while building her own business include how to price your work, how to set up accounts, how to write grants, and how to photograph your work. As an artist, she places a strong emphasis on continuing to improve one's technique.

She feels it's important for felters to pay attention to their felt during the process, to watch the different textures that develop. Being able to "sculpt" by shaping

This striking lace vest and hat were made with Merino wool.

and "paint" with color and surface design allows limitless opportunities to create beautiful textiles from a natural and historical material. (*See* Resources.)

10

Working Large: Garments

Making your own highly textural, tactile felt clothing can be both exciting and challenging. The possibilities are endless, with the level of difficulty ranging from simple to complex. It's fairly straightforward to turn your felt yardage into simple clothing such as a shawl, a wrap, or even a tank dress. If you have sewing skills, the constructions can move beyond these free-form styles to become beautifully tailored garments.

Hand-felted clothes are very much a reflection of the felt medium in general. It's easy to make simple ones, yet the technique can grow excitingly complex once you begin to construct clothing. You learn through the process itself, using the wool behavior to guide and shape your garments. Once you've acquired the basic skills, you can explore on your own. We'll start you off by creating some great-looking, basic three-dimensional garments and show you how to handle them on your felting table.

One of the biggest challenges you'll face is how to manage the sheer size of the projects. Logistically, things get rather more complicated when you need to flip over a resist package that is 6' by 9' and composed of only one sheer, delicate layer of fiber on each side. This chapter will explain why garment templates are so large and offer tips for working with them.

A New Agreement

Throughout this book, I've presented the idea of feltmaking as an agreement between you and the wool or fiber you're working with. This includes thinking about the character and qualities of the fiber, considering the shape you'd like to achieve, and so forth. No doubt you've also developed a sense of your own hands and how they relate to the wool. You've determined whether you're a vigorous or light felter, you're aware of the pressure in your hands when you touch the wool, and you know whether you tend to lay out a wool layer thickly or thinly. All of these things have

This striking example shows how much a felted garment can shrink after fulling. Felter Carol Ingram gently felted four pieces for this jacket (collar, body, two sleeves), then sewed them together (front and back shown *left*). The entire piece was fulled in the dryer for short intervals, alternating with stretching and drying (the result shown *right*). Materials used: Merino wool roving, Border Leicester wool, Merino prefelts, cotton muslin, printed cotton gauze, and tussah silk.

come through experience. Now it's time to make a few adjustments in how you approach the projects.

It's amazing to think that the same basic process that can produce felt tough enough to be a rug can also produce felt delicate enough to be a featherweight scarf. These widely diverse results depend a fair amount on the kind of wools you use and how thick or thin the layers are. Making garments involves working with very thin layers of wool or fiber and working much bigger than you have so far. You can do it! But you'll be far happier with your results if you understand this shift in thinking before you jump right into making a tank top or dress. If that's just your style, go for it — at best, it will work nicely. At worst, it won't work, and you can use the material for prefelts.

However, it can be very frustrating to spend so much time on layout and materials only to have delicate seams fall apart. Part of the bargain when working big is that the mistakes can also be big, so give yourself time to get up to speed. Learn how to handle big sheets of plastic, large expanses of thin, wet wool, and 4'- to 5'-long seams. Even with your best efforts, disappointments will no doubt happen to you at some point. My advice then is to walk away from the table, go make a cup of tea, and gather up some old crayons and gold stars. Make yourself a pretty little badge that says, "Now I'm initiated" or "I survived the tank top of '07."

Why So Large?

Why is the template so large? The answer lies in the matter of drape. Felt that is thick enough to be a placemat or bath mat is going to be too stiff to work as clothing. What you want to achieve is felt that will drape well across the body. This requires laying out very thin layers of felt. The following now come into play:

- The less fiber you use in a given space, the higher the shrinkage rate. This happens because the fibers have farther to travel to find each other and lock down. When using Merino top in one layer, we generally figure on a shrinkage rate between 50 and 60 percent.

- When comparing pure wool to a blend of wool and nonfelting fiber (such as Tencel), the blend will always shrink more. Why? Because the nonfelting fibers are like filler: They don't have scales and are not going to do the job of entangling. So, wool fibers that are searching for other wool fibers must keep moving through the filler until they encounter more wool and can lock down. This explanation is simplified, but it helps us understand why Merino/Tencel will always shrink more than the same amount of 100 percent Merino. You can compensate for this by using more (a thicker layer) of the blend, so it will effectively shrink less. In this case, you can generally go by a 50 percent shrinkage rate, but as always, make a sample to be sure.

So, you can't rely on your earlier shrinkage rate experiments from chapter 5. Three nice, even layers of Merino wool are not going to be the same as one layer of Merino wool. This time, the felt is going to shrink more and your garment will be too small. You must start with a larger pattern to compensate for the shrinkage that happens when felting only one layer. Because so much depends on your pattern, your clothing size, the wool you use, and how you lay it out, we will not be providing template sizes and shrinkage rates for the projects in this chapter.

Because the layers are also very thin, you now have a new concern: fragility. The strength of traditional felt lies in the countless fiber-to-fiber unions that occur *in all directions*. Felted fibers in a three-dimensional volume (a layered pile) are very strong, but the same fibers lying side by side on plastic in a single sheer layer do not have the same inherent strength. The felt strengthens when fibers find each other and begin to entangle, something that takes longer than in a three-dimensional volume.

Equipment Notes

The equipment you choose when making large, thin felt should be sturdy enough to support the project, but thin and delicate enough not to disturb the fine layers. For the projects in this chapter, use the same materials as for nuno felting (*see page* 210) with a couple notes:

- For resists, anything heavier than 1 or 2 mil plastic tends to push too strongly against fragile seams. (Some felters like to use cotton fabric resists; personally, I find them fussy to use with so little fiber.)
- A large nonslip rug mat is a good choice for many large items since it's light and bendable. In some cases it won't offer enough support for the project, and

LOGISTICS REGARDING SIZE

A common mistake is to assume you can't create long or big clothing because you don't have a big enough table or a large enough room to work in. Scrolling the project back and forth is the key. (*See* Scrolling *on page* 217.) This not only keeps the equipment manageable in your hands, but it also protects the felt. By exposing only a small portion of the project during folding and turning, you minimize gravity's effect. Sealing and immobilizing the project in the two working sheets of plastic also helps when you turn it over or move it around.

Work smart. Think of a way to work with the equipment and the project to adapt it to your space. This is true innovation, and at times like this, a creative maker is likely to discover other new things about her felt beyond the boring logistics of the table size.

bubble wrap will be a better choice. You may find that you like to begin in bubble wrap and move to a rug mat. Hard mats are usually reserved for finishing the felt in the late fulling stages, if they are used at all.

- Larger-diameter rolling bars, such as large pool noodles or even trash cans, are the best choice for large felt projects. (*See pages* 30–31.)

Using a Sprayer

Because the fibers are laid out so finely and deliberately, you would never pour a stream of water directly onto them, since they would wash apart. For clothing, it's best to use a pump sprayer of hot, soapy water. Make the water hot this time. The wool layers for garments are so thin that they cool off right away, so don't add to the problem by using cool or tepid water. The pump sprayer quickly covers a lot of area, which is why it works so well on large garment projects.

Wetting out large projects with a pump sprayer was a brilliant idea shared by feltmaker Alexa Ginsburg at a meeting of the Northeast Feltmakers Guild one year. Every felter present at the meeting was eager to try it, and many of us became hooked. Alexa didn't get much felting done, as she watched her clever equipment pass from one felter to the next, but we're all grateful to her for solving a big problem: how to quickly wet out something so big.

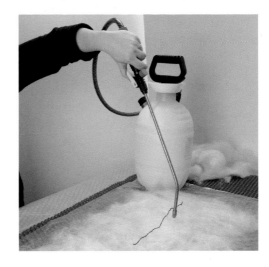

This kind of sprayer's intended purpose is pesticide application, and you can find it at most hardware or garden stores. The sprayer delivers a fine mist that is perfect for wetting thinly laid wool. Thicker wool piles are still more quickly wetted out with the usual method (pouring and spreading out from the center), because the sprayer mist is so fine that it doesn't penetrate very fast. But for more delicate felts and even nuno, the pump sprayer is a miracle tool. Here are some tips for its use:

- Buy a new, clean sprayer and clearly designate it for felting only, so someone in the household doesn't use it for another purpose.
- Use hot water and only liquid soap (any tiny particles will clog the nozzle head).
- If the spray begins to spurt and dribble out unevenly, unscrew the nozzle head to clear out any fibers or other particles.
- When wetting wool, hold the spray wand directly above it, not at an angle.
- Use short, quick bursts to lock down important areas of the wool when you wet it out. Wetting corners, design

elements, and edges first will stabilize your piece on the working plastic. Then proceed to the center.

Making Garment Patterns

In feltmaking, it's highly advisable to learn to make your own patterns. Felt is unlike sewing because factors like wool type, the exact amount of wool (the number of layers or the thickness of those layers), and the feltmaker's technique each play a significant role in the size and shape of the finished garment. Although there are more variables, there is also much more leeway than with sewing. You can impact the shape, size, and quality of the felt in a way that is not possible when working with a manufactured fabric.

Making your own garment patterns is not difficult if you go slowly and think about what you're doing. Most feltmakers I know use a sewing pattern and size it up. But some garments lend themselves to this more easily than others. Also, since a sewing pattern is composed of unassembled parts of the garment, you have the extra step of either assembling the pattern pieces or figuring out a way to convert the pattern to a three-dimensional seamless method. Since I was never trained as a seamstress, I've always made my own patterns by learning the shrinkage rates of my wools, measuring at many points across a garment, and sometimes using an existing piece of clothing as a guide. Of course, the forgiving nature of the felt has much to do with my success!

Creating large seamless garments requires patience and skill. For example, a nuno-felted evening dress made of superfine wool and lightweight silk might begin somewhere around 16' to 18' long, if it's made with the seamless method. This is because the fabric is doubled over (two 8' sides) and then shrunk down (from about 8' to 9' to 4' to 6'). It's easy

THREE WAYS TO MAKE FELTED GARMENTS

What are some of the pros and cons for felting separate pieces and sewing them together versus making seamless felt in three dimensions?

Seamless 3-D: Using a resist to create a garment without seams

- requires the highest feltmaking skill level
- more difficult to manage while felting
- no need to sew anything later

Basted: Hand-sewing felted but not fulled pieces of felt together

- quicker to felt
- some finessing needed when basting
- basting adds stability during critical parts of the process

Sewn: Hand-sewing or machine-stitching fulled pieces of felt together

- fastest method (flat, no resist)
- more steps required to assemble the garment
- can use multiple yardages, including nonfelt
- can create very custom fit

HOW TO MAKE A GARMENT TEMPLATE

To construct your own patterns, you'll need the following materials:

- a long tape measure (at least 10') and a retractable metal tape measure

- a yardstick

- a marker

- 4 mil plastic for the template

- scissors

- a calculator

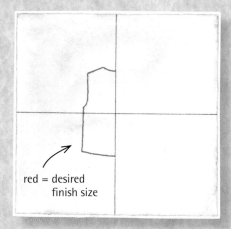

red = desired finish size

It can be helpful to use two different colored markers: one for the finished size and another for the upsized template. Both are drawn on the same plastic, one inside the other. Use a cloth tape measure for body measurements and a retractable heavy-duty metal tape measure (which can double as a straight edge) for the patterns. Be sure to have lots of plastic on hand (rolls of 25').

Pattern drafting is beyond the scope of this book, so we'll assume that you will make or obtain a pattern for the finished garment size. We recommend tracing a garment that fits. You can use a traditional sewing pattern as a jumping-off point, but beware that complex patterns with multiple pieces and seam allowances can be misleading when you are making felted garments.

green = template size

Once you have a suitable pattern, fold it in half vertically. For the template, use a piece of plastic that is double the size of your pattern — to allow for shrinkage, you will need lots of room on all sides to size up.

Draw two centerlines on the plastic, bisecting the plastic in both directions. Align your folded pattern on one side of the line and trace it. *Remember:* Felt is very forgiving and can be moved, stretched, and spot fulled, so it doesn't make sense to draw a lot of details. A scalloped edge, for example, is something you would shape yourself rather than draw in the pattern.

To size up the pattern, measure from the center of the template outward to key points where the shape changes (at the neckline, shoulder, armhole, bottom edge). Use as many key points as you need to size up the pattern accurately; there is no steadfast rule. Write down each measurement and calculate a new one based on the shrinkage rate of the wool. (*See page* 132.) Use that measurement to plot a new point in a straight line from the center through the old point.

Once you've plotted all points and connected the dots, fold the plastic along the centerline and trace the other side of the pattern. It may seem like a lot of work to make a garment template, but once you've plotted a successful pattern, it can be used indefinitely.

to understand that advanced skills are required to create such a dress, but could you make the same thing by sewing?

Well, yes. Almost, anyway. You can make a gorgeous nuno dress much more simply by felting two long, flat pieces, then sewing them together. A trained eye will be able to find your sewn seam, but no one else will know the piece was not felted in three dimensions. This is particularly true of nuno felt: Its highly textured surface will instantly hide the seam.

I often use a hybrid approach. This involves felting the garment partway (to the felting stage), then basting it together very evenly and fulling it as one piece. Many times the basting thread will completely disappear (especially if it's nuno felt) or can easily be pulled out later if it shows. There is still skill involved in coaxing the sides together as you are fulling so it will appear as if the garment is totally seamless. Loose basting stitches are intended to *support* the joining in a structural way without *defining* the tension of the join. This can sometimes be a stumbling block for new feltmakers who also sew, since they naturally think of using a sewing machine or seaming pieces together securely without slack. But with experience, you'll learn to anticipate movement in the seam as the fulling process continues toward completion.

CORRECTING PATTERN MISTAKES

Every pattern you make will be different, but the beauty of making felt garments is that the felt can be stretched or spot fulled to alter minor mistakes. By using a garment steamer, you can sometimes alter more major shaping mistakes. Remember that steam relaxes felt, so to some degree, you can reverse the process in areas you've already fulled or even overfulled.

Don't forget, though, that the clock is always ticking on your wool journey, and every time you change your mind, the wool has a harder and harder time changing. The farther along in the process you are, the more difficult it is to change a particular part of your garment shape. Work intelligently by keeping track of the whole garment at every step. Don't get caught up in overworking one area at a different rate or without regard to the felt as a whole.

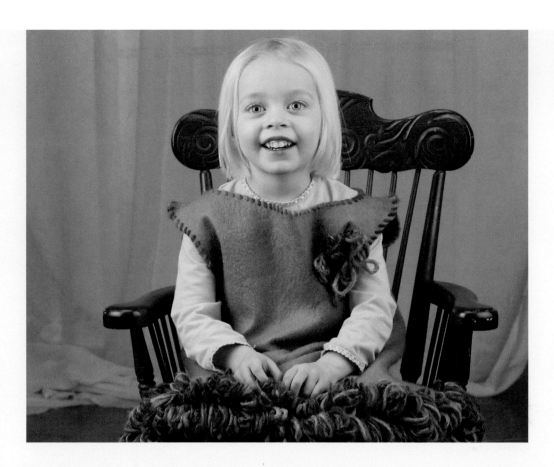

Little Girl's Dress

The Merino is soft and the style is free and open, making this a perfect first garment project. You can even invite your young lady to choose the colors and let her help during the later rolling stage. Add any cheerful trim or decoration you wish — sew a big felted daisy onto the front or add some prefelt flower shapes for pockets as a variation. This little dress feels so good against the skin that the felter who helped make it was seen wearing it as an adult baby doll top!

What You Need

- basic felting supplies (*see page* 20)
- a 5' x 5' nonskid rug mat or bubble wrap
- a piece of tulle, somewhat smaller than the bubble wrap
- two working sheets of 2 mil plastic the same size as the tulle
- an extra sheet of 2 mil plastic, at least 5' x 5', for the template/resist
- a pump sprayer or spray bottle filled with warm, soapy water
- 6–8 oz. of Merino roving in your choice of color(s)
- yarn for embellishment (I used a wool/acrylic boa scarf and unraveled a portion of it for the stitching)

Project Notes

- This dress was made using the closed resist, and design outside methods (*see chapter 6*) and assumes that you are reasonably familiar with the process. I won't walk you through the steps but will provide notes that apply to the project.

- Use a little girl's dress of an appropriate size as a basis for the template, then upsize to allow for a 50 percent shrinkage rate. When sketching the neck and armhole areas, sketch only a shallow curve. You can shape these areas later. Draw the bottom hem as an arc, which reflects the way it will drape on the curves of the body.

- When laying out the wool, aim for two very sheer layers in alternate directions.

- When flipping your (wet) work, use a second sheet of working plastic to seal in your project before turning it over.

- If you prefer to crochet your own edging, make a foundation row by threading some yarn through an embroidery

needle and sewing a blanket stitch with evenly spaced loops along the edge.

Cutting the Resist Package

Exactly how you cut your felt open to retrieve the resist matters quite a bit. You want to cut as little as possible until the felt is more stable. Cutting open the bottom, the neck, and the armholes of your garment at the end of the felting stage before any fulling has begun is like throwing a handful of firecrackers into your nicely gathered sheep herd! Suddenly everyone's scattering off in different directions and you've lost control. It's much better to keep the felt whole for as long as you can. Cut open only one area at a time so you can monitor how the rest of the felt responds.

You can start by cutting a small opening along the neckline that is just big enough to get your hand in without distorting the felt. Right away, seal the cut you've made by felting the raw edge closed. (*See* Cutting and Sealing *on page*

139.) Before you reach in to retrieve the resist, roll the felt for an extra minute or two to make sure the felt is a little stronger. Since the pressure against the seams has been released by your first cut, it's all right to leave the plastic in there for a little while. After 3 to 4 minutes of light fulling, remove the resist with one hand while protecting the seams with the other.

In theory, the felt should be fulled as a single closed pouch for as long as possible to achieve the most even fulling across the garment. However, trying on the piece for fit is also important, to check things like the slope of the shoulders and the curve of the hem. When the size is near the finished measurement and it's time to try it on, cut any remaining uncut openings and immediately seal the raw edges with soap glue.

Finishing

Rinse the garment well to remove all soap. Some feltmakers will then soak their felt in water with vinegar or lemon juice added. This is meant to readjust the pH, which was altered by the use of soap. Some believe this practice locks down the wool fibers a little tighter and even gives an all-felt surface (one that has no embellishments) a slight sheen.

IS IT SAFE TO WASH FELT?

It's natural to think of something handmade as delicate, which means the last thing you want to do is dress up a toddler in felt. Plus, we're used to thinking that it's not safe to wash wool, because it will shrink. But if you've pounded, kneaded, and fulled your felt for hours, using both hot and cold soapy water, it has already shrunk as much as it possibly can — and it's hardly delicate.

However, you shouldn't just toss felt into a washing machine or dryer — especially a top loader with a central agitator, which could distort the shape and evenness of your felt. But handmade felt can certainly take a good washing in your sink. Use the mildest soap you can find and be sure to rinse it very thoroughly in water (any temperature is fine). Lay it out flat to dry, smoothing with your hand. Iron it if a very smooth, professional finish is important to

you; otherwise, you can smooth it while it's damp and it will look fine.

Nuno felt is structurally very sturdy due to the stabilizing fabric inside. Just be careful with any embellishments. Cobweb is the most delicate of all felt because it's made of so few fibers and they become fragile when wet. It is best washed when trapped flat in a mesh bag or netting. The thing to avoid is having parts of it fold over on itself, causing the folds to felt into ridges. Use tepid water and a small amount of soap.

So wash and wear without fear — and pass the word to anyone lucky enough to receive your felted gifts. Wool and felt are time-honored fabrics that feel good and have been used throughout the ages, for kids and everyone else.

North Woods Camp Vest

This vest, designed and made by Roz Spier, was inspired by a favorite camping place in the woods — where there's a fire in the stove, a hot meal ready, and a bright quilt on the bed. Fascinated with color, Roz likes to ask herself the question, "Does it glow?" This one surely does! The color blocks are formed by using prefelts.

What You Need

- basic felting supplies (*see page* 20)
- a 5' x 5' piece of bubble wrap or nonskid rug mat
- two working sheets of 2 mil plastic about the same size as the bubble wrap
- a sheet of 4 mil plastic for the template/resist
- a separating zipper in a coordinating color
- 8–9 oz. of Merino roving in one of more colors (Roz used two dark brown layers and one red)
- prefelts or prefelt sheets to cut as you go

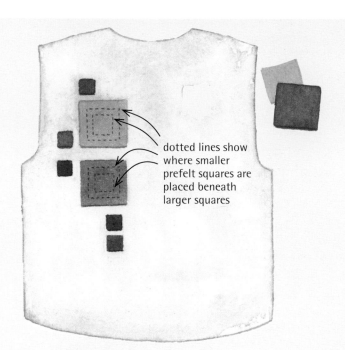

dotted lines show
where smaller
prefelt squares are
placed beneath
larger squares

Project Notes

- This vest was constructed with three layers of wool, so the Merino shrinkage rate will be close to 40 percent. Whether you use the design inside or the design outside method is entirely a matter of your preference. Design outside can be useful for keeping track of prefelt placement. Roz placed prefelts in the center of the template for the back and to the sides on the front (to leave space for a zipper). Remember to stack your prefelts appropriately – on your first layer, lay out the smaller squares first; on the last layer, lay out the smallest squares last.

- Since felt doesn't unravel like fabric, the zipper can be sewn directly on the front felted edges without a need to fold anything under. Just make sure the two sides of the zipper and the vest are aligned.

Using Prefelts

Roz offers the following tips for creating a design with prefelts.

- Use simple motifs, ones you can draw with your eyes closed.

- Use single motifs or repeats, layered or overlapping.

- Throw in an "ugly" color – it creates a jolt that enlivens all of the other colors.

- For balance in the design, use larger pieces of subdued colors and smaller ones of bright colors.

- Create depth by laying a bright color under one neutral or two dark layers.

- Take into consideration that colors will dull in the process of felting and fulling.

- Look at your design from a distance.

- Gently baste prefelts to hold them in place, if needed.

- Brush up the backs of firmer prefelts to loosen fibers for better attachment.

White Shell Top

Part of the ensemble on page 271, this lovely piece is made from viscose and Merino. It is graceful enough to be worn alone or as a shell under pretty summer blouses. Viscose is a long, cellulose fiber and its presence in this Merino blend makes the felt very strong. This strength is especially helpful when making the seams. The true elegance is in the detail — a barely visible structure within the field of white created by purposefully laying the fiber just a bit unevenly.

What You Need

- basic felting supplies (*see page* 20.)
- a 5' x 5' piece of bubble wrap or nonskid rug mat
- two working sheets of 2 mil plastic about the same size as the bubble wrap
- an extra sheet of 2 mil plastic for the template/resist
- 4 oz. of white Merino/viscose roving (or another blend if you have tested the shrinkage rate)

Project Notes

- Merino/viscose, Merino/Tencel, and Merino/silk blends can all be used for this project. The shrinkage rates will vary with each blend, so be sure to make a large sample swatch first. There will also be differences in the sheen and smoothness of each blend. Silk feels smoother, but the Tencel and viscose blends are more durable.

- When laying out the fiber, make sure you have covered all areas of the plastic. However, allow the roving to be a little bit thicker and thinner in areas (*see below*). This will create the subtle grid texture within the felt.

HORIZONTAL OR VERTICAL RAYS?

Here's a bit of information vital to garment making: The felt will shrink most in the direction in which the fibers are laid (parallel to the fibers) and be most elastic in the direction perpendicular to them. If you intend to use only one layer to make a very drapable garment, you will need to alter your pattern to accommodate the *preferential shrinkage* in one direction. You cannot always predict how much longer (if laying fiber vertically) or wider (if laying fiber horizontally) to make the pattern until you try it. This is part of the reason garment-making skills in feltmaking develop over time.

Spring Green Tank Top

Unbelievably comfortable even in August, this little top is perfect whether paired with jeans at an evening barbecue or dressed up for a candlelight dinner on the patio. When an apprentice and I codesigned this top, the single layer of wool (laid out vertically) made it shrink up far shorter than we had anticipated. Our attempts to reshape the bottom area only hardened it far sooner than the top area. The result was an oddly shaped top that didn't leave much to the imagination when on the body! When a friend and I redesigned the piece by adding silk, the look became a signature design of the studio.

Project Notes

- Now's your chance to experiment with preferential shrinkage (when the one layer of wool shrinks more in the direction it's laid). In this case, you generate the shrinkage in length on purpose because you will be adding silk at the bottom. For future projects, it's a good idea to keep track of the before and after measurements, so you will know just how much your pattern is affected by preferential shrinkage.

- Hand-dyed silks can be hard to find (*see* Resources), so you won't have as many color choices as you will for wool. Unless you're a dyer, it's easier to choose the silk color first, then select the wool to match.

- After fulling and before rinsing, cut the window holes in the sternum area. Immediately seal the seams closed. (*See* Cutting and Sealing *on page* 139.) Rinse, reshape, and iron. Hang to dry.

Attaching the Silk

- *To finish this garment,* add a double layer of 5 mm hand-dyed silk to the bottom. Hand-dyed silk of this weight has the perfect combination of weight-lessness and discreet coverage. Use another fabric if you like; just make sure it breathes and is comfortable against the skin.

- *Sewing the silk.* Position the selvage of your silk fabric along the bottom edge that will be visible. Otherwise finish that edge with a small lingerie or roll hem. Fold the silk in half lengthwise, so it will be a double thickness — and not quite so transparent! Since silk is very slippery, tape or pin it closed while you're working with it. Turn the tank top inside out and pin the folded side of the silk on the tank. Check that the length is even all the way around. Fold back and overlap the seam as shown for a slit that is fairly well hidden in the folds. Sew the silk to the top, then remove any tape or pins.

right side

wrong side

- If you're an advanced feltmaker, you may prefer to challenge yourself by felting the silk bottom portion directly to the top, using a multiple resist approach. Think carefully about how to do this and make a sample first. (*See the* Tulip Skirt *on pages* 271–272.)

Advanced Garment Design

The next project uses the same basic tank pattern as the Spring Green Tank Top (*see page* 266), but it introduces two new concepts: the effect on shrinkage rate when using a lot of prefelt on a background and using different shrinkage rates within one pattern.

BEFORE YOU START

Here are some basic considerations to keep in mind:

- Make a large sample. The bigger it is, the more accurate it will be regarding drape and shrinkage. Use the sample's measurements to guide you, but be aware of some other effects outlined below.

- Typically, felters who make garments lay a background of only one thin layer. Orient that layer vertically on your template because you can adjust an incorrect length in a design much more easily than an incorrect width.

- Shrinkage is greatest in the direction the fiber is laid, in this case vertically. The less fiber you use, the stronger this preferential shrinkage becomes, so if you lay a very thin one-layer garment, expect it to shrink a lot more in length (vertically) as compared to the width (horizontally). A 10 percent difference in length and width shrinkage should be enough of a correction to even things out.

- Prefelt designs reduce the shrinkage rate. If you plan to lay prefelts over much of the felt's surface, they will essentially act as an additional layer. How much will they impact the shrinkage? No one knows; it's different every time. Don't despair; just make a guess, say 5 to 8 percent.

Needle-punch prefelts come in different weights, and this project uses a medium weight equivalent to one thick layer or two thin layers of loose wool. Please note that these prefelts are different from "felting fabric" (also called embellishment prefelt), which is much thinner. You can use felting fabric, but you will need to double its thickness throughout the design to keep it strong and visible. Thin prefelts quickly melt into the background wool, so they are better suited for more subtle embellishments on fine scarves or nuno pieces.

We already know that thinner layers of wool make the felt shrink more. We also know that if wool is laid in one direction, that will be the direction in which it shrinks the most. Prefelts act as a sort of stabilizer in garment design, keeping the shrinkage rates from increasing so drastically, especially if they are used heavily all over the garment. But how much? And what if you use a lot of prefelts (slowing shrinkage) but put them on a background of only one thin vertically or horizontally oriented layer (increasing shrinkage)? Ah, that's the million-dollar question! You don't know exactly, but you do know enough to predict some of the effects. Don't worry too much about the exact numbers; there is always leeway in felt. And that, along with some experience, will be enough.

Pacific Rim Tunic

This pattern was inspired by artist Keith Haring and some African printed cloth, but it ended up with a name unrelated to both! I first sketched the embellishments as free-form angular shapes, but I found it faster to fold up the prefelt, cut out elaborate shapes, then open them up (like cutting paper snowflakes). This made the design symmetrical and gave it a native Alaskan or Hawaiian feel. But after felting and fulling, the top more closely resembled a Chinese print. Calling it Pacific Rim seemed to cover it all.

Project Notes

- Add extra length to your tunic pattern to allow for later cutting an irregular hemline along the bottom.

- Use the polyester curtain for this project. The thin background wool requires a gentle covering even though you're using thicker prefelts.

- Use the closed resist and design inside methods in order to continue the design elements around the body. Remember to leave a few minor design elements hanging over the edge of the template. This is the point of using the design inside method.

- As with all of the garment projects, cut an opening in the middle of the neck a few inches long to release the pressure from the resist inside, but do not remove it right away. Let the felt get a little stronger and then reach in.

- When the felt is dry, cut the unusual hem and neckline. The prefelts help to stabilize the felt, so if you've fulled long enough, you may not have to worry about felting the edges closed.

- For a more fitted garment, add darts at the bustline.

What You Need

- basic felting supplies (*see page* 20.)
- a 5' x 5' piece of bubble wrap or nonskid rug mat
- two working sheets of 2 mil plastic about the same size as the bubble wrap
- an extra sheet of 2 mil plastic for the template/resist
- a piece of polyester curtain about the same size as the bubble wrap
- a pump sprayer filled with warm, soapy water
- a needle and thread for hand sewing the silk
- 6–7 oz. of Merino roving in background color, plus 2 oz. more for a sample
- 2 square yd. of medium-weight needle-punch prefelt, or make your own
- 5 yd. of thin wool yarn in a complementary color

Tulip Skirt

This is the last piece of the Merino/viscose ensemble, designed to accompany the white Shell Top. I used the same silk that I used in the Monet Shawl to coordinate the garments, allowing the pretty colored flare of the "tulip" at the bottom to pull the outfit together. While shaping the skirt, you can stretch and full the back area to accommodate your shape. Add a simple elastic waistband to complete the skirt.

What You Need

- basic felting supplies (*see page* 20.)
- a 6' x 9' piece of bubble wrap or nonskid mat
- two working sheets of 2 mil plastic about the same size as the bubble wrap
- an extra sheet of 2 mil plastic for the template/resist
- a piece of polyester curtain about the same size as the bubble wrap
- a pump sprayer filled with warm, soapy water
- 12–14 oz. of white Merino/viscose or Merino/Tencel roving
- 1 oz. of extra cut-up bits of roving to help the silk attach
- 19" x about 50" strip of 5 mm hand-dyed silk (or any open-weave silk with a pleasing pattern)

Project Notes

- Merino/viscose and Merino/Tencel blends work especially well for skirts because they wear well and will keep their shape nicely.

- Select a skirt pattern that is a simple A-line, with allowance at the waistline to fold it over for an elastic waistband. Or, instead of elastic, you could use a fancy ribbon as a drawstring.

- The upper portion of the skirt is made entirely from the Merino blend, and a band of silk fabric is added at the bottom. The upper half of the silk fabric is felted into the wool, but the bottom half hangs freely.

- This skirt is fast and easy to make using the design inside, open resist method. The silk at the bottom of the skirt will remain open. Felt the sides and waist together in the usual way, with rays and seams.

- To make the template, determine the length you want the skirt to be *without* the silk along the bottom. This measurement should include the extra needed at the top for the elastic waistband. Upsize your selected pattern according to the appropriate shrinkage rate (*see page 257*) and make the template. Plot where the silk band will be: Half will lie on the felted portion of the skirt, and the other half will extend below it. (As you can see by looking at the photograph of the skirt, the upper half of the scarf will shrink considerably, while the lower portion will remain unchanged.)

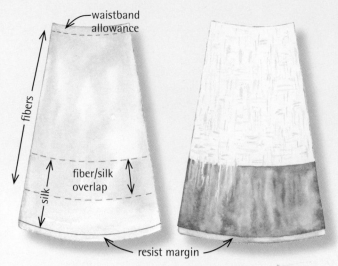

- *Important:* The resist needs to be a couple of inches longer than the template so it extends beyond the silk fabric at the bottom. This prevents the free-hanging silk sides from sticking to each other when wet (which can compromise the shape of the project during fulling).

- It's much easier to lay out the skirt if the silk fabric is cut into two pieces: one for the front and one for the back. This will result in fashionable slits on each side of the silk portion of the skirt. When you've determined how long the silk needs to be to go all the way around the skirt bottom (mine was 50"), cut the length in half (25").

- To make the skirt, lay out two layers of fiber on the template, including where the upper half of the silk will be. (The lower half will hang freely, so don't lay any fiber there.) Next, carefully position one length of the silk fabric with half of it on the fibers and half of it below. To make sure the silk attaches and felts in well, lay out *very small* bits of chopped roving on top of the fabric (only on the half that overlaps the wool fibers). From here, follow the usual procedure for making seamless felt.

What You Need

- basic felting supplies (*see page* 20)
- a 5' x 8' piece of bubble wrap or nonskid rug mat
- two working sheets of 2 mil plastic about the same size as the bubble wrap
- a 5' x 9' piece of tulle netting about the same size as the bubble wrap
- an 8" x 8" piece of tulle netting to rub against the main piece during felting and fulling
- a pump sprayer filled with warm, soapy water
- a steam iron and a pressing cloth or flour-sack-style dish towel
- a sewing machine (recommended) or a needle and thread to sew the sides, neckline, and sleeves
- four balls (110 yd/100 meters per ball) of ribbon yarn (we used Lion Brand *Incredible*, #520–206 Purple Party)
- 2.25 oz. of Merino roving in a complementary color (dark colors blend in better)

Ribbon Tunic

This project requires patience, but the reward is a fabric with a unique felted texture that moves well and feels great on the body. By far the longest part of making this tunic is ironing and laying the ribbon. If you work with one or two other people, the layout part of the process goes much faster. One person can cut the ribbon yarn and lay the strips over a drying rack. A second person can run the ribbon yarn under an iron and hang the ironed strips on a second drying rack. (Note: When using nylon yarn, use a pressing cloth or a very low setting to prevent melting.)

Project Notes

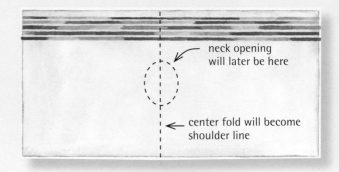

neck opening will later be here

center fold will become shoulder line

- If you don't have a pump sprayer, wet the felt by pouring small amounts of water at a time onto your hand and letting it dribble onto the fibers. (*See pages* 215–216.)

- These instructions are for a sleeveless garment, but many fabrics would work well with ribbon felt if you want to add sleeves for year-round wear. *Note:* I highly recommend making a top before attempting a dress! (*See page* 276.)

- You can use two different types of ribbon yarn for this project, but there is a trade-off. Yarns with some silk content catch faster and are less fussy to work with but are quite expensive. Less expensive acrylic yarns work, but you must make sure the yarn attaches well to the wool early on in the process; they also take longer to full. We Used 100 percent nylon yarn.

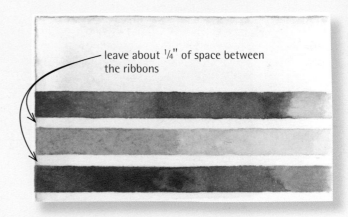

leave about ¼" of space between the ribbons

close-up of ribbon layout

- Set up two drying racks or two or three chairs as hanging stations. Measure and cut strips of yarn approximately 60" in length from two of the balls of yarn and drape them over the first drying rack. Do this for half of the ribbon yarn (two balls). Using an iron setting appropriate to the yarn, run the cut ribbon yarn under the iron to remove all creases. Hang the ironed yarn strips close together on a second chair or rack.

- For the template size, start as usual by first deciding your desired finished size. The tunic will be made in one long piece that will be folded in half. A neckline will be cut into the fold, with either side

becoming the front and the back. It helps to cut a test pattern from inexpensive fabric to determine how wide and how long you want the tunic to be. Figure out the shrinkage rate by making a felted and fulled sample of the materials you will be using, then upsize the test pattern accordingly. (*See page* 257.)

- Lay the ironed ribbon yarn lengthwise on the working plastic, leaving a space of no more than ¼" between the ribbons. Keep the strips in as straight a line as possible, and be sure to leave a couple of inches of space along the sides of the template. If you lay ribbon right up to the edge, it will fall off when you wet it.

- Using very sheer bits of wool, lightly cover the ribbons with a single layer going in the same direction as the ribbons. You should still be able to just see the ribbon yarn through the fibers, but there must be complete and even coverage, especially if you're using acrylic yarns.

- Prepare the rest of the ribbon yarn as you did the first half, and lay a second layer of ribbon on top of the wool. Don't worry about lining up the second layer of ribbons with the first layer of ribbons (or with the gaps between the ribbons). Things will shift slightly anyway as you felt, and the ribbon–wool–ribbon sandwich will make a nicely sturdy fabric.

- Lay the tulle over the entire project, taking care not to let the rough edges of tulle catch on any wool or yarn. Wet it out with warm, soapy water, then roll the entire project (including the bubble wrap) up with a large pool noodle in the center and secure it with ties. Gently roll for about 5 minutes, then open the roll to check it. Some small creasing is normal, but if there are any big creases that are folded back on themselves, reach under and adjust the ribbon. Roll up the project from the opposite side and roll for about 15 minutes, this time using medium pressure. Check again to make sure the tulle isn't felting into the fabric.

- Before moving on to fulling, make sure all of the ribbons have been captured by working the pieces by hand. Using your small piece of working tulle, rub *in the direction of the ribbons,* removing any excess cold water and replacing it with warm, soapy water as you go. This tulle-on-tulle action pulls up fibers through the ribbons, locking them down better. Work one region and then lift the main tulle and check to see if the ribbon is staying down.

- Once the fabric is holding together securely, move on to the fulling stage. Keep it wrapped initially in tulle to protect it, and roll the tulle-covered felt in a warm, damp towel or in a bamboo mat. Open the roll often and reverse your rolling to full from all directions. Continue this process for a few minutes.

- Now full more rigorously. Scrunch the fabric with your hands and rub it on the bubble wrap *in the direction of the ribbons.* Take it to the sink and work in a shallow dishpan with a couple of inches of very hot water in the bottom. Drop it from a foot or two above and work it hard in the dishpan. You should begin to see the straight ribbons shrinking and feel the fabric tighten.

- When the wool has migrated through the ribbons and the fabric feels finished, take it to the table. Holding the felt above your head, throw it down hard a couple of times. Use all of your force when you do this. Do this only for a few moments and then rinse the felt well in warm water. Stretch out the rectangular shape and leave the felt to dry.

- Final assembly is easy. Before cutting and sewing, check the fit of the circumference by folding the yardage in half and pinning the sides together. Carefully step into the tube and pull it

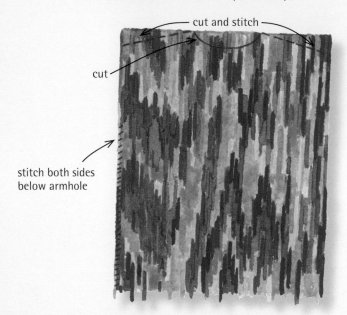

cut and stitch

cut

stitch both sides
below armhole

up around the body as far as possible. If the yardage is too wide, mark how much to take it in along the sides. Then, working with the still-folded fabric, cut a very shallow arc for a neck hole (you can cut it deeper later). Sew the sides from the bottom edge up to about 8" to 9" from the top (leave the top open for the armholes). You will most likely wish to slope the fabric on the top of the shoulders and finish the neckline, so consult a sewing book or seamstress for finishing techniques to refine the design as desired.

Variation
Ribbon Dress

If you're still game after making a tunic, you might want to try a full-length dress (the procedure is the same.) The template for this dress was just under 10' long, so laying the ribbons was quite a challenge. If you're wondering, "Why bother?" I'll tell you: The feeling of ribbon yarn felt fabric on the body is worth it. The shimmering ribbons draw your eye vertically, so the dress is slimming.

When developing this fabric, I experimented with only one layer of ribbon yarn with wool instead of the ribbon–wool–ribbon sandwich. The result was a fabric inclined to holes and weak spots. I recommend spending the extra time on two ribbons layers, since this is a very special piece of felt!

Jorie Johnson

If there is one feltmaker whose work embodies the perfect balance of technical excellence, sophistication, and pure artistic beauty, it is Jorie Johnson of Kyoto, Japan. The owner of award-winning design label Joi Rae, Johnson is a Boston native and daughter of a wool merchant. Jorie provides the international feltmaking community with a visible benchmark of what is possible in the medium. Be it clothing, rugs, or accessories, the quality of her felt is unparalleled, the result of careful and deliberate feltmaking procedures combined with a sympathetic respect for the material.

Jorie's international reputation keeps her busy, but she still finds time to teach feltmakers in Japan, the United States, and other countries, in addition to being an author, researcher, and artist. Johnson believes that the felt she makes should be functional, and her modern missives are firmly rooted in an understanding of the relevance of wool to various cultures through time, including our own. Her modern felt can be seen as an evolution of the two-dimensional survival felts that provided housing and protection in central Asian and other cultures in ancient times. By setting an example of well-made and functional wearable art, Jorie offers both feltmakers and nonfeltmakers alike the thrill of seeing where the feltmaking medium is headed in the future.

Elegant felted fabric, created by Jorie Johnson, is featured in this jacket designed and sewn by Japanese costume designer Mari Hotta. Silk fabric was first dyed using a shibori wrapping technique, then felted into a Merino wool base. Surface embellishments were added using needle-felting. *Shibori Origami Jacket*, silk georgette.

11

Feltmaking in Your Community

The alchemy of felt is simple to achieve and magical to watch, which makes the medium an appealing one to share with others. Anyone can learn it, and it's portable enough to take to school classrooms, demonstrations, and various group activities. As a bonus, feltmaking also holds enough secrets and hidden complexities to provide more advanced artists with an endless challenge. This dual personality works well in teaching situations where different skill levels are involved. And for community fund-raising projects or theater and costume design, felt shines as a versatile medium that delights everyone involved.

Teaching Feltmaking

If you plan to teach kids, the most important thing is to be sure you are working with wool that felts! This is the most common problem behind failed classroom projects. Because feltmaking is not well understood, many teachers aren't aware that not all wools felt. Also, because funds are often tight, it's common for teachers to accept donated wool with the intent of using it for felting projects. If you plan to teach felting, the single best piece of advice is to work with a wool you know will felt quickly and neatly. The magic of feltmaking will be that much more apparent to the children, and everyone will leave amazed and smiling.

Most teachers understand the importance of working with color. Kids love to choose their favorite colors, and fortunately, many colors of wool are available. It's simple to add some wool yarn or some other embellishment as well. Children love *glitz* (a metallic spinning fiber) and *angelina fiber* (a synthetic tinsel), both of which provide sparkle. But beware: These fibers migrate into everything, much like glitter!

A number of beginning feltmaking books are available, and many of the projects intended for adults can be done with children, depending on age and attention span. Feltmaking activities are fun and engaging on their own, but you can also take them to the next level by coordinating with other teachers. A math teacher could build a lesson on measurements and shrinkage rates, or a social studies teacher could broaden the scope with information about countries that have been making felt for hundreds of years.

One-Day Kid Projects

Outlined below are some suggested projects for feltmaking with elementary-school children, including supplies you will need and some tips for the classroom.

THINGS YOU NEED

- *Wool.* A couple of ounces of wool per child is usually enough. Have extra on hand, especially in colors kids prefer. Test the wool first to make sure it felts easily.
- *Pet brushes.* Two small cat or dog brushes serve as paddles to mix colors by brushing them together. Instruct children to brush gently across the tines (don't let the tines grip each other). The brushes should almost float past each other, barely touching.
- *Nylon stockings and knee-highs.* Kids can bring clean ones to class, donated by moms.
- *Liquid soap.* Liquid soap is easier than bar soap to handle and pass around. However, make sure you control the bottle or you will end up with way too many suds and failed projects.

- *Shallow sheet pans.* Use these to contain water.
- *A few feet of stair treading or ribbed vinyl shelf lining.* These help to harden cords after they've first been felted gently by hand.
- *Towels and sponges.* For obvious reasons!
- *Scissors, wool yarns, thin shiny threads, and strings.* Think creatively about what might be used for embellishment and finished decoration.

THINGS TO MAKE

Coiled snake baskets. Instruct children to make several cord snakes (*see pages 45–48*) and weave them into a small, simple basket. Use pipe cleaners to construct a little frame as shown, and then weave in the cording. Tuck and tie any loose ends with more pipe cleaners or yarn, as needed. The baskets will be more decorative than sturdy but are colorful and fun to make.

Rainbow strips. Using their hands or pet brushes, children can make a range of shades by mixing varying amounts and colors of Merino wool. Have each child build a long, fluffy band of colors, then lay the bands side by side in a large square (about 12" by 12"). There's no need to be fussy about alternating layers of wool; just make sure there are enough short pieces of fluffy fibers for the felting magic to happen. Felt the square, then turn it 90 degrees to the left or right and

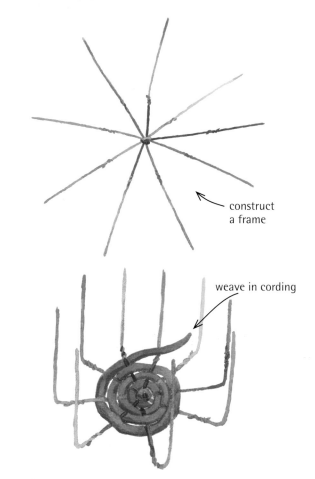

construct a frame

weave in cording

coiled snake baskets

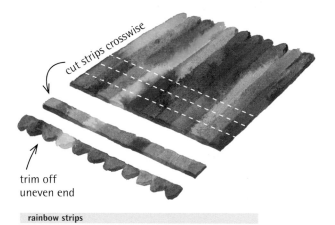

cut strips crosswise

trim off uneven end

rainbow strips

cut across the bands to make multicolored strips of felt. Let each child have a strip or two, and help them tie or sew the bands into a long belt or multiple colored bracelets, pet collars, or key rings.

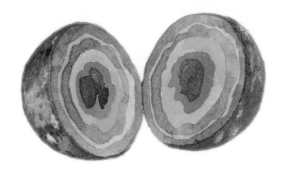

Felted balls and geodes. Everyone loves this project, including adults! Here are the instructions for making them:

- Wad up a central core of colored wool.
- Wrap thin webs of wool around the ball. How thin? Tell kids they must be able to see their neighbors through each web layer they put on the ball.
- Wrap each layer completely around the ball and back onto itself, so it will stick. Think of each piece of wool like an athletic bandage. Wrap the layers tightly enough to keep the center from springing open and to keep as much air out of the wool ball as possible.
- When the ball is about the size of a baseball (for the smallest hands) or a softball (for older kids), stuff it into an inexpensive ladies' knee-high nylon stocking. Push one ball down into the toe and tie the stocking off like a sausage. Continue stuffing the stocking with more balls, each one separated from the next by a knot, until the stocking is full. (*See illustration on page* 59.)
- Submerge the stocking in soapy water and squeeze it to saturate the wool. Let the children gently work the wool through the stocking for a few minutes, until the balls feel slightly firm and you see hairs poking through the nylon.

- Cut open the stocking and let each child finish hardening the ball in his or her hands, using increasing pressure. If you intend to cut the balls open like geodes, they must be very hard. Use scissors or an electric knife to do this.

Prefelt ornaments. Have the children make a number of colored prefelts, blending colors of wool in the layers. Cut out little 2" shapes such as circles, stars, hearts, diamonds, and suns. Cover a pre-existing plastic ball (softball size) or Styrofoam ball with loose wool and arrange the shapes. Add thin little strips of additional wool if desired for stripes. *Carefully* put the balls into the nylon stocking as described above and felt them. Sew a decorative cord at one end so the ornament can be hung.

Felting in a baggie. For a fast way to felt a patch of wool, have the kids layer a design that will just fit inside a small, plastic, zipper-type bag. Squirt a very small bit of soapy water into the bag, just enough to saturate the wool when the water is worked in. Press out the air, seal it, and let the kids gently work the wool by pressing down and rubbing it. When the wool hangs together, take it out and let

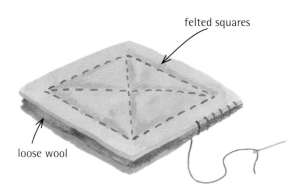

felted squares

loose wool

them finish the swatch in their hands to experience the feel of the shrinking wool.

Sewing and quilting. Thick felts are a great fabric for sewing and quilting. Stuff bits of extra wool between two sheets and, using yarn and a craft needle, quilt the pieces together. Instant hot pad!

Felting with Older Students

Most high school students can handle any adult project, but time is often the determining factor. Be sure to go through any project you intend to do with students a time or two yourself. Don't make the common mistake of assuming that once you've seen wool felt, you can skip ahead to any project — the process, experience, and results are often variable.

Students at this age are exploring their creative identities in addition to establishing independence. Be open to their interpretation of the process and let them experiment with the wool. For example, students may prefer to work in black and white. Let them try to "paint" by laying down tiny bits of wool at a time to build an image and then see what emerges after felting. Or encourage students to use the wool as a base to create

a small, personal sculpture that incorporates meaningful bits of their lives, such as jewelry, buttons, strips of paper, or fibers from old clothing.

As an insightful instructor, you can encourage exploration of felt as a medium. This can be explored from within: *How does the felt speak as a medium? What feeling does it invoke?* Or explore it from the outside: *How does it respond to wax, to paint, to cutting? Can you felt things within it?*

Teaching Adults

Adults can handle all skill levels, of course, but here is one observation worth passing on: Many adults are afraid of being wrong, which is sometimes expressed as a fear of exploring their own creativity. Felt is a fantastic medium for breaking down these barriers because it works at least to some degree every time. Nuno felt, in particular, has the effect of stunning the maker with its beautiful texture and explosion of color. Even hesitant beginning efforts will be well rewarded.

Most adults who take felting classes are very project oriented, although some are not and some will obviously fall in between. It sounds simple, but remembering this basic fact will greatly help the instructor and the energy of the class. With experience, a teacher learns about the pace of the class and where problems arise. Naturally you will want to keep things moving in a timely fashion and set limits around deviation from the main project. But allow some room within these boundaries. Some people are simply there to experience the wool and absorb things in their own way and should be allowed to do so. Adults, especially those who have been making art for years, know how they learn best, and as long as you are clear with them about the trade-off between playing around and finishing the project, allow them to discover their own dialogue with the wool.

The students who are more "linear" may be open to experiencing the wool but are probably more focused on producing a finished project. Time and money are in short supply for all of us, and people need to feel they made the right choice by spending a weekend in your class. Work with these students to teach them the steps, but help them to connect the dots by pausing to feel the wool at stages throughout the process. The best workshops are led by instructors who pause to occasionally explain *why* something is happening. In other words, never forget that you are the ambassador for the wool. Use its inherent and amazing qualities as your guide and both you and your students will be mutually thrilled.

Community Projects

Felting works beautifully as a community project. Not only can everyone participate, but the process is relatively unknown, so you will be sure to draw a large, curious crowd. One project that is always popular is a large rug. A project of this size and scope takes a lot of energy from a number of people working together. Since people can stop to rest at any point in the process, this becomes an ideal project for a situation where people may be dropping in to participate for only part of the time. The story of one such project, offered below, can serve as an example for anyone interested in leading a similar group event.

Felt by All

In the fall of 2002, I organized a community feltmaking event on the common green of the small New England town of Amherst, Massachusetts. I'd become involved in teaching and volunteering for the newly formed nonprofit Foundation for Fiber Art, located in downtown Amherst. That November was also to mark the first fund-raising auction for the Fiber Art Center (FAC), and I saw a perfect chance to take advantage of a number of opportunities at the same time. Why not introduce people to feltmaking, make a large rug to donate to the auction, and hold the event

Before attempting a rug, test the wool or wool mixtures to make sure they will felt well. *Flying through Dreamtime* was made with a Harrisville wool mixture; the finished size measures about 4' x 5'.

right on the highly visible common during a well-attended fall festival?

GETTING ORGANIZED

With the help of other volunteers from the FAC, I set a date for the event to take place during the town's popular Apple Harvest Festival. We made sure to schedule at least two other volunteers who could be present at all times during the event. That left me free to guide the project, with one person talking to passersby and the third person taking care of logistics. I made a few posters explaining related things (such as why wool fibers felt) so interested onlookers could quietly take in information while watching the process.

I arranged for a local Celtic band to play for the event in exchange for publicity. Although we had set up a large tent for protection in case of rain, the weather turned out to be beautiful that day. We were able to spread out a large plastic tarp in the sunshine to serve as a base for laying down the wool background. I donated about 7 pounds of wool; about 5 to 6 pounds were needed for the base of the rug and the rest was used for the design.

DESIGN

I thought it would be fun to let the public vote on the design for the rug, so I created two options. Simple designs works best, in the interest of keeping things moving; almost no one expects the rug-making process to take so long! FAC volunteers chose the base color and began laying down strips of wool batting, which immediately attracted a lot of people. Some of these folks began to join in, while others voted on the pattern for the rug. Eventually, a modified design that incorporated elements from both of my examples emerged — and the design layout began.

BUILDING THE RUG

As the hours went by, many people stopped to look at or feel the wool. Some had never felt loose wool in their hands before. Adults stood transfixed by a 6' by 7' blanket of bold, bittersweet orange color lying in the bright sun. Men, in particular, seemed fascinated by the poster describing the physical process of interlocking scales. Soon the Celtic band began to play, filling the south end of the common with its lively music and bringing even more people.

WETTING AND FELTING

After the wool was laid down, a large polyester curtain was spread over the rug to protect the design. Everyone was invited to help wet the pile with watering cans full of warm, soapy water. Bare feet of all ages walked across the soft curtain, plunging the warm water down into a lofty dry wool batting that was originally stacked 13" thick.

Appropriately, the band played traditional *waulking* songs from the British Isles. "Waulking" is the old name for fulling: soaking and shrinking woven woolen cloth. Traditionally, music and singing were part of the process to keep the rhythm of the process going and to lighten the work. Our musicians commented that they never dreamed they would experience people acting out the centuries-old lyrics they were singing! For me personally, watching people of all ages, from children to seniors, dancing to the music around the rug was definitely the climax of the project.

ROLLING AND FULLING

To roll and full the rug, we used a large, patio-sized plastic blind with the hardware end cut off. The hard work began and the crowds thinned out, but the devotees stuck it out. We finished the day exhausted, with a rug that held together but needed a lot more fulling to be durable. I took it home and worked on it off and on for a week or two before I decided to speed things up and crammed it into my washing machine. Big mistake!

Although I left it in for only a few minutes, the central agitator overfelted the center of the rug, causing it to pucker. At the time, I didn't know that I could have fixed it by steaming the center, which would have allowed the scales to relax and the center to flatten. Luckily, I managed to flatten it fairly well, and I figured it would flatten out completely with use. But don't make the same mistake I did. Just keep rolling the rug, even if it takes a long time and you have to stop and rest. Allow *at least* six hours of rolling for a rug that size; feltmakers who make rugs would consider that a mere warm-up! Stop and stretch it out periodically as is discussed earlier in this book. The end result will be worth it.

FINISHING

Since the rug strongly resembles an Aboriginal or tribal design, I named it *Flying through Dreamtime*. (*See page* 285.) Another FAC volunteer created a computer-printed fabric label (quilters often label their work this way) and sewed it on for us. The rug was now ready for auction. The highest bidder, who took the rug home, was well deserving, since she was one of two volunteers who worked through the entire process. The community felting event was a big success. Not only did the FAC receive attention and an auction donation, but we were able to work within the foundation's mission of "increasing awareness of fiber art." The wide interest resulted in new students for me, the band got some publicity, and a good time was "felt by all."

New York felt rug maker Theresa May O'Brien has apprenticed under master feltmaker Mehmet Girgic of Turkey. (*See page* 125.) Here, Theresa has used a combination of loose wool prefelts and muslin cotton to create a lightweight, washable rug. This is called the Osman technique, named in honor of the Ottoman patterns.

Rug Making

Rug making is a special category within feltmaking, because it's one of the few circumstances where the value of hand-made felt is acknowledged. Collectors of fine textiles understand and appraise the felt rugs from various regions of Turkey, the Middle East, and central Asia. Each region has distinctive designs or characteristics, such as a particular style of stitching, a positive–negative cutout patterning (called *mosaic pattern*), certain regional colors, or a particular regional design. A detailed look at these amazing rugs is beyond the scope of this book.

Felt rugs are certainly doable if you have endurance; but a high-quality felt rug is in a different category. Much depends on the unseen structure of the wool inside the rug. Making felt rugs of collectable value requires years of study; there are special methods to ensure that all areas of the felt are even and very densely fulled. You should not be able to alter the shape at all on such a rug, even if you pull with all of your strength. The key to this durability lies in fulling slowly over a long period of time, usually a day or two.

Fortunately, you can make a rug that is perfectly functional and certainly beautiful in less time than that. When making something new, always evaluate the equipment you are using to see if it makes sense. Some rug makers prefer the plastic dog-kennel-style mats; these mats are made of smooth plastic, so the wool and designs can be laid directly on them without being disturbed.

When they're using a more traditional bamboo mat or anything with slightly larger slats, such as a plastic window blind, felters often substitute a prewetted tight cotton sheet (or other nonwool, densely woven material) for the working sheet of plastic. This is because the fabric will allow excess water to drain away, whereas the working plastic might hold too much in.

When working with such a large volume of wool (which is often on the coarse side, chosen for its durability), it's useful to underwet the wool at first and let any extra soapy water be plunged out of the mat during initial rolling. Otherwise, the weight of the water is likely to distort the wool or make it difficult to handle. Adding more water after a couple of minutes of rolling is much easier than removing a watery mess.

Rugs are most frequently constructed in reverse, with the design laid down first, followed by the wool (any asymmetrical patterns or lettering should be reversed, as if to be read backward). There is a good reason for this: surface distortion. The wool on the outside of the roll is always distorted less during the process of rolling than whatever lies on the inside of a roll. Often the prefelt or roving design is laid out on the mat and then soap is dribbled on the back of these elements to help them adhere easily to the background wool. Some felters use rolling bars or pool noodles; others do not. The key is to check the rug often as you first begin felting.

Fulling steps are the same as described in chapter 5, but fulling is somewhat more difficult since you are working a large piece of felt. To manage the size, frequently fold the rug in half as you roll it. Keeping it wrapped in a wet towel can also help keep it contained. If you're serious about learning to make rugs, the best advice is to take a rug-making workshop from someone with experience. Often, there are so many things that you "don't know you don't know" until you take a class in this technique. If you are making a rug for a group project, you needn't worry too much about perfect edges and totally even felt so much as fulling the rug long enough to make sure it's durable.

This *Family Handprint Rug* was made by Nan Crawford, founder of Felting Frenzy. (*See* Resources.) The background was lightly felted, then handprints were traced and names were added using pencil roving and a felting needle. Dyed locks were tacked into the handprints, then the entire piece was wet felted and fulled by Nan and family members.

Community Rug

It's fun to customize a rug pattern for a specific community event, but keep it general if you intend to sell it for fund-raising. Floral patterns are a great choice, and many colored prefelt sheets can be made or purchased ahead of time to allow people to cut their own flower and add it to the garden motif. Use the instructions below as a general guideline for determining how much wool, prefelt, and other materials you'll need for the big rug. Be sure to test the wool you plan to use. It's difficult to predict exactly how much you will need until you are practiced with one wool over time.

What You Need

2–3 lbs. of wool for a rug about 3' x 4', or 4–6 lbs. of wool for a thicker, larger rug

For any size of rug:

- a large plastic blind or dog-pen mat that is slightly larger than your layout
- a large prewetted polyester curtain, cotton sheet, or any type of nonwool fabric that is tightly woven as a protective underlayer and/or overlayer (not necessary with a dog-pen mat)
- liquid soap and access to water
- a watering can
- a pool noodle, if desired
- tarp(s) to lay down in your work space
- chairs (so you can sit and roll with your feet, if desired)
- extra towels

Project Notes

Rather than walk you through steps for this project, we will assume that you already know the feltmaking basics. If you've never felted before, we recommend that you gain some experience by making smaller felted objects as described earlier in this book before tackling this larger-scale project. Below are some guidelines and suggestions for rug making.

Suitable wools to use:

- For coarse, durable rugs: Karakul, Navajo Churro (outer coat), Icelandic (you can shave the finished rug if it's too hairy)

- For tight, strong rugs: Coopworth, Shetland, Romney, Norwegian C-1, Corriedale

- For very soft luxury rugs (not for high foot traffic): Merino, alpaca, llama

Wools to avoid:

- down breeds (these will not felt or will take too long to full)

- short-fiber "chopped" fleece blends (these will pill too easily)

Other tips:

- Our best advice for this project is to be sure to make a sample of the wool you intend to use. For one thing, a sample will give you the shrinkage rate, so you can more accurately determine how much wool you will need. It will also give you an idea of how long it takes the wool to become saturated and how much soap you will need. If you are using prefelts in your final design, include some in your sample to keep it accurate.

- It's a common mistake to overwet the wool. Water has a tendency to sink down through a pile of lofty dry fleece and puddle underneath where you can't see it. Add water slowly at first. You can always add a bit of soap, roll that in, and then open the roll to add water a second time. Rolling a small amount flattens and wets the lofty pile enough for you to see how much water is really there — usually more than you think!

- Use masking tape to outline the layout.

- Make sure you have close access to water; keep a hose nearby if possible.

- When first wetting out the fleece, make sure people step up and down vertically rather than sliding their feet across the curtain, which will smear your design.

- Work in teams while rolling and try a variety of methods. For instance: sitting on the ground and rolling with your arms; rolling with your feet while sitting in a line of chairs; and walking in a line with your arms around each other's shoulders.

- Work with music or make up songs or chants while rolling.

- Don't forget to rinse the rug thoroughly at the end.

- Block the finished rug (hold down the corners with weights) to keep it squared and allow a few days for it to dry.

- Finish the project by creating an attractive label that describes the event.

- Rugs can be hung like quilts for display. Sew a sturdy aluminum bar across the back, use Velcro strips, or create a sleeve to insert a strong dowel. (*See page* 293.)

Felting Costumes for Theater

In general, because feltmaking is so time consuming and the projects shrink so drastically in size, it's much faster and easier to sew large costumes from fabric rather than felt them from scratch. But there are a few notable exceptions.

Hats

Hats are relatively easy to make. Unlike a whole felted garment, even an elaborately shaped hat can be made fairly quickly. And because fabulous hats can often bring costumes to life, they are a good choice for costume making.

With a clear picture of your desired shape and some shaping and steaming skills from chapter 7, you can create a very fancy period costume hat. The Shakespearean-style hat on this page was shaped from a simple eggplant-shaped resist that was about 2½' by 4' in size. The wool is a blend of an ochre Norwegian C-1/Pelsull blend felting batt and brown Merino roving. Keep in mind that any hat that has a lot of weight, either from attachments or from its own extended shape, will need to fit very snugly on the head to stay in place.

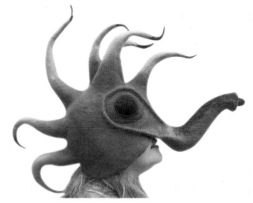

The Shakespeare Hat (top) strikes the perfect dramatic note for a theater production. Cathy Roger's mask (below) was made around a 3'-square plastic resist. The curled projections were formed through extensive steaming and stretching. *Amazon Love*, Merino wool.

Masks

Masks fall into the same category as hats but can be even more central to a character's identity. Well-known feltmaker Beth Beede has loaned many of her intriguing and fantastic felted masks to dramatic productions at Smith College and even to a Broadway show in New York City. As with rugs, we've only just touched on felted mask making in this book, but you have all of the skills you need if you follow the techniques in chapter 7 on advanced shaping by hand and with steam. Work from a two-dimensional resist or use the Beede Ball technique (*see* Resources) on a 16" or 18" ball for a large, round shape. Either way, try on the mask frequently as you work it. Shaping the detailed features requires a lot of felt and the shrinkage is always much higher than one expects. Maskmaker Linda Van Alstyne (*see page* 295) suggests cutting open the back of the head if needed and adding horse hair, husks, or some other material to cover the opening.

Cobweb

Another time to use felt for the theater is when a costume must be ethereal or dreamlike. Cobweb felt is a good choice for simple ragged shawls or mysterious white gossamer-style costumes. When learning to felt at my lakeside studio, I made a large, 4'-long, black cobweb shawl that I soon discovered had too many holes that kept growing bigger as the shawl was worn. Luckily it was headed for a better life, reborn as the Magic Crow Wing costume with the help of my neighbor's granddaughter, who visited during a July week at the lake. We shared some lovely late afternoon moments, with her flapping around next to the water, arms hooked into the holes of the felt, the wings spread wide and floating aloft on the breeze off the lake.

In recent years, Hollywood has called on a few feltmakers to create extraordinary costumes for movies in the fantasy genre, notably the *Lord of the Rings* trilogy. No doubt as handmade felt becomes better known and appreciated, we will see more of it in everyday fashion, in theater and film, and in home decor.

Framing and Finishing

One of the most common questions among felters is "How do I hang my felt artwork?" There is no clear consensus among feltmakers as to one single method. Many feel that felt should not be displayed under glass, which diminishes the experience of its texture. Others feel that it *should* be displayed under protective glass, particularly if it will hang in a public venue. This debate boils down to the question of whether or not the felt should be touched. Conventional wisdom tells us that art should generally go untouched, but many people who make felt actually desire their work to be touched by the viewer.

If the felt is to be glassed, use acid-free mat material and mount it conservation-style (sewn to the mat, not glued). The highest-quality glass is museum glass, which is nearly invisible to the viewer, but it is very expensive. A good alternative is conservation UV glass, which minimizes fading from sunlight and fluorescent lighting. In my opinion, glass shadow boxes should be avoided because they are often too dark. Felt absorbs a tremendous amount of light, and it is already enough of a challenge to light the work well when it is hanging on the wall.

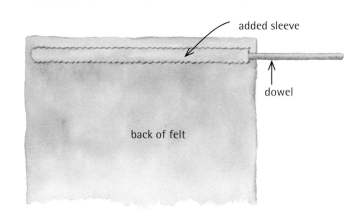

added sleeve

dowel

back of felt

If you decide to leave the work unglassed, there are a number of ways to hang it. Even well-fulled felt is subject to some slight drooping over time from gravity and air moisture, so many felters prefer to sew a flat felt onto a stretched canvas or other framed structure that is usually covered first in fabric. Others take a cue from quilters and sew a sleeve near the top of the work across the back, where a dowel can be inserted. Velcro is a natural to use with felt because it so easily grabs the surface fibers. Use it alone on a hanging bar or along an entire frame for extra reinforcement.

If you are not opposed to coating the back of your felt, experiment by mixing water in varying amounts with gel matte or some other textile medium. Be sure, of course, to test this first on a similarly thick piece of felt of the same composition, and you may even want to wait for a period of time to see if humidity has an effect. Coating the felt will stiffen a piece without a frame and minimizes moth and insect damage to the dark, back side of the piece where these pests prefer to hide.

Other Care

Natural electrostatic charges can cause a buildup of dust particles on felt, making it a virtual magnet for lint and pet hair. For the most part, you can hand wash felt in warm water and leave it to air-dry. For items too large to wash, gently vacuum them. If you're concerned about surface design, lay a piece of tulle or fine netting over the piece and keep it taut as you vacuum through it. Vacuuming prevents dust mites and other allergens from building up on the felt. Felt that is well fulled is quite durable, so you'll be enjoying the fruits of your labors for years to come.

The Future of Felt

As awareness and appreciation of hand-felted works grows, so does the number of questions about how to evaluate the quality of the work. Recently, there has been a sudden flood of nuno felt into the marketplace, and it is showing up in shops and galleries everywhere. I've been asked by some gallery personnel how they should evaluate the hand-felted work, since there is no well-known precedent in the United States. It will take some time for the standards to be recognized, but

a few helpful guidelines exist for both makers and buyers. They mostly boil down to one simple but important thing: Felt is *deceptively* simple. This means that it's easy to make a great-looking, hand-felted scarf without understanding much about its durability or the nuances of the material.

For Buyers

Well-made felt is valuable as a collectable textile, although that reputation is not yet well established in this country. As the field of fiber arts gains recognition, awareness of feltmaking and quality felt will follow.

When buying clothing in particular, understand that the degree to which the piece has been fulled is the most underestimated and least understood aspect of felt. If the felt feels soft and puffy, it will likely pill or break down within a few months of wear. Felted surfaces should be drapable but firm and relatively tight. Gently stretch the felt to see if it grows — a sign of underfelting.

Look at the felt's surface and general quality and then get to know the expertise of the artist by asking questions about the material. Go beyond the trendy look of texture or the fact that it's something new. It's the buyer's responsibility to question whether the piece will stretch out or break down over time.

For Makers and Sellers

If you've worked your way through the projects and chapters in this book, no doubt you are making high-quality felt. By now you will understand that it takes time to become an accomplished feltmaker, even though it seems like the magic happens so easily. And because the medium is new to the American public, first impressions about the value of felt are still being formed, so your work may carry an extra importance. Artists, shoppers and buyers, craft jurors — all of these people are still forming opinions about the medium, so maintain high standards for your felt. Quality felt does not bag out, change shape, pill, fluff up, or bleed color. Make sure you adequately test for these potential problems if you plan to sell your work in a shop or gallery.

It is a fantastic time for feltmakers in the United States. We have a rare opportunity before us — the privilege of establishing high standards for our medium right from the beginning of its public awareness. The more feltmakers who join in this effort, the more the message of quality and value will be heard.

Linda Van Alstyne

Feltmaker Linda Van Alstyne of Middle Grove, New York, is known for her unique felted masks and high-quality handmade felt. Also a physical therapist, Linda is aware of how the movement of her hands and body will affect wool fibers. She is a self-admitted technical felter who values hard, well-fulled felt, and she credits Beth Beede with helping her learn the shaping process. She challenges, "I would love to someday see handmade felt that is hard enough to work on a lathe!"

Balancing Linda's quest for technical excellence is her love of fantasy and play. Her masks always seem to breathe life into some waiting character, many of them with interesting dualities: a kindly ogre or a misshapen medicine man. Linda's masks are a wonderful example of how one can use the malleability of the felt to form custom features and faces straight from the imagination of the maker.

Linda's masks are generally felted on a resist, with layers added to form features. Steaming and stretching are used to shape the felt. *Oscar* (left) and *Yoda's Cousin* (right), both made from Merino wool and found objects.

Glossary

Alkaline. *See* pH.

Batt. A wool preparation in which fibers are carded into flat sheets.

Beede Ball felting. A technique created by Beth Beede for forming vessels and hats out of felt; wool is wrapped around a collapsible ball and felted, then the ball is removed.

Brush end. A dry, unfelted end of a felted cord or spike, used to attach the cord or spike to another felted object.

Carding. A process for combing wool into thin, even layers.

Carved felt. Thick, multicolored layers of wool that have been felted, with outer layers cut away to expose the colors within the felt.

Closed resist method. A seamless felting technique where the resist is entirely enclosed within the felt; used to create bags, garments, and other three-dimensional items.

Clouding. A technique for randomizing the fiber orientation when laying out fleece, where open tufts of wool roving are fluffed and allowed to fall onto a dry wool layout before felting; used in nuno felting.

Cobweb felt. A type of felt where very small amounts of wool fibers are used to create an extremely sheer felt that contains intentional holes.

Combed top. A commercial preparation that straightens and combs wool fibers and makes them all the same length.

Crimp. The natural kinks in the structure of the wool fibers.

Design inside method. A process where the two halves of a project are assembled on either side of a resist with the surface design facing in (toward the resist).

Design outside method. A process where the two halves of a project are assembled on either side of a resist with the surface design facing out (away from the resist).

Drawing. A process that thins out wool roving for spinning.

Drum carder. A machine designed for carding (processing) large quantities of wool; two drums with intermeshed tines are turned, usually with a hand crank.

Dry felting. *See* Needle felting.

Elasticity. The ability of wool fibers to expand and contract without breaking or separating.

Entangling. *See* Tangling.

Featherweight felt. A term referring to very thin felt; includes cobweb and other ultra-thin felts without holes.

Felt on a ball. *See* Beede Ball felting.

Feltability. The degree to which fibers will felt.

Felting. A word that can refer to either fulled knitting or traditional feltmaking; also the first stage of feltmaking where the fibers begin tangling together.

Feltmaking. An ancient process that involves working loose wool fibers into a sturdy fabric called felt; also known as wet felting or traditional felting.

Fiber arts. Creative projects made from synthetic and natural fibers, which can include wool, cotton, linen, silk, and paper.

Fleece. The woolly pelt of a sheep.

Free lace. *See* Yarn felt.

Fulled knitting. Knitted fabric of wool yarn that is then shrunk in a washing machine to create a durable fabric; commonly called felted knitting.

Fulling. The second stage of feltmaking, when the wool fibers shrink and lock together to form felt.

Grain. A directional term describing how a wool is carded, or the dominant fiber direction in a felt.

Grid felt. *See* Yarn felt.

Guard hair. Long, coarse, water-repellent hairs that overlay and protect the soft under-coat of a sheep or other mammal.

Hand card. A tool used to card wool by hand, consisting of a pair of paddle-style brushes with metal tines.

Hat on a ball. *See* Beede Ball felting.

Kemp. Naturally occurring fibers in a sheep's coat that act as spacers to keep fleece from becoming matted.

Laminated felting. *See* Nuno felting.

Lanolin. Grease secreted by a sheep's glands that is present in unwashed fleece.

Lasts. Shoe forms; commonly used in making felt slippers.

Locks. *See* Staples.

Materiality. The physical characteristics of a given material, such as drape, sheen, roughness, elasticity, hairiness, body, and surface contour.

Mosaic pattern. A positive–negative cutout patterning used in ancient feltmaking, especially Shyrdak rugs from Kazakhstan

Needle felting. A technique where dry, loose wool fibers are poked with a barbed needle to mat (entangle) them into a shape; used to attach embellishments or create three-dimensional figures; also known as dry felting.

Nuno felting. A technique that involves felting loose fibers into preexisting cloth, usually silk or cotton; also known as laminated felting.

Open resist method. A seamless felting technique where one or more edges of the resist are not enclosed.

Outer coat. The outer layer of hair that protects an animal from the elements by repelling water and keeping the undercoat dry and fluffy.

pH. A chemical measure of acidity or alkalinity; solutions with a pH of less than seven are considered acidic, while those with a pH greater than seven are considered basic (alkaline). A pH of 7 is considered neutral.

Picking. A process that opens up the staples in sheared wool.

Plied. When two or more drawn rovings are twisted together to form yarn.

Prefelt. A fragile but coherent piece of felt that has not yet begun to shrink; the result at the end of the first step of felting.

Preferential shrinkage. When fibers are laid primarily in one direction within a felt, causing it to shrink more in that direction.

Rays. The ends of the fibers, especially roving fibers.

Resist. A physical barrier placed between two layers of loose fiber to keep them from felting to each other; usually a nonfelting material (plastic, cardboard, tightly woven cloth); used to create seamless, three-dimensional felt.

Roving. A wool preparation where fibers are combed in one direction and slightly twisted into a rope form; this is one step beyond a sliver in wool processing, where the rope is not twisted and therefore weaker.

Ruching. A textural term describing nuno felt; derived from a sewing term that refers to tightly gathered pleats.

Scrolling. A method of laying out wool on plastic or bubble wrap, then rolling up the ends as needed to work in a confined space.

Seamless felting. Creating three-dimensional felt by joining the edge fibers of two sides that are separated by a resist; results in an invisible felted seam that appears seamless. (*See* Open resist method *and* Closed resist method.)

Sheen. A shiny appearance created by light reflecting off smooth wool fibers (ones with unopened scales).

Shock fulling. A process that uses a washing machine, dryer, or violent action such as throwing or beating to full the felt, which causes fibers to immediately but unevenly lock down.

Singles. One strand of tightly spun roving; two or more are plied together to create yarn.

Skirting. A process that removes undesirable parts of the fleece after shearing.

Sliver. *See* Roving.

Staples. The individual locks of wool in a sheep's fleece.

Surface design. Any embellishment such as yarn, prefelt, or dye used to create a pattern on the felt.

Tangling. The action that occurs as scales on the wool fibers open and lock together.

Tencel. A man-made fiber sometimes combined with Merino wool in a blend.

Traditional felting. *See* Feltmaking.

Undercoat. Fibers that lie next to the skin of a sheep and provide insulation by trapping the animal's body heat.

Wet felting. *See* Feltmaking.

Wetting out wool. Gradually adding warm, soapy water to wool fibers until they are saturated, causing their scales to open.

Wool preparations. The process of cleaning and preparing wool for use in fiber arts.

Working sheet. A sheet of plastic (usually 4 mil but sometimes 2 mil or 1 mil) that is laid on top of a rolling mat and on which the wool fibers are laid.

Yarn felt. Felted fabric made of wool yarn and sometimes small amounts of roving; different methods include free lace, lattice felt, and grid felt.

Yield. The fleece that remains after skirting and cleaning.

Resources

Books

British Sheep & Wool. Edited by J. Elliot, D. E. Lord, and J. M. Williams. The British Wool Marketing Board, 1990.

Dutch Felt. Ria van Els-Dubelaar. Zijdar, 2005.

Fabulous Felt Hats. Chad Hagen. Lark, 1995.

Felt: New Directions for an Ancient Craft. Guinlla Pateau Sjöberg; translated by Patricia Spark. Interweave, 1996. Originally published by Tova, 1994.

Feltmaking: The Whys and Wherefores. Sheila Smith and Freda Walker. Dalefelt Publications, 2005. Originally published 1995.

Feltmaking: Traditions, Techniques and Contemporary Explorations. Beverly Gordon. Watson-Guptill, 1980.

Feltmaking and Wool Magic: Contemporary Techniques and Beautiful Projects. Jorie Johnson. Quarry, 2006. Originally published in Japanese by Jorie Johnson, 1999.

In Sheep's Clothing: A Handspinner's Guide to Wool. Nola Fournier and Jane Fournier. Interweave, 1995.

Nineteenth Century Hat Maker's and Felter's Manuals. Suzanne Pufpaff, 1995. Pamphlet on hat-making history.

Nunofelt: Feltmaking Using Wool and Silk. May Jacobsen Hvistendahl. N. W. Damm & Son A. S., 2004.

Vild Med Filt. Marianne Brostøm. Klematis, 2004.

Watercolor Felt Workbook. Patricia Spark. Fine Fiber Press, 2006.

To supplement this list, we highly recommend a visit to the Feltmaker's List FAQ *at www.peak.org/~spark/feltlistFAQ for an extensive library of feltmaking information.*

Artists Featured in This Book

Andrea Graham
613-386-1869
www.andrea-graham.com

Beth Beede
For Beth's method of felting a hat on a ball, visit Pat Spark's website:
www.peak.org/~spark/
patshatonaball.html

Chad Alice Hagen
828-252-6830
www.chadalicehagen.com

Jorie Johnson
Joi Rae Textiles
+81-75-611-3800
www.joirae.com

Lori Flood
The Spinster's Treadle
304-284-0774
www.spinsterstreadle.com

Mehmet Girgic
0090332-350-28-95
www.thefeltmaker.net

Nan Crawford
540-854-4916
feltingfrenzy@earthlink.net

Nicole Chazaud Telaar
Festive Fibers
603-835-2247
www.festivefibers.com

Pat Spark
spark@peak.org
www.peak.org/~spark/spark.html

Polly Stirling
Wild Turkey Felt Makers
pollyfelt@earthlink.net
www.wildturkeyfeltmakers.com/
PollyStirling.html

Roz Spier
Feltworks by Roz Spier
Hartford Artists' Studio
www.spierhead.com/feltbyroz

Sharon Costello
Black Sheep Designs
518-797-5191
www.blacksheepdesigns.com

Theresa May O'Brien
607-433-7615
www.woodscapeartistry.com

Clubs and Organizations

International Feltmakers Association
www.feltmakers.com

North American Felters Network
www.peak.org/~spark/feltmakers.html

Northeast Feltmakers Guild
www.northeastfeltmakersguild.org

Dyeing

Dharma Trading Co.
800-542-5227
www.dharmatrading.com
Undyed silk and cotton and wool dyes

Feltmaker' List FAQ
www.peak.org/~spark/dyeingfelt.html
Pat Spark's information on dyeing, wool, fleece, and felt

General Bailey Homestead Farm
877-471-9665
www.generalbaileyfarm.com
Information on acid, solar, Kool-Aid, natural, and mordant dyes

Pro Chemical & Dye
800-228-9393
www.prochemical.com
Technical help and safety information

Thai Silks
800-722-7455
www.thaisilks.com
Dyed and undyed silk and cotton

Felt Rugs

Felt
+44-0-20-8772-0358
www.feltrugs.co.uk
Woolen shyrdaks (felt rugs) from Kyrgyz

Peace Industry
415-255-9940
www.feltrugs.org
Examples of felted rugs

Feltmaking Sources and Classes

Blacksheep Designs
518-797-5191
www.blacksheepdesigns.com
Felting supplies, glass washboards, tools, kits, books, and videos

The Bug-guy
877-207-9640
www.bug-guy.com
Pest control and bug identification

Columbus Washboard Company
740-380-3828
www.columbuswashboard.com
Glass washboards

eBay
www.ebay.com
Shoe lasts, fiber, and many other supplies and materials

Felting Frenzy
Nan Crawford
540-854-4916
feltingfrenzy@earthlink.net
Kits and workshops for felted rugs and wall hangings, made by needle felting on a prefelted background, then wet felting the final piece

Fine Fiber Press & Studio
541-917-3251
www.peak.org/~spark/fine.html
Feltmaking tools, undyed prefelt, books, and classes

French Soaps
888-511-7900
www.frenchsoaps.com
Olive-oil soaps

Hat Block
www.hatblock.com
Extraordinary handmade Italian hat blocks

Hat Shapers
www.hatshapers.com
Lightweight hat blocks in a variety of shapes, as well as stiffeners and other hat-making supplies; owner Carol Marston is very helpful with questions

Hats by Leko
800-817-4287
www.hatsupply.com
Nontoxic gelatin sizing/stiffener and hat-making tools and supplies

Home Infatuation
877-224-8925
www.homeinfatuation.com
Woven plastic mats

In the Swim
800-288-7946
www.intheswim.com
Solar pool cover (bubble wrap)

Kartehuset
+45-6599-1919
www.kartehuset.com
Polystyrene shoe lasts

Lisa Souza Knitwear and Dyeworks
925-283-4058
www.lisaknit.com
Luxury hand-dyed fiber blends

Lori Flood Felted Fibers
The Spinster's Treadle
304-284-0774
www.spinsterstreadle.com
Felting fibers, felting supplies, and felting soap

Lowe's
800-445-6937
www.lowes.com
Nonslip rug mats

Magpie Designs Felting Studio
Chris White
413-256-6031
www.magpiefelt.com
Classes, lectures

Manny's Millinery Supply Co.
212-840-2235
www.mannys-millinery.com
Stiffeners, ribbon, and wire

Miriam Carter
603-563-8046
mcarter@cheshire.net
Merino batts

New England Felting Supply
413-527-1188
www.feltingsupply.com
Merino and Norwegian batts, dyed prefelts, hand-dyed silks, local fleece, and classes

Outback Fibers
800-276-5015
www.outbackfibers.com
Prefelts, silk fibers, kits, superfine Merino combed top

R. H. Lindsay Co.
617-288-1155
www.rhlindsaywool.com
White Merino top and other natural colored wools

Scottish Fibres
+44-0-131-445-3899
www.scottishfibres.co.uk
Polystyrene shoe lasts (also called moulds)

Simple Shoemaking
Sharon Raymond, shoemaker
413-59-1748
www.simpleshoemaking.com
Soling kits for indoor and outdoor shoes,
soling service

Spirit Trail Fiberworks
703-309-3199
www.spirit-trail.net
Exotic and rare breed fibers

Susan's Fiber Shop
888-603-4237
www.susansfibershop.com
Glitz, cotton, silk, wool, and other fibers

Tandy Leather Factory
800-433-3201
www.tandyleatherfactory.com
Leather lacing and stitching

Universal Mercantile Exchange
800-921-5523
www.umei.com
General handbag supplies and other
fashion supplies

Wendy Hallman
503-407-5413
www.justpokingaround.com
Custom, needle-felted animal portraits

Wingham Wool Work
+44-0-1226-742926
www.winghamwoolwork.co.uk
Fibers, dyes, dyed wool and roving, felting needles, shoe lasts, hat blocks, wool
batts, prefelt, classes, and felting machine
rental

Woodland Woolworks
800-547-3725
www.woodlandwoolworks.com
Felting needles and dyes

Woodscape Artistry
www.woodscapeartistry.com
Plastic Turkish rug mats, Turkish soap,
and Turkish wool

Fiber Processing and Felting Machines

ABC Ranch
573-492-6472
www.abcranch.com
Fiber processing

Belfast Mini-Mills Ltd.
902-659-2202
www.isn.net/~minimill
Flat-style felting machine

Felt Crafts
800-450-2723
www.feltcrafts.com
Roller-style wet and needle felting
machines and other educational supplies

The Felt Lady
www.yurtboutique.com
Building plans for felting machine,
milling service

Stonehedge Fiber Mill
231-536-2779
www.stonehedgefibermill.com
Fiber processing

Zeilinger Wool Co.
877-767-2920
www.zwool.com
Wool processing mill

Sheep and Wool

Chart of Some Felting Wools
www.peak.org/~spark/feltingwool.html

Maryland Sheep & Wool Festival
410-531-3647
www.sheepandwool.org
Held annually in May

NYS Sheep & Wool Festival
www.shcepandwool.com
Held annually in October

Oklahoma State University
www.ansi.okstate.edu/breeds/sheep
Excellent encyclopedia of sheep breeds

METRIC CONVERSIONS

For those of you using metric measurements, here are some basic conversion formulas:

Multiply inches x 2.54 to get centimeters

Multiply feet x .305 to get meters

Multiply yards x .9144 to get meters

Tregellys Fiber Farm
Ed & Jody Cothey
Hawley, Massachusetts
413-625-6448
www.tregellysfibers.com
Wonderful place to see unusual fiber animals; tours and weaving studio

Wild Fibers Magazine
207-594-9455
www.wildfibersmagazine.com
Quarterly magazine offering outstanding photography of fiber animals and cottage industry.

ABOUT THE *Author*

CHRISTINE WHITE is the owner of Magpie Designs Felting Studio, where she works with students and fellow fiber artists to develop both functional and artistic felt. Founder and past director of the seven-state Northeast Feltmakers Guild, Christine curates and juries handmade felt and also lectures and writes about felting and wool. She is co-owner of New England Felting Supply, a retail supply house dedicated to the field of feltmaking. Christine lives in western Massachusetts.

Index

Photography Credits

John Arrighi: 16 top; Tim Barnwell: 87 bottom; Beth and Larry Beede: 5 bottom; Larry Beede: 205 left; Andrea Graham: 61 bottom; Mark Graham: 61 top; You Kobayashi: 277 bottom; M. Kowalczyk: 252 right; Jason Landrigan, Exposure Photo Studio: 295 center and right; Rick Lee: 249 left; Lisa Mahoney: 277 top; Tom McColley: 249 right; Kortney Meyers: 41 top; Theresa May O'Brien: 125 and 287; Steve Omlar: 16 bottom; Clifton Page: 117 right; Dean Powell: 167 right; Pat Spark: 41 bottom; Geoffrey Stirling: 231; Thomas Telaar: 167 left; Bill Van Allstyne: 295 left; Christine White: 6, 252 left and center. 291 bottom; Nancy D. Wood: viii (background), 91, 193, 289.

Other Storey Titles You Will Enjoy

101 Designer One-Skein Wonders, edited by Judith Durant.
More patterns for every lonely skein in your stash.
256 pages. Paper. ISBN-13: 978-1-58017-688-0.

Felt It!, by Maggie Pace.
Hats, shawls, belts, bags, home accessories — the perfect introduction to the magic of felting, for all levels of knitters.
152 pages. Paper. ISBN-13: 978-1-58017-635-4.

Kristin Knits, by Kristin Nicholas.
Hats, mittens, scarves, socks, and sweaters — inspired designs for bringing your knitting alive with color.
208 pages. Hardcover with jacket. ISBN-13: 978-1-58017-678-1.

Knit One, Felt Too, by Kathleen Taylor.
Twenty-five spectacular projects to transform items, knit large and loose, into thick, cozy, felted garments or accessories.
176 pages. Paper. ISBN-13: 978-1-58017-497-8.

The Knitting Answer Book, by Margaret Radcliffe.
Answers for every yarn crisis — an indispensable addition to every knitter's project bag.
400 pages. Flexibind with cloth spine. ISBN-13: 978-1-58017-599-9.

Making Felted Friends, by Sue Pearl.
Twenty-five irresistible projects in a creative, malleable medium, using both wet and needle-felting techiniques.
128 pages. Paper. ISBN-13: 978-1-58017-685-9.

Sew What! Fleece, by Carol Jessop & Chaila Sekora.
Thirty cozy projects in the perfect fabric choice for the Sew-What woman — fleece.
160 pages. Hardcover with concealed wire-o. ISBN: 978-1-58017-626-2.

These and other books from Storey Publishing arc available
wherever quality books are sold or by calling 1-800-441-5700.
Visit us at *www.storey.com.*